Star Magic

Star Magic

Matthew Petchinsky

Star Magic: Harness the Power of the Universe
By: Matthew Petchinsky

Introduction: Unveiling the Mystical Force of Star Magic

In the vast expanse of the universe, stars have long held a captivating allure. They serve not only as guiding lights in the night sky but also as symbols of hope, destiny, and the mystical forces that govern the cosmos. From ancient civilizations to modern spiritual practices, the stars have been revered as sources of powerful energy, capable of influencing our lives in ways both profound and subtle. *Star Magic: Harness the Power of the Universe* is an invitation to explore this cosmic energy, uncovering the secrets of the stars and learning how to harness their power to manifest desires, heal the soul, and transform one's life.

Throughout history, the stars have guided sailors across oceans, inspired poets and philosophers, and been worshipped as celestial deities. Their positions in the sky, their movement, and their brilliant light have fascinated humankind, leading to the creation of myths, legends, and magical practices centered around their power. The ancient astrologers of Babylon, the star-gazing priests of Egypt, and the mystics of the East all understood that the stars were more than mere points of light; they were reservoirs of cosmic energy, channels through which the universe communicated its mysteries. In this book, we will delve into these ancient practices and explore how we can apply this age-old wisdom in our modern lives to create our own magic.

At its core, Star Magic is about forming a connection with the cosmos. It is the art of aligning ourselves with the universe's rhythm, tapping into the unique energies of different stars, and using that energy to shape our realities. By understanding the stars' influence on our thoughts, emotions, and actions, we open up a world of possibilities for personal growth and transformation. Whether you are new to the world of magic or a seasoned practitioner, this guide will offer you valuable insights into the celestial forces at play and how to work with them to create the life you desire.

In these pages, you will embark on a journey through the starry realms, learning how to recognize and harness the different types of stellar energy. Each star carries its own vibration, and each constellation its unique power. We will explore the energies of fixed stars, wandering planets, and the elusive, ever-changing astrological patterns that dictate cosmic influence. You will learn to identify the stars' roles in various aspects of life, from love and relationships to career and spiritual awakening. The book will introduce rituals, meditations, and spellwork that channel stellar energy, guiding you in developing your own personal practice of Star Magic.

By tapping into the magic of the stars, you will unlock hidden potential within yourself. This book aims to show that the stars are not distant, unapproachable beings. Instead, they are intimately connected to us, influencing our physical, emotional, and spiritual states. Star Magic teaches that by consciously aligning with these cosmic forces, we can amplify our intentions, deepen our understanding of our true selves, and navigate life's challenges with greater wisdom and grace.

One of the key aspects of Star Magic is learning to work with specific stars and constellations that resonate with different areas of life. For instance, the fixed stars such as Sirius, Aldebaran, and Regulus have been associated with particular qualities and powers, which can be invoked in rituals to bring about change and growth. Understanding the stars' characteristics allows us to select the right energy for the desired outcome, whether it be attracting abundance, fostering love, or protecting against negativity.

In addition to star-specific work, this book will also explore how to use celestial alignments, such as planetary conjunctions, eclipses, and meteor showers, to enhance your magical practice. These cosmic events are moments of heightened energy when the veil between the physical and spiritual realms becomes thin, offering powerful opportunities for manifestation and transformation. You will learn how to synchronize your magic with these celestial occurrences, maximizing the potency of your intentions.

Star Magic: Harness the Power of the Universe will serve as your guide to the cosmic dance of the stars. It is structured to provide both practical tools and spiritual insights, offering step-by-step instructions for star rituals, meditations, and spells, as well as deepening your understanding of the stars' esoteric meanings. This knowledge will empower you to become an active participant in your own destiny, harnessing the universe's boundless energy to shape your path.

As you progress through this guide, remember that Star Magic is not about rigid rules or dogma. It is a deeply personal practice that evolves with your unique connection to the cosmos. You are invited to experiment, explore, and develop a relationship with the stars that feels authentic to you. The magic of the stars is as vast and infinite as the universe itself, and within its light, there is a power waiting for you to uncover.

So, look up to the night sky, feel the stars' ancient light on your skin, and know that you are part of this grand cosmic tapestry. Within you lies the potential to wield the stars' energy, to manifest your desires, to heal, and to transform. Let this book be your companion on this celestial journey, guiding you in unlocking the mystical force of Star Magic. With the stars as your allies, you will discover the magic that resides not only in the universe around you but also within your own soul.

Chapter 1: Understanding Star Magic

Stars have been gazed upon with awe and reverence throughout history, seen not just as beautiful points of light in the sky, but as sources of mystical energy and cosmic wisdom. Many cultures believed that stars held secrets to the universe's workings, influencing both the collective and individual destinies of humankind. The practice of Star Magic revolves around the idea that these celestial bodies are reservoirs of potent energy, each star and constellation carrying its unique vibration and influence. In this chapter, we will lay the foundation for understanding Star Magic, exploring how it differs from other forms of magic, its core principles, and how to begin forging a connection with the universe through the stars.

The Essence of Star Magic

Star Magic is a magical system that centers on the idea of harnessing stellar energy to create change, manifest desires, and align one's life with the cosmic rhythm. While other magical systems may draw upon the elements (earth, air, fire, and water), the energies of plants, or the power of intention alone, Star Magic specifically taps into the celestial forces emanating from the stars and their cosmic movements. It is a practice that sees the stars as living entities, each radiating specific frequencies that can be worked with to influence personal energy fields and life circumstances.

Unlike astrology, which focuses on the influence of planetary positions on human behavior and fate, Star Magic goes deeper into actively interacting with these celestial energies. It is about recognizing that the stars are not distant or detached from us; they are vibrant sources of power that we can consciously connect with and utilize in our magical practices. This dynamic relationship with the stars allows practitioners of Star Magic to access a range of energies, from the soothing and nurturing vibrations of lunar phases to the intense and transformative power of stellar constellations.

Star Magic also stands apart from traditional ceremonial or folk magic in that it encourages a more expansive and cosmic perspective.

While many forms of magic are rooted in earthly energies and symbols, Star Magic invites you to look beyond the confines of our planet and into the vast expanse of the cosmos. This focus on the celestial realm provides a unique way to understand and influence the energies that permeate every aspect of existence.

The Basic Principles of Star Magic

Star Magic operates on several fundamental principles that define how it works and how it can be practiced:

1. **Cosmic Resonance:** Each star, constellation, and celestial event emits a unique vibration or energy frequency. Just as every individual has their own vibrational signature, so too do the stars. Star Magic is based on the idea of resonance—the ability of these stellar energies to affect and harmonize with our personal energy fields. By aligning ourselves with specific stellar vibrations, we can influence our thoughts, emotions, actions, and even our physical well-being.
2. **Celestial Connection:** Central to Star Magic is the belief that humans are intrinsically connected to the universe. We are made of stardust, the remnants of ancient stars that exploded eons ago, and this cosmic heritage gives us a natural link to the stars' energies. When practicing Star Magic, we are essentially re-establishing this connection, opening ourselves to the guidance, wisdom, and power of the cosmos. This connection is fostered through meditation, ritual, and a mindful awareness of celestial movements.
3. **Stellar Influence:** The stars' positions and movements have a direct impact on the energy available to us. For example, the rising of certain stars heralds new beginnings, while others bring closure or transformation. The phases of the moon, the appearance of constellations, and the occurrence of celestial events such as eclipses and meteor showers all represent opportunities to harness

different types of energy. Understanding these influences is key to effectively working with Star Magic.

4. **Intentional Alignment:** In Star Magic, intention is the tool that directs stellar energy. The stars provide a vast pool of potential power, but it is through our intention that we shape and channel this energy towards our desired outcome. By aligning our intentions with the appropriate celestial energies, we can amplify the effectiveness of our magical practices. This alignment can involve timing rituals with specific star risings, invoking constellations' qualities, or attuning to the moon's phases.

5. **Sacred Reciprocity:** In working with Star Magic, there is an emphasis on respect and reciprocity. The stars are not merely tools to be used; they are ancient beings with their own consciousness. When we call upon their power, we do so with reverence and gratitude. This principle of sacred reciprocity reminds us to offer something in return, whether it be a symbolic offering during a ritual or simply a moment of heartfelt thanks to the cosmos.

Creating a Connection with the Stars

To practice Star Magic effectively, building a connection with the stars is essential. This process is not about understanding the stars solely from a scientific perspective but forming a spiritual and energetic bond with these celestial entities. Here are some ways to start creating this connection:

1. **Stargazing as a Ritual:** One of the simplest yet most profound practices in Star Magic is stargazing. Spend time outside at night, looking up at the stars. Allow yourself to be mesmerized by their light, feeling their presence as more than just distant objects. As you gaze, focus on the energy each star radiates. Notice how some stars seem to pulse with a particular vibration or how certain constellations evoke specific emotions within you. This practice is a

form of communion, where you open your senses to the stars' energies and begin to establish a personal relationship with them.
2. **Learning the Stars and Constellations:** Knowledge is a key component of any magical practice. Take time to learn about the stars and constellations visible in your region. Understanding the myths and stories associated with each constellation will provide insight into the types of energy they embody. For example, the constellation Orion is associated with strength and hunting prowess, while the Pleiades, often referred to as the Seven Sisters, are linked to themes of unity, grace, and feminine power. As you learn about these celestial bodies, you will start to sense which energies resonate with you and how you might incorporate them into your magic.
3. **Star Meditation:** A powerful way to connect with stellar energy is through meditation. During a star meditation, you visualize yourself surrounded by the stars, feeling their light and energy filling your body. Imagine each star as a source of specific power—perhaps one star represents healing, another abundance, and yet another protection. As you breathe in, draw this energy into yourself, allowing it to merge with your own. This practice not only strengthens your connection with the stars but also attunes you to their various frequencies.
4. **Astrological Timing:** An important aspect of Star Magic is knowing when to work with certain stellar energies. Astrological timing involves aligning your magical practices with celestial events, such as new moons, full moons, eclipses, or the rising of specific stars. By timing your rituals to coincide with these cosmic occurrences, you harness the natural amplification of energy that they provide. For example, a ritual for new beginnings may be more potent when performed during the new moon or the heliacal rising of a star associated with fresh starts, such as Sirius.
5. **Creating a Star Altar:** Setting up a star altar in your home is a physical way to honor the stars and create a space where their

energy can reside. Decorate your altar with star symbols, crystals that resonate with celestial energy (such as clear quartz or selenite), and items that represent the constellations or stars you wish to work with. Light candles to mimic the stars' light, and use this altar as a focal point for your star rituals and meditations.

The Relationship Between Stars and Personal Power

In Star Magic, the stars are seen as mirrors to our inner potential. Just as the stars shine brightly in the night sky, each of us possesses an inner light that can be nurtured and amplified through our connection to the cosmos. The stars offer guidance and energy that can enhance our personal power, helping us to manifest our desires, overcome challenges, and transform our lives. By working with the stars, we become co-creators with the universe, actively participating in the weaving of our fate.

Star Magic teaches that our personal power is not separate from the universe; it is a reflection of the cosmic energies that flow through us. When we connect with the stars, we are tapping into the boundless potential of the cosmos, aligning our intentions with the universe's rhythm. This alignment allows us to draw upon the strength of Orion, the compassion of the Pleiades, or the transformative power of eclipses, integrating these energies into our own being.

As you continue your journey into Star Magic, remember that this practice is both an art and a science. It requires knowledge of the stars, an understanding of cosmic cycles, and the cultivation of an intuitive relationship with celestial forces. Through dedication and exploration, you will uncover the secrets of the stars and learn to wield their magic to shape your destiny. The stars are not mere spectators to our lives; they are our partners, offering their energy and wisdom as we navigate the path of personal transformation. With the stars as your allies, the possibilities for magic, growth, and self-discovery are infinite.

Chapter 2: The History of Star Magic

The night sky, filled with stars that shimmer like precious jewels, has captivated humanity for millennia. Throughout history, various cultures have looked to the heavens for guidance, wisdom, and mystical power, developing complex systems of star-based magic to align themselves with the cosmos. From the Egyptians, Greeks, and Mayans to ancient Druids and the mystics of the Far East, the practice of Star Magic has been integral to humanity's spiritual and cultural evolution. This chapter delves into the rich history of Star Magic, exploring how ancient civilizations revered the stars, incorporated them into their rituals, and built monumental structures to align with celestial events.

The Egyptians: The Stars as Portals to the Divine

In ancient Egypt, the stars were more than mere points of light in the sky; they were portals to the divine realm and symbols of eternal life. The Egyptians believed that the stars held the souls of the gods and the spirits of the deceased, serving as a gateway between the physical world and the afterlife. Egyptian Star Magic was deeply intertwined with their religious beliefs, architecture, and cosmology.

One of the central stars in Egyptian Star Magic was Sirius, known as Sothis in their culture. Sirius held immense importance because its annual heliacal rising—when the star first becomes visible just before dawn—coincided with the flooding of the Nile River. This event marked the start of the Egyptian New Year and was considered a time of rebirth, fertility, and renewal. In response to this celestial event, the Egyptians performed rituals and ceremonies to honor the gods and ensure the prosperity of their lands. The alignment of Sirius with the Nile's inundation reinforced their belief in the stars as powerful forces that influenced earthly life.

The Egyptian priests, known as astronomer-priests, were masters of Star Magic. They meticulously tracked the movements of stars and planets, using this knowledge to align temples, pyramids, and other sacred structures with celestial bodies. The Great Pyramid of Giza, for instance, was aligned with the constellation of Orion, representing Osiris, the god of the afterlife and resurrection. By orienting their monumental architecture with specific stars, the Egyptians believed they were creating a direct connection to the divine, enabling them to channel stellar energies during rituals and ceremonies.

Moreover, the Egyptian Book of the Dead, a collection of spells and incantations for the afterlife, often referenced the stars. It was believed that by aligning oneself with the stars' power, particularly with Orion and the circumpolar stars that never set, the deceased could attain immortality. This belief in the stars as guides to the afterlife is a testament to the profound role of Star Magic in Egyptian culture, shaping their religious practices, architectural designs, and views on life and death.

The Greeks: The Mythology and Magic of the Stars

The ancient Greeks were equally fascinated by the stars, weaving their myths, philosophy, and magical practices into the fabric of the cosmos. They personified the stars and planets as gods and heroes, each with its own stories, attributes, and powers. For the Greeks, the stars were divine actors in an ongoing cosmic drama, influencing human fate and destiny.

Greek philosophers and astronomers, such as Pythagoras and Ptolemy, were deeply engaged with the study of the stars. They developed early systems of astrology and star-based magic that would later influence the magical practices of Western esotericism. The Greeks viewed the stars as part of the celestial sphere, a divine and unchanging realm that contrasted with the ever-changing, imperfect world below. By studying the stars' movements, they believed they could uncover universal truths and gain insight into both cosmic and human affairs.

In Greek Star Magic, the constellations played a significant role. Each constellation was associated with specific myths and magical properties. For example, the constellation of Andromeda, associated with the myth of the princess chained to a rock, was often invoked in protective spells and rituals. Similarly, the constellation of Perseus, the hero who saved Andromeda, was believed to embody the qualities of courage and strength. By calling upon the stars in their rituals, Greek practitioners of Star Magic sought to embody the virtues and powers of these celestial figures.

The Greeks also practiced a form of magical timing known as *katarchic astrology*, where specific actions, such as rituals, journeys, or even the founding of cities, were aligned with favorable celestial configurations. They believed that by timing these events with the stars' movements, one could harness the most auspicious energy to ensure success and protection. This integration of celestial timing into daily life demonstrated the Greeks' belief in the stars' profound influence over human fate.

Additionally, temples in ancient Greece were often aligned with celestial phenomena. The Temple of Apollo at Delphi, a major center of prophecy and magic, was oriented towards the rising sun on specific days of the year, reflecting Apollo's association with the light and truth of the sun. By constructing sacred spaces in harmony with celestial events, the Greeks believed they could draw down the stars' power, creating sanctuaries where the divine could manifest.

The Mayans: Masters of Celestial Magic

The Mayans of Central America were extraordinary astronomers and mathematicians who built their civilization around the cycles of the stars, planets, and celestial events. Star Magic in the Mayan culture was not merely a spiritual or religious practice; it was a complex system that intertwined with their calendar, agriculture, architecture, and even their political power.

For the Mayans, the stars were living entities that directly influenced the world below. They meticulously observed the stars' positions, tracking the cycles of Venus, the Pleiades, and other celestial bodies with astonishing accuracy. Venus, in particular, was associated with the god Kukulkan (also known as Quetzalcoatl), and its movements were used to time major events, including wars and rituals. The Mayans practiced a form of Star Magic that involved aligning their actions with these celestial cycles to ensure harmony and success.

The Mayan pyramids and temples were marvels of astronomical alignment. Structures like El Castillo at Chichen Itza were designed to align with celestial events such as the equinoxes and solstices. On the spring and autumn equinoxes, a shadow in the shape of a serpent appears to slither down the steps of El Castillo, representing the descent of Kukulkan. This event was a powerful demonstration of Star Magic, as it showed the alignment between earthly structures and the cosmic forces governing the universe.

Mayan Star Magic also incorporated a complex calendar system, including the Tzolk'in, a 260-day ritual calendar that linked human activities with celestial movements. Mayan priests, or *ah k'in*, used these calendars to determine the most auspicious times for planting crops, performing ceremonies, and engaging in political or military endeavors. By aligning their actions with the stars' cycles, the Mayans sought to maintain balance and order in both the human and natural worlds.

Rituals and ceremonies were central to Mayan Star Magic. These often took place in sacred cenotes (natural wells) or atop pyramids, where the priests would perform offerings to the gods in conjunction with celestial events. For example, during significant astronomical events such as solar eclipses or the heliacal rising of specific stars, rituals were conducted to invoke the gods' favor and protection. Through these practices, the Mayans believed they were directly interacting with the divine forces that shaped the universe.

Other Ancient Star Magic Traditions

Beyond Egypt, Greece, and the Mayans, many other cultures practiced forms of Star Magic. The Druids of ancient Britain revered the stars and their movements, constructing stone circles like Stonehenge that aligned with celestial events, including the summer solstice. These stone circles were believed to be sites of magical power, where the Druids performed rituals to connect with the cosmic energies of the stars.

In Mesopotamia, the Babylonians were pioneers in celestial divination. They meticulously recorded the stars' movements, developing one of the earliest forms of astrology that influenced magical practices across the ancient world. Babylonian magicians used star charts to predict events, perform rituals, and create talismans imbued with the stars' power. This practice of star-based divination laid the groundwork for many Western astrological and magical traditions.

In China, the Daoist practitioners of star magic used the stars to connect with the divine order of the universe, known as the Dao. They studied star patterns, eclipses, and planetary movements to harmonize their lives with the cosmos, believing that the stars governed not only human fate but also the natural and spiritual worlds.

The Legacy of Star Magic

The star magic of ancient civilizations left a profound legacy, influencing magical practices, astrology, and cosmology throughout history. The Egyptians' reverence for Sirius, the Greeks' mythological constellations, and the Mayans' celestial calendars were not isolated practices but parts of a universal human quest to connect with the stars' mystical power. Through rituals, architecture, and astrological systems, these cultures wove Star Magic into the fabric of their spiritual and everyday lives, setting the stage for future generations to explore the magic of the cosmos.

Today, modern practitioners of Star Magic draw inspiration from these ancient traditions, blending their wisdom with contemporary practices. The stars continue to be seen as sources of cosmic energy and guidance, offering their light to those who seek to align with the universe's rhythm. By understanding the historical roots of Star Magic, we can appreciate its enduring power and learn to wield it with the same reverence and skill as the ancients. As we continue our exploration of the stars, we honor the legacy of those who came before us, recognizing that the magic of the stars is as timeless and infinite as the cosmos itself.

Chapter 3: Mapping the Stars—An Astrological Overview

Astrology is the ancient art and science of studying celestial bodies and their influence on human life. At its heart, astrology is about recognizing the interconnectedness between the cosmos and our daily experiences. For practitioners of Star Magic, astrology provides a detailed map of the sky, illustrating how the stars, planets, and constellations exert their energy upon the Earth. In this chapter, we will explore the fundamentals of astrology, focusing on how the stars are positioned in the sky, the roles of constellations, zodiac signs, and planetary movements, and their significance in Star Magic practices.

Understanding the Celestial Map

When we look up at the night sky, we see a vast tapestry of stars, planets, and other celestial phenomena. For centuries, astrologers have studied this tapestry to decipher the cosmic patterns that influence our lives. The sky is divided into sections based on the positions of stars and planets, each carrying its unique vibration and energy.

In astrology, the sky is conceptualized as a circular band called the *ecliptic*, representing the apparent path of the Sun as it moves through the sky over the year. This circle is divided into 12 sections, each corresponding to one of the zodiac signs. Along this path, we find the constellations, which are star groupings that form recognizable patterns and are rich with mythological significance. Additionally, the positions and movements of planets through these constellations create dynamic influences that practitioners of Star Magic can harness for various purposes.

The sky is also divided into *houses*, which represent different areas of life (such as relationships, career, and personal growth). Understanding the interplay between the zodiac signs, constellations, planetary positions, and houses forms the foundation of astrological practice. For Star Magic practitioners, mapping these celestial influences is essential to aligning magical work with the most powerful cosmic forces available at any given time.

The Constellations: Patterns of Myth and Magic

Constellations are groups of stars that have been named and mythologized by various cultures throughout history. In Western astrology, 88 official constellations are recognized, but only 12 correspond to the zodiac signs that dominate astrological studies. Each constellation carries distinct energies and symbolic meanings, offering practitioners of Star Magic different avenues to tap into specific cosmic vibrations.

- **Orion:** Perhaps one of the most well-known constellations, Orion represents the mythical hunter and embodies themes of strength, pursuit, and adventure. In Star Magic, invoking the energy of Orion can aid in rituals aimed at courage, leadership, and the pursuit of goals. When Orion rises in the sky, it signifies a time to take action and pursue one's ambitions with determination.
- **The Pleiades:** Known as the "Seven Sisters," the Pleiades constellation holds associations with mysticism, grace, and spiritual wisdom. In various cultures, it symbolizes unity, femininity, and celestial guidance. Star Magic practices often call upon the Pleiades during rituals focused on intuition, emotional healing, and connecting with higher realms of consciousness.
- **Draco:** The dragon constellation, Draco, winds its way across the northern sky and is steeped in myths of dragons, guardianship, and transformation. Its energy is intense and protective, making it an ideal focal point in Star Magic rituals designed to protect, transform, or delve into esoteric knowledge.

Each constellation has a season, a time when it becomes most visible and exerts its strongest influence. By aligning magical practices with these seasons, practitioners of Star Magic can harness the specific energies associated with each constellation to enhance their spells, rituals, and meditations.

The Zodiac Signs: Gateways to Cosmic Energy

The zodiac is a 12-part division of the sky, each section associated with a specific constellation and carrying distinct characteristics and energies. In astrology, the zodiac signs represent archetypal patterns of behavior and cosmic influences that shape our personalities, experiences, and destinies. Understanding the zodiac signs is crucial for Star Magic, as they provide the energetic framework through which planetary and stellar forces are interpreted and utilized.

Here is a detailed overview of each zodiac sign and its influence on Star Magic:

1. **Aries (March 21 - April 19):** The first sign of the zodiac, Aries, is ruled by the element of fire and is associated with Mars, the planet of action and desire. Aries energy is bold, pioneering, and assertive. In Star Magic, Aries is ideal for rituals focused on new beginnings, courage, and overcoming obstacles. When the Sun or planets are in Aries, it's a powerful time for initiating projects and setting intentions that require a fearless approach.

2. **Taurus (April 20 - May 20):** An earth sign ruled by Venus, Taurus embodies stability, sensuality, and a connection to the material world. Its energy is slow, steady, and nurturing. Star Magic practices aligned with Taurus involve grounding, prosperity, and enhancing physical well-being. When Taurus is prominent in the sky, it's an excellent time for rituals related to abundance, self-care, and creating a secure foundation.

3. **Gemini (May 21 - June 20):** Ruled by Mercury, the planet of communication, Gemini is an air sign known for its adaptability, curiosity, and intellect. In Star Magic, Gemini's energy is perfect for spells and rituals focused on communication, learning, and flexibility. When planets transit through Gemini, it's a time to seek knowledge, communicate ideas, and explore new possibilities.

4. **Cancer (June 21 - July 22):** A water sign ruled by the Moon, Cancer is associated with emotions, intuition, and nurturing. Its energy is sensitive, protective, and deeply connected to the cycles of the Moon. In Star Magic, Cancer is ideal for rituals related to emotional healing, protection, and enhancing psychic abilities. During Cancer's prominence, especially around the New Moon or Full Moon, it's a time to focus on self-care, family, and home.
5. **Leo (July 23 - August 22):** Leo, a fire sign ruled by the Sun, represents vitality, creativity, and self-expression. Its energy is confident, bold, and radiant. Star Magic practices that draw on Leo's energy include rituals for confidence, artistic endeavors, and personal empowerment. When the Sun transits Leo, it's a potent time to shine, celebrate achievements, and engage in acts of generosity.
6. **Virgo (August 23 - September 22):** An earth sign ruled by Mercury, Virgo is known for its analytical, practical, and service-oriented nature. Its energy is meticulous, health-focused, and detail-oriented. In Star Magic, Virgo is excellent for rituals aimed at health, organization, and cleansing. When planets transit Virgo, it's an optimal period for refining plans, purifying spaces, and setting intentions for wellness.
7. **Libra (September 23 - October 22):** Ruled by Venus, Libra is an air sign that represents balance, harmony, and partnership. Its energy is diplomatic, fair, and beauty-oriented. Star Magic practices associated with Libra include spells for relationships, harmony, and artistic pursuits. When Libra's influence is strong, it's an ideal time for rituals focused on love, justice, and equilibrium.
8. **Scorpio (October 23 - November 21):** A water sign ruled by Pluto and Mars, Scorpio embodies intensity, transformation, and mystery. Its energy is passionate, secretive, and deeply emotional. In Star Magic, Scorpio is ideal for rituals that involve deep healing, transformation, and uncovering hidden truths. When plan-

ets transit Scorpio, it's a powerful time for exploring the subconscious, releasing old patterns, and embracing change.

9. **Sagittarius (November 22 - December 21):** Ruled by Jupiter, the planet of expansion, Sagittarius is a fire sign known for its adventurous, philosophical, and optimistic nature. Its energy is expansive, explorative, and truth-seeking. Star Magic practices that resonate with Sagittarius include rituals for travel, spiritual growth, and abundance. When Sagittarius energy is present, it's a time to seek new horizons, broaden the mind, and embrace life's journey.

10. **Capricorn (December 22 - January 19):** An earth sign ruled by Saturn, Capricorn represents discipline, ambition, and structure. Its energy is focused, determined, and practical. In Star Magic, Capricorn is ideal for rituals related to career, long-term goals, and building structures. During Capricorn's influence, it's a time to set realistic plans, work on self-discipline, and honor commitments.

11. **Aquarius (January 20 - February 18):** Ruled by Uranus and Saturn, Aquarius is an air sign associated with innovation, independence, and humanitarianism. Its energy is forward-thinking, unconventional, and progressive. Star Magic practices aligned with Aquarius include rituals for change, innovation, and community work. When planets are in Aquarius, it's a period to embrace new ideas, technology, and social causes.

12. **Pisces (February 19 - March 20):** A water sign ruled by Neptune, Pisces is connected to intuition, dreams, and spirituality. Its energy is compassionate, mystical, and imaginative. In Star Magic, Pisces is ideal for rituals focused on intuition, spiritual growth, and creative endeavors. When Pisces is prominent, it's a time to explore the subconscious, connect with the divine, and express empathy.

Each zodiac sign offers unique energy that practitioners of Star Magic can draw upon to enhance their work. Aligning magical practices with the zodiac's influence allows for a deeper connection with cosmic rhythms and more potent results.

Planetary Movements: Navigating the Cosmic Dance

The planets' movements through the zodiac signs are another crucial aspect of Star Magic. Each planet represents specific energies and influences different aspects of life. For instance:

- **The Sun** symbolizes vitality, self-expression, and identity. Its movement through the zodiac highlights areas where we shine and express our inner power.
- **The Moon** governs emotions, intuition, and subconscious desires. The Moon's phases (new, waxing, full, waning) mark different stages of growth, manifestation, and release, serving as a calendar for Star Magic rituals.
- **Mercury** rules communication, intellect, and travel. When Mercury is in retrograde, it's known to cause disruptions in communication and technology, making it a time for introspection rather than new beginnings.
- **Venus** governs love, beauty, and harmony. Its movements influence relationships, creativity, and matters of the heart. Rituals involving love and attraction are particularly powerful when Venus is in favorable positions.
- **Mars** represents action, desire, and courage. Mars' transits energize and motivate, offering a time to pursue goals and confront challenges.
- **Jupiter** symbolizes expansion, abundance, and spiritual growth. When Jupiter is prominent, it's an auspicious time for rituals related to prosperity, learning, and adventure.
- **Saturn** is the planet of discipline, structure, and karma. Its influence is about setting boundaries, achieving mastery, and facing life's lessons.

- **Uranus** embodies innovation, change, and freedom. Its energy disrupts the status quo and invites radical shifts, making it potent for transformation rituals.
- **Neptune** governs dreams, spirituality, and illusion. Neptune's influence is ideal for magical practices involving intuition, mysticism, and creativity.
- **Pluto** represents transformation, power, and the subconscious. Its movements through the zodiac signify periods of profound change, making it a potent influence for deep magical work, healing, and rebirth.

By tracking planetary movements and their interaction with zodiac signs, practitioners of Star Magic can time their rituals, spells, and meditations to align with the most supportive cosmic energies. This practice of astrological timing enhances the efficacy of magical work, allowing for greater resonance with the universe's rhythm.

Conclusion

Mapping the stars through astrology offers a profound understanding of the cosmic forces that influence our lives. By recognizing the power of constellations, zodiac signs, and planetary movements, practitioners of Star Magic can attune themselves to the universe's vast energies. This alignment is key to unlocking the stars' full potential, creating a magical practice that is both deeply personal and cosmically guided. With this astrological overview, you now possess the tools to navigate the celestial map, forging a connection with the stars that will enhance your magical journey.

Chapter 4: The Power of the North Star—Guidance and Direction

Throughout history, the North Star has been a symbol of guidance, direction, and constancy in the night sky. For ancient travelers, navigators, and mystics, it served as a steadfast beacon, unchanging while the rest of the celestial sphere rotated around it. Known formally as Polaris, the North Star has become deeply rooted in mythology, spirituality, and magic, representing an unerring guide that can lead one back to their true path. In the practice of Star Magic, the North Star's energy can be harnessed for finding clarity, making decisions, and navigating the complexities of life. This chapter explores the magical significance of the North Star and provides practical ways to use its powerful energy for guidance and direction.

The North Star: A Cosmic Anchor

Polaris, commonly known as the North Star, is located almost directly above the Earth's North Pole. This unique position means that, unlike other stars that appear to move across the sky throughout the night, Polaris remains relatively fixed, marking the northern direction. This celestial stability has made the North Star a crucial navigational tool for centuries, guiding sailors, travelers, and explorers across land and sea.

In spiritual and magical contexts, the North Star embodies the concept of a "cosmic anchor." It is a symbol of constancy and an embodiment of true north—the direction that represents one's inner compass, purpose, and higher calling. While the world around us is in constant flux, the North Star remains a reliable guide, reminding us of the importance of staying true to our path. This steadfastness is what gives the North Star its immense power in Star Magic practices.

The energy of the North Star is associated with qualities such as:

- **Guidance:** Providing insight and direction, helping individuals navigate life's uncertainties and choices.

- **Clarity:** Illuminating the path ahead, revealing truths that might otherwise remain obscured.
- **Purpose:** Acting as a reminder of one's inner purpose and the importance of pursuing it despite distractions and obstacles.
- **Stability:** Offering a sense of stability and grounding, even in times of chaos and transformation.

By tapping into the North Star's energy, practitioners of Star Magic can align themselves with their true direction, access inner wisdom, and cultivate the courage to move forward confidently.

The Magical Significance of the North Star

In many mythologies, the North Star holds a revered place as a celestial guide. It has been seen as the "star of the sea" for mariners, a marker of the axis mundi (the world axis) in shamanic traditions, and even a cosmic eye of the universe that watches over and guides souls. Its unwavering presence has inspired stories of divine guidance and the pursuit of one's destiny.

In Star Magic, the North Star is considered a powerful conduit of guidance and insight. It represents the idea that within the vastness of the universe, there is a point of certainty—a fixed star that can guide one through life's complexities. By focusing on the North Star, practitioners believe they can gain access to a higher perspective, allowing them to see their life path more clearly and make decisions that are in alignment with their true purpose.

The North Star's position at the center of the sky's rotation also symbolizes the power of stillness. In Star Magic practices, this stillness is seen as a state of inner clarity and wisdom. Just as Polaris remains constant while all other stars appear to move around it, those who attune to the North Star's energy can find a sense of calm and focus amidst life's chaos. This practice encourages individuals to become their own "north star," cultivating inner strength and stability as they navigate their journey.

Using the North Star's Energy for Guidance

Connecting with the North Star's energy involves more than simply observing it in the night sky. It requires mindful intention and a willingness to open oneself to the cosmic guidance it offers. Here are several ways to use the North Star's energy for finding direction in life, making decisions, and staying aligned with your true path:

1. North Star Meditation: Finding Your Inner Compass

One of the most direct ways to connect with the North Star is through meditation. This practice helps you center yourself, gain clarity, and align with the North Star's guidance. Here's how to perform a North Star meditation:

- Find a quiet, dark place where you can view the North Star in the sky. If it's not visible due to weather or location, visualize it in your mind's eye.
- Sit or lie down comfortably, and take a few deep breaths to ground yourself.
- Focus your gaze on the North Star. As you look at it, imagine its light growing brighter and more focused, forming a direct line from the star to your heart.
- Close your eyes and visualize this line of light as a guide, connecting your inner compass to the cosmos. Feel its stabilizing energy anchoring you.
- Reflect on a situation or decision in your life where you seek guidance. Ask the North Star to illuminate the path that aligns with your true purpose.
- Sit in silence, allowing insights, images, or feelings to arise. Trust that the guidance you receive is in harmony with your higher self.
- When you are ready, open your eyes, express gratitude to the North Star for its guidance, and carry this clarity into your life.

Performing this meditation regularly can help you stay connected to your inner compass, making it easier to navigate through life's challenges and decisions with confidence.

2. North Star Ritual for Decision-Making

The North Star can be invoked in rituals designed to gain clarity when faced with difficult choices. To harness its energy for decision-making, try this simple yet powerful ritual:

- Begin by choosing a night when the North Star is visible.
- Set up a small altar outdoors (or near a window) facing north. Include items that represent clarity and guidance, such as a white candle, a compass, or a piece of clear quartz.
- Light the candle and focus your gaze on the North Star. Say aloud, "North Star, beacon of guidance, grant me the clarity to see the right path."
- Write down the choices or decisions you are contemplating on small pieces of paper. Fold them and place them on the altar.
- Hold a piece of clear quartz in your hand. Close your eyes and focus on the light of the North Star filling the quartz with its steady energy.
- When you feel ready, pass the quartz over each piece of paper, sensing which one resonates with the energy of the North Star. Pay attention to any feelings of warmth, tingling, or inner knowing.
- Once you have identified the choice that feels aligned with the North Star's guidance, extinguish the candle and thank the North Star for its assistance.
- Reflect on your chosen path and take steps in that direction, trusting that you are guided by the light of the cosmos.

3. Setting a North Star Intention

In Star Magic, setting an intention is akin to aligning your inner compass with your true path. The North Star can be a powerful ally in solidifying this intention. Use this practice to establish a clear direction or goal:

- Choose a specific goal or intention that aligns with your life's purpose or something you wish to achieve.
- Go outside on a clear night when the North Star is visible. Bring a candle, paper, and pen with you.
- Light the candle and sit facing the North Star. Write your intention on the paper, phrasing it as a clear statement, such as, "I align with my true path in pursuing my career in healing others."
- Fold the paper and hold it close to your heart. Close your eyes and focus on the North Star's light. Imagine it shining down on you, filling you with a sense of purpose and direction.
- As you feel the light strengthening your intention, visualize your goal coming into alignment with the universe's rhythm, moving steadily towards fulfillment.
- Keep the paper somewhere special, such as on your altar or in a sacred box, as a reminder of your commitment to stay on the right path.

By setting your intention under the guidance of the North Star, you infuse it with cosmic energy, enhancing your resolve and focus in bringing it to fruition.

4. Using the North Star for Navigating Life Transitions

Major life transitions, such as changes in career, relationships, or personal development, can leave us feeling disoriented and uncertain. In such times, the North Star can be called upon as a source of stability and guidance. Here's how to work with its energy during transitions:

- Create a North Star talisman using a simple object, like a small stone or piece of jewelry. Hold the object under the North Star, asking it to imbue the talisman with its guiding light.
- Carry this talisman with you during times of uncertainty, holding it whenever you need clarity or reassurance.
- When facing a difficult choice or feeling lost, hold the talisman and close your eyes. Visualize the North Star shining within the talisman, offering you a beacon of light in the darkness. Breathe in its energy and ask for the direction you seek.
- Trust that the guidance you receive will help you navigate your transition in alignment with your highest good.

Staying Aligned with the North Star's Path

The North Star serves as a reminder that even amidst life's uncertainties and changes, there is a constant source of guidance available to us. In Star Magic, maintaining a connection with the North Star's energy is a practice of self-reflection, alignment, and trust in the universe's guidance. By regularly incorporating the North Star into your magical practice, you reinforce your inner compass, helping you stay true to your path.

Remember, the power of the North Star lies not in dictating a specific route but in illuminating the possibilities that align with your soul's journey. It provides clarity, direction, and the strength to navigate life's challenges with purpose and confidence. As you continue to work with the North Star's energy, you will find that your decisions become more aligned, your path clearer, and your connection to the cosmos deeper.

In the ever-changing landscape of the night sky, the North Star remains a constant, reminding you that no matter how tumultuous life becomes, there is always a guiding light to lead you home to your true self. Embrace this celestial guide as a symbol of your inner wisdom, and let it illuminate your journey in the magical practice of living your most authentic path.

Chapter 5: Harnessing Constellation Energy

Constellations have been revered for millennia as both navigational guides and symbolic representations of divine power. In Star Magic, each constellation is seen as a cluster of stars radiating unique energies and attributes. By understanding the nature of these constellations and the mythologies behind them, practitioners can tap into their energies for various magical purposes, whether for protection, creativity, love, or spiritual growth. This chapter explores how to harness the energy of major constellations, breaking down their associated powers and providing practical methods for drawing upon their cosmic influence.

The Magic of Constellations

Constellations are more than just beautiful patterns in the night sky; they represent archetypal energies and stories that resonate within the human psyche. Ancient cultures across the world associated the stars with gods, heroes, animals, and symbols of power, each carrying specific qualities and magical properties. These stories formed the basis of constellational magic, where people invoked the power of the stars to influence their lives and surroundings.

In Star Magic, harnessing constellation energy involves connecting with the stars' collective essence and channeling their vibrations for particular needs. Each constellation carries distinct energies based on its mythological background, elemental nature, and astrological influence. By understanding these characteristics, you can intentionally draw on their power to enhance your magical practices.

The following sections outline some of the most prominent constellations, their associated powers, and how to harness their energies for different purposes.

Orion: The Hunter's Strength and Protection

Associated Powers: Strength, courage, protection, pursuit of goals
Mythological Background: Orion, one of the most recognizable constellations in the night sky, represents a mighty hunter from Greek mythology. He was known for his immense strength, bravery, and pur-

suit of grand adventures. After his death, the gods placed him among the stars as a tribute to his hunting prowess.

Harnessing Orion's Energy: Orion's energy is potent for protection, courage, and the pursuit of goals. To draw on this energy:

1. **Orion's Belt Meditation:** Locate Orion in the sky, focusing particularly on Orion's Belt—the three bright stars that form a straight line in the center of the constellation. Visualize the stars radiating a protective light that surrounds you, filling you with courage and strength. As you breathe in, imagine this light forming a shield around you, offering protection against negativity and fear. This meditation is especially useful before embarking on new challenges or when you need an extra boost of bravery.
2. **Hunter's Ritual:** During Orion's peak season (usually from November to February), create a talisman for strength and protection. Use natural materials like a small stone, arrowhead, or a piece of wood. Hold the item under Orion's light, saying, "Hunter of the stars, grant me your strength and protection. Guide my steps as I pursue my path." Keep this talisman with you as a symbol of Orion's protective and empowering energy.

The Pleiades: Mystical Wisdom and Nurturing Love

Associated Powers: Intuition, emotional healing, spiritual wisdom, nurturing love

Mythological Background: The Pleiades, often called the "Seven Sisters," are a cluster of stars that have been prominent in many cultural mythologies. In Greek mythology, they were the seven daughters of Atlas and Pleione, transformed into stars by Zeus to protect them from Orion's pursuit. Their energy is associated with the nurturing and mystical aspects of femininity, as well as a deep sense of unity and spiritual connection.

Harnessing Pleiades' Energy: The Pleiades' energy is perfect for enhancing intuition, emotional healing, and nurturing love. Here's how to connect with their mystical power:

1. **Pleiades Water Blessing:** To invoke emotional healing, prepare a bowl of water under the Pleiades' presence in the sky (usually visible in the fall and winter months). Place a piece of rose quartz in the water to represent love and healing. Hold your hands over the bowl and say, "Sisters of the stars, grant me your wisdom and healing. Pour your love into this water, so it may nurture my soul." Use this blessed water to wash your face or hands, symbolizing a cleansing of emotional wounds and an infusion of nurturing energy.
2. **Nurturing Love Spell:** For spells related to self-love or nurturing relationships, draw a small seven-pointed star (heptagram) to symbolize the Seven Sisters. Light a pink candle and place it beside the heptagram. Focus on the candle's flame, imagining the Pleiades' energy wrapping around you or your loved ones, filling the space with warmth and compassion. Chant, "Pleiades of love, stars of grace, nurture this heart and bless this space." Allow the candle to burn down safely as you keep the heptagram as a reminder of their loving guidance.

Draco: The Guardian's Power and Transformation

Associated Powers: Protection, transformation, wisdom, spiritual ascension

Mythological Background: Draco, the dragon constellation, is known in many cultures as a guardian of treasures and sacred knowledge. Its serpentine shape spirals around the northern celestial pole, evoking the image of a dragon guarding cosmic secrets. In mythology, dragons often symbolize transformation, power, and the boundary between the material and spiritual worlds.

Harnessing Draco's Energy: Draco's energy is ideal for protection, transformation, and exploring esoteric knowledge. To harness its power:

1. **Dragon's Breath Protection:** On a clear night when Draco is visible, light a green or black candle to represent the dragon's energy. Visualize the constellation glowing with a protective light. Breathe in deeply, imagining that you are drawing in the dragon's protective power, and breathe out, forming an energetic barrier around yourself. As you exhale, say, "Guardian of the stars, Draco, encircle me with your might. Shield me from harm, grant me your insight." Repeat this several times, each time strengthening the protective energy around you.
2. **Transformation Sigil:** Use Draco's shape—a coiling serpent or dragon—as the basis for a sigil that represents transformation. On a piece of paper, draw a spiral or coiled line. Within this symbol, write your intention for change or personal transformation. Place this sigil on your altar or carry it with you as a focus for Draco's transformative energy.

Leo: The Lion's Courage and Creative Power

Associated Powers: Courage, creativity, self-expression, leadership

Mythological Background: The constellation Leo is linked to the myth of the Nemean Lion, a creature of immense strength and pride, slain by the hero Hercules. Leo embodies qualities of nobility, confidence, and creative power, shining brightly in the sky with its distinctive "sickle" shape.

Harnessing Leo's Energy: Leo's energy is perfect for boosting confidence, creativity, and personal leadership. Here's how to draw on its influence:

1. **Lion's Roar Ritual:** To empower your voice and self-expression, perform this ritual under Leo's constellation, which is most visible in spring and early summer. Stand tall, facing the direction

of Leo in the sky. Visualize a golden lion within you, ready to unleash its power. As you take a deep breath, imagine the constellation's stars filling you with radiant light. On the exhale, let out a vocalized sound—a roar, hum, or chant—releasing any fears that hold back your creative potential. Affirm, "I roar with the strength of Leo, my voice rings true, my light shines bold."

2. **Creative Spark Candle Spell:** Place a gold or yellow candle on your altar, surrounded by symbols of creativity (such as a paintbrush, pen, or musical note). Light the candle and focus on Leo's position in the sky, feeling its vibrant energy fill your creative space. Say, "Leo, heart of the stars, ignite my passion, inspire my art." Let the candle burn as you engage in a creative activity, allowing Leo's energy to flow through your work.

Andromeda: Liberation and Overcoming Obstacles

Associated Powers: Liberation, resilience, overcoming challenges, freedom

Mythological Background: Andromeda, in Greek mythology, was a princess chained to a rock as a sacrifice to a sea monster, only to be rescued by the hero Perseus. The constellation represents themes of struggle, liberation, and the journey to freedom.

Harnessing Andromeda's Energy: Andromeda's energy is excellent for spells and rituals focused on liberation, breaking free from constraints, and overcoming obstacles:

1. **Chain-Breaking Ritual:** Under Andromeda's constellation, perform a ritual to break free from a personal limitation or fear. Take a piece of string or thread and tie knots in it, each representing a challenge or barrier you wish to overcome. Hold the string up towards Andromeda in the sky, saying, "Andromeda, star of liberation, help me break these chains of limitation." Visualize the stars' energy flowing into the knots. When ready, untie each knot slowly, releasing the constraints one by one. Dispose of the

thread by burying it or burning it safely, symbolizing the release of those obstacles.
2. **Liberation Sigil:** Create a sigil for freedom using Andromeda's star pattern as inspiration. Draw the outline of the constellation, and within it, write a word or symbol that represents your intention for liberation. Charge this sigil under Andromeda's light, allowing its energy to amplify your desire for freedom.

The Southern Cross: Faith and Guidance

Associated Powers: Faith, guidance, navigation, hope

Mythological Background: The Southern Cross is a prominent constellation in the southern hemisphere, often used for navigation and symbolic of finding one's way. Its cross-shaped pattern has been seen as a symbol of faith, spiritual guidance, and the promise of hope in difficult times.

Harnessing the Southern Cross's Energy: To draw on this constellation's energy for guidance and faith:

1. **Faith Candle Ritual:** Place a white candle on your altar to symbolize the light of the Southern Cross. Light the candle and focus on the constellation in the sky, feeling its guiding presence. Say, "Southern Cross, beacon of faith, guide me through darkness, light my way." Close your eyes and reflect on a situation where you need hope or direction. Allow the constellation's energy to fill you with the reassurance that you are on the right path.
2. **Guidance Talisman:** Create a simple talisman using a small cross or star symbol. Charge it under the Southern Cross's light, asking it to guide you whenever you feel lost or uncertain. Carry this talisman with you, holding it in times of need to connect with the constellation's steadying energy.

Conclusion

The constellations serve as gateways to specific energies, each radiating a unique cosmic influence that can be harnessed in Star Magic practices. By understanding the myths, qualities, and vibrations associated with each constellation, you gain access to a wealth of magical tools for protection, creativity, love, transformation, and guidance. As you work with these stellar powers, remember that the constellations are not just distant lights in the sky; they are living symbols of the universe's wisdom, ready to offer their energy to those who seek it. Embrace the stars as your allies, and let their light illuminate your magical path.

Chapter 6: Star Magic and the Moon Phases

In the practice of Star Magic, the Moon serves as an essential intermediary between the stars and Earth, amplifying and transforming stellar energy as it moves through its monthly cycle. The Moon is intimately connected to our emotions, intuition, and inner worlds, and its phases significantly influence the potency and nature of magical workings. Whether it's waxing, full, waning, or new, each phase of the Moon can enhance, alter, or direct the energies drawn from the stars. Understanding how to align your Star Magic rituals with the lunar cycle enables you to tap into this powerful synergy, creating more profound and effective outcomes in your magical practices.

This chapter explores the relationship between the Moon's phases and stellar energy, offering detailed insights into how each phase interacts with star magic rituals. By learning to work in harmony with the Moon's changing light, you can amplify your intentions, align with cosmic rhythms, and manifest your desires more effectively.

The Moon's Role in Star Magic

The Moon acts as a mirror, reflecting the light of the Sun and the stars, and serving as a conduit for celestial energy. Its cycle—from the dark new moon to the brilliant full moon and back again—marks the ebb and flow of universal energies, influencing the effectiveness of magical workings. In Star Magic, the Moon's phases are seen as a dynamic force that can enhance or redirect the stellar energies you harness during your rituals.

By understanding the nature of each lunar phase and its interaction with the stars, you can time your rituals to coincide with the most supportive cosmic forces, thereby maximizing the power of your intentions. Let's explore each phase of the Moon in detail and how it can be integrated into Star Magic practices.

The New Moon: Setting Intentions and Connecting with Hidden Star Energies

Key Characteristics: New beginnings, introspection, setting intentions, connecting with hidden or subtle star energies

Star Magic Focus: The new moon is a time of darkness, when the Moon is not visible in the sky. This phase symbolizes new beginnings, making it an ideal time for setting intentions and planting seeds for future growth. In Star Magic, the new moon's darkness is also seen as a veil that reveals subtle stellar energies, those that are often hidden or overshadowed by the brightness of the full moon.

How to Use New Moon Energy in Star Magic:

1. **Setting Intentions:** The new moon is the perfect time to align with stars that represent fresh starts, renewal, or hidden potential. Choose a constellation or star that embodies the qualities you wish to cultivate. For example, connect with Sirius, the star associated with rebirth and renewal in ancient Egyptian culture. During the new moon, focus on your intentions and visualize the chosen star's energy infusing your new beginnings with its power.

2. **Hidden Star Meditation:** The new moon's darkness allows you to connect with stars and constellations that symbolize mystery, intuition, and the unseen. Spend time meditating under the new moon's sky, imagining yourself surrounded by the stars' subtle energy. This is an opportune moment to work with constellations like the Pleiades, which embody mystical wisdom and spiritual guidance. Visualize their energies illuminating your path as you set intentions for the lunar month ahead.

3. **New Moon Star Ritual:** Create a ritual during the new moon that involves writing down your intentions on a piece of paper. Choose a star associated with your goal (e.g., Polaris for guidance, Leo for courage) and light a small candle to represent this star's energy. Hold the paper over the candle's light, saying, "Under the new moon's veil, I call upon [Star Name] to guide this intention

to fruition." Fold the paper and place it on your altar, allowing it to rest there as the moon grows.

The Waxing Moon: Growth, Manifestation, and Drawing in Stellar Energy

Key Characteristics: Growth, expansion, attraction, building momentum

Star Magic Focus: The waxing moon phase occurs as the moon moves from new to full, gradually increasing in light. This phase is associated with growth, attraction, and the gathering of energy. In Star Magic, the waxing moon amplifies the energy of stars related to abundance, creativity, and the forward momentum of your goals.

How to Use Waxing Moon Energy in Star Magic:

1. **Amplifying Stellar Energy:** During the waxing moon, work with stars and constellations that embody growth, power, and expansion. The constellation of Leo, with its association with courage and creativity, is particularly potent during this phase. To draw on Leo's energy, stand outside in the waxing moonlight and visualize Leo's stars shining brighter as they pour their courage and creative power into you.
2. **Growth Rituals:** Choose a star or constellation that resonates with your current intentions. For example, if you are working on a creative project, connect with the star Aldebaran in the constellation Taurus, known for its association with abundance and success. Write your intention on a piece of paper and place it under a crystal that represents growth, such as green aventurine. As the moon waxes, periodically hold the crystal and recite your intention, feeling the star's energy amplifying your desire.
3. **Waxing Moon Star Meditation:** Use this phase to meditate on the concept of growth. Find a quiet place outdoors or near a window where the waxing moon is visible. Close your eyes and imagine the energy of the stars flowing into you, growing brighter

and stronger with each breath. Visualize your intention as a seed within you, being nourished and expanding under the combined power of the moon and stars.

The Full Moon: Illumination, Amplification, and Stellar Power

Key Characteristics: Peak energy, illumination, culmination, manifestation

Star Magic Focus: The full moon represents the peak of the lunar cycle, radiating the maximum amount of light and energy. It is a time of illumination, manifestation, and the revelation of truths. In Star Magic, the full moon's brilliance magnifies the energies of stars, making it an ideal phase for rituals that require heightened power and focus.

How to Use Full Moon Energy in Star Magic:

1. **Amplifying Star Power:** During the full moon, work with stars and constellations that symbolize power, protection, and the culmination of intentions. Orion, the mighty hunter, is an excellent constellation to invoke during the full moon for protection and strength. Stand in the full moonlight and envision Orion's stars pouring their energy into you, strengthening your resolve and surrounding you with a protective aura.
2. **Manifestation Ritual:** On the night of the full moon, create a sacred space where you can focus on your desires. Choose a star that aligns with your intention, such as Regulus in Leo for success and recognition. Write your goal on a piece of paper and place it under the full moon's light, along with a symbol representing the chosen star. As you meditate, say, "Under the full moon's gaze, I call upon [Star Name] to manifest this desire with power and grace." Leave the paper and symbol out overnight to absorb the moon and star energy.
3. **Full Moon Star Bath:** Prepare a bath during the full moon, adding herbs or essential oils that correspond with the star you

wish to connect with (e.g., rosemary for mental clarity when working with the constellation Gemini). Place crystals or star symbols around the bath. As you soak, imagine the moonlight and star energy permeating the water, filling you with illumination and the strength to manifest your intentions.

The Waning Moon: Release, Transformation, and Clearing Star Energy

Key Characteristics: Release, banishment, transformation, letting go

Star Magic Focus: The waning moon phase occurs as the moon decreases in light, moving from full to new. This phase is associated with releasing, banishing, and clearing out old energies. In Star Magic, the waning moon's influence aids in working with stars related to endings, transformation, and purification.

How to Use Waning Moon Energy in Star Magic:

1. **Release Rituals:** During the waning moon, work with stars and constellations associated with transformation and letting go, such as the constellation Scorpio. To tap into Scorpio's energy for release, write down what you wish to let go of (e.g., fears, bad habits) on a piece of paper. Stand outside or near a window, focusing on Scorpio in the sky, if visible. Burn the paper safely, visualizing Scorpio's stars assisting you in transforming and purifying your energy.
2. **Cleansing with Stellar Energy:** Choose a star associated with purity and cleansing, like Spica in the constellation Virgo. Place a bowl of water outside under the waning moon's light, and hold a piece of quartz over the water, saying, "Spica of the stars, cleanse this water with your purity." Use this water to wash your hands or sprinkle around your space, allowing the combined energy of the waning moon and Spica to clear away negativity.

3. **Waning Moon Star Meditation:** Sit quietly under the waning moon's light, and imagine the energy of stars flowing through you, carrying away what no longer serves you. Visualize stars like Algol (in the constellation Perseus), known for its association with transformation and endings, assisting in removing obstacles and clearing your path for new beginnings.

Integrating Moon Phases into Your Star Magic Practice

Working with the Moon's phases in conjunction with stellar energies allows you to harness the natural ebb and flow of cosmic forces. Here are some additional tips for integrating moon phases into your Star Magic practice:

- **Create a Lunar Star Calendar:** Track the Moon's phases alongside the positions of stars and constellations. This calendar can help you plan rituals, meditations, and magical workings according to the most favorable lunar and stellar alignments.
- **Set Up a Moon-Star Altar:** Dedicate a space on your altar to represent both the Moon and stars. Include symbols for each lunar phase, such as a crescent for the waxing moon or a circle for the full moon. Add star imagery, crystals, and other items that correspond with the stars you work with regularly. Change the altar setup with each moon phase to reflect the energy you wish to invoke.
- **Lunar Journaling:** Keep a journal to document your Star Magic practices during different moon phases. Record your intentions, rituals, feelings, and the outcomes of your workings. Over time, you will begin to see patterns in how the Moon's phases influence your connection with stellar energies, allowing you to refine and deepen your practice.

Conclusion

The Moon's phases play a vital role in amplifying or shifting the energies of the stars, providing an ever-changing landscape of cosmic power for your magical workings. By aligning your Star Magic practices with the lunar cycle, you can enhance your rituals, attune to the natural flow of energy, and bring your intentions into harmony with the universe's rhythm. Whether you seek to set new intentions under the new moon, manifest your desires with the full moon, or release old patterns during the waning moon, the Moon acts as a powerful partner in your star magic journey, reflecting and channeling the vast energies of the stars directly into your life.

Chapter 7: Using Celestial Events—Solar Eclipses, Meteor Showers, and More

In the realm of Star Magic, celestial events like solar eclipses, meteor showers, and planetary alignments are considered windows of heightened cosmic energy. These occurrences alter the usual flow of stellar and planetary forces, offering unique opportunities for practitioners to connect with the universe and amplify their magical workings. The energies released during these events can be potent catalysts for transformation, illumination, and manifestation. Harnessing the power of these cosmic phenomena requires preparation, intention, and an understanding of the specific influences each event brings.

This chapter will explore how to prepare for and make the most of these celestial events in your Star Magic practice, offering rituals, meditations, and magical workings that align with their distinct energies.

The Power of Celestial Events in Star Magic

Celestial events create shifts in the energetic field of the universe, temporarily altering the dynamics of how cosmic forces interact. These moments can magnify intentions, reveal hidden truths, cleanse old energies, or open pathways to new possibilities. The ancients recognized the significance of these events, using them to mark important transitions, perform rituals, and seek guidance from the cosmos.

In Star Magic, celestial events are seen as cosmic signals, invitations from the universe to tune into specific energies that may not be as accessible at other times. By attuning to these events, you align your magical practice with the broader movements of the cosmos, creating a harmony between your intentions and the natural flow of universal energy.

Solar Eclipses: Times of Transformation and Revelation

Key Characteristics: Transformation, endings and beginnings, revelation, shadow work

Star Magic Focus: Solar eclipses are some of the most powerful celestial events in Star Magic. During a solar eclipse, the Moon passes between the Earth and the Sun, temporarily obscuring the Sun's light. This celestial phenomenon symbolizes a moment of transition, where the usual light of consciousness (the Sun) is shadowed, allowing hidden truths and deeper aspects of the self to surface.

How to Harness Solar Eclipse Energy:

1. **Preparation:** Solar eclipses occur a few times a year, so it's crucial to mark these dates on your calendar and prepare in advance. Spend the days leading up to the eclipse reflecting on areas of your life where you seek transformation or where hidden aspects may need to be brought to light. Set intentions for the kind of change or revelation you wish to experience.
2. **Solar Eclipse Ritual:** On the day of the eclipse, find a quiet outdoor location where you can observe the event safely. Bring a candle (preferably black or dark blue) to represent the eclipse's energy and a clear quartz crystal for amplifying your intentions. As the eclipse begins, light the candle and say, "Sun shadowed by Moon, reveal what lies within. I embrace transformation and open to the hidden truth." Sit quietly and meditate, allowing the eclipse's energy to wash over you. Hold the quartz in your hand, imagining it absorbing the transformative energy of the eclipse. Keep the crystal on your altar afterward as a reminder of the insights gained.
3. **Eclipse Meditation:** Solar eclipses are ideal for shadow work—exploring the hidden parts of the psyche that often remain in the background. As the Moon covers the Sun, close your eyes and visualize the darkness within you. Imagine the stars above you illuminating this inner darkness, revealing fears, de-

sires, or hidden talents that have been overshadowed by everyday consciousness. Reflect on what you see and how it relates to your current path. This meditation can lead to powerful insights and the release of old patterns.
4. **Post-Eclipse Integration:** After the eclipse, take time to journal about your experiences and insights. Solar eclipses often trigger periods of change that unfold over the following months. Use this time to integrate any revelations and take actionable steps toward transformation.

Lunar Eclipses: Releasing and Emotional Clearing

Key Characteristics: Release, emotional clearing, completion, heightened intuition

Star Magic Focus: A lunar eclipse occurs when the Earth passes between the Sun and the Moon, casting a shadow over the Moon. This event represents a time of emotional release, the culmination of cycles, and the clearing of stagnant energy. Lunar eclipses amplify the Moon's natural influence over our subconscious, making it an opportune time for deep emotional work and the completion of ongoing processes.

How to Harness Lunar Eclipse Energy:

1. **Preparation:** In the days leading up to a lunar eclipse, identify what you wish to release from your life. This could be negative emotions, old habits, limiting beliefs, or anything that no longer serves you. Write these on small pieces of paper to be used during the eclipse ritual.
2. **Lunar Eclipse Ritual:** On the night of the eclipse, create a sacred space outdoors where you can observe the Moon. Bring a white or silver candle and a small bowl of water. As the eclipse begins, light the candle and say, "Moon in shadow, I call upon your light to cleanse and release." One by one, take the pieces of paper and dip them into the water, imagining the energy of the lunar eclipse dissolving the negativity or attachments written on them. After-

ward, dispose of the paper and water safely, symbolizing the release of these energies.
3. **Emotional Clearing Meditation:** During the eclipse, close your eyes and visualize the Moon's energy washing over you. As the shadow covers the Moon, imagine it drawing out emotional blockages and old energy. When the shadow begins to recede, picture the stars filling the Moon with new, purified light. Breathe in this energy, feeling a sense of release and renewal.

Meteor Showers: Inspiration, Cosmic Wisdom, and Manifestation

Key Characteristics: Inspiration, cosmic messages, wish-making, sudden insights

Star Magic Focus: Meteor showers occur when the Earth passes through the debris left behind by comets. As these meteors burn up in the atmosphere, they create beautiful streaks of light across the sky. In Star Magic, meteor showers are seen as moments of cosmic inspiration and a time for wish-making. They symbolize sudden insights, flashes of creativity, and the arrival of messages from the stars.

How to Harness Meteor Shower Energy:

1. **Preparation:** Meteor showers have set annual dates (such as the Perseids in August and the Geminids in December). Mark these dates on your calendar, and plan to spend time outdoors under the stars. Before the shower, meditate on what you wish to manifest or the insights you seek from the cosmos.
2. **Meteor Shower Ritual:** During the peak of the meteor shower, lie on a blanket under the stars and relax. Bring a piece of paper and a pen to write down any inspirations or ideas that come to you. As you watch the meteors, silently make a wish or set an intention with each one you see. Whisper, "Stars in motion, cosmic flame, hear my wish and call my name." When the shower concludes, write down the wishes or insights that arose during the

experience. Keep this paper on your altar to remind you of the wishes cast during this celestial event.
3. **Cosmic Inspiration Meditation:** Meteor showers are ideal for connecting with higher wisdom and creative energies. As you watch the meteors, close your eyes and imagine their energy entering your mind, sparking new ideas and illuminating hidden knowledge. Allow yourself to be open to sudden flashes of insight, trusting that the universe is communicating with you through this celestial display.

Planetary Alignments: Harmonizing Energies and Amplifying Intentions

Key Characteristics: Harmonization, focus, amplification of specific energies

Star Magic Focus: Planetary alignments, or conjunctions, occur when two or more planets appear close together in the sky. These events create a blending of planetary energies, offering a unique opportunity to work with amplified cosmic forces. Different alignments bring various influences based on the planets involved, whether for love (Venus and Mars), communication (Mercury and Jupiter), or transformation (Saturn and Pluto).

How to Harness Planetary Alignment Energy:

1. **Preparation:** Research upcoming planetary alignments and their associated astrological influences. Determine what you want to work on or enhance in your life, and align your intentions with the energies of the planets involved in the conjunction.
2. **Planetary Alignment Ritual:** On the night of the alignment, set up an altar with symbols representing the planets involved (e.g., a rose quartz for Venus, a candle for Mars). Light candles of colors associated with the planets, and place a piece of paper in the center with your intention written on it. Say, "Planets aligned, energies entwined, grant my wish, my stars combined." Visualize

the combined energies of the planets infusing your intention with their power. Allow the candles to burn down safely as you meditate on the alignment's energy.
3. **Harmony Meditation:** During the alignment, find a quiet place outdoors. Sit comfortably and visualize the planets involved shining brightly in the sky, their energies intertwining and descending toward you. Imagine this combined energy filling your body, bringing harmony and focus to your intentions. Breathe deeply, feeling the alignment's power amplifying your inner strength and resolve.

Equinoxes and Solstices: Balance, Renewal, and Transition
Key Characteristics: Balance, renewal, transitions, seasonal changes
Star Magic Focus: The equinoxes (spring and autumn) and solstices (summer and winter) mark the changing of the seasons and are times of natural balance and transition. In Star Magic, these events represent opportunities to realign with the Earth's rhythms and the universe's cycle of light and darkness.
How to Harness Equinox and Solstice Energy:

1. **Preparation:** Equinoxes and solstices are predictable events that occur every year. Reflect on the seasonal themes they embody (growth for spring, harvest for autumn, introspection for winter, and abundance for summer) and how they resonate with your current path.
2. **Balance Ritual for the Equinox:** During the spring or autumn equinox, find a quiet spot outdoors. Bring two objects representing balance (e.g., a feather for air and a stone for earth). As the Sun sets or rises on the equinox, hold the objects in each hand, saying, "Equal day, equal night, balance my life, align my sight." Visualize the stars above you harmonizing with the Earth's energy, bringing balance into your life.

3. **Renewal Ritual for the Solstice:** During the summer or winter solstice, create a fire or light a candle. Write down what you wish to release (winter solstice) or what you wish to celebrate and grow (summer solstice). Burn the paper in the flame, saying, "Solstice fire, grant my desire, renew my soul, make me whole." Use the starry sky as a backdrop, imagining the stars amplifying the energy of renewal and transition.

Conclusion

Celestial events like solar and lunar eclipses, meteor showers, planetary alignments, and solstices are powerful moments that offer unique energies for your Star Magic practice. By preparing for and harnessing these events, you align your intentions with the broader movements of the cosmos, creating rituals and meditations that resonate with the universe's dynamic flow. These events serve as cosmic milestones, reminding us of our place in the vast celestial dance and offering opportunities for transformation, renewal, and manifestation. Embrace the power of these celestial occurrences, and let them become beacons of magical energy that guide your path through the star-filled journey of life.

Chapter 8: Working with the Fixed Stars

In the vast expanse of the night sky, certain stars hold a special place in the hearts of stargazers, astrologers, and magicians alike. These are the fixed stars, celestial bodies that appear to maintain their relative positions in the sky. Unlike the planets, which wander across the zodiac, fixed stars remain steadfast, marking their place with a constancy that has been recognized for millennia. Each fixed star carries a unique energy, mythology, and astrological influence, making them powerful allies in Star Magic rituals. This chapter delves into the significance of key fixed stars such as Aldebaran, Regulus, and Sirius, and explores how to harness their power in your magical practices.

The Nature and Significance of Fixed Stars

Fixed stars are some of the brightest and most ancient celestial bodies visible to the naked eye. They were used by ancient astronomers and astrologers to map the heavens, navigate the seas, and mark the passage of time. While they do move, their shifts are so minuscule over human lifetimes that they seem fixed in position, hence their name. Their relatively constant placement in the sky makes them anchors of specific energies, each star radiating its distinct influence.

In Star Magic, fixed stars are seen as cosmic beacons that embody the essence of certain qualities, archetypes, and spiritual truths. Working with these stars allows practitioners to tap into powerful forces that can aid in protection, manifestation, guidance, and spiritual growth. Each star has its own characteristics, symbolism, and magical associations, offering a variety of energies to draw upon in ritual work.

Key Fixed Stars and Their Energies

Let's explore some of the most prominent fixed stars, their mythological backgrounds, magical significance, and how to harness their power in Star Magic practices.

1. **Aldebaran: The Eye of the Bull**

   - **Location:** In the constellation Taurus
   - **Key Characteristics:** Power, success, courage, leadership
   - **Mythological Background:** Aldebaran, one of the four Royal Stars of Persia, is known as the "Eye of the Bull." In ancient mythology, it was associated with the archangel Michael, the warrior angel of protection. It represents strength, determination, and the unwavering focus of the bull.
   - **Magical Significance:** Aldebaran's energy is powerful for rituals involving success, leadership, protection, and courage. Its fiery essence provides a boost of strength and determination, helping you to overcome obstacles and pursue your goals with unwavering focus.

How to Work with Aldebaran:

1. **Courage Ritual:** To harness Aldebaran's energy for courage and strength, perform this ritual on a night when the star is visible. Set up an altar with symbols of power, such as a bull figurine or a piece of red jasper. Light a red candle to represent Aldebaran's fiery essence. As you focus on the star in the sky, say, "Aldebaran, Eye of the Bull, grant me your strength and courage. Help me face my challenges with the power of your light." Imagine the star's energy pouring into the candle flame, filling you with a sense of boldness and resolve. Allow the candle to burn down safely as you meditate on your intention.
2. **Success Meditation:** Sit in a quiet place where you can see Aldebaran or visualize it in your mind. Close your eyes and picture its glowing red light radiating towards you. As you breathe in, imagine this light filling you with the energy of success and de-

termination. Focus on a specific goal you want to achieve and see Aldebaran's light illuminating the path toward it. Repeat this meditation whenever you need to boost your confidence and motivation.

2. Regulus: The Heart of the Lion

- **Location:** In the constellation Leo
- **Key Characteristics:** Honor, ambition, success, authority, fame
- **Mythological Background:** Regulus, also one of the four Royal Stars, is known as the "Heart of the Lion." It has been associated with nobility, leadership, and the divine right of kings. In ancient Persia, it was linked to the archangel Raphael, representing healing and guidance.
- **Magical Significance:** Regulus embodies qualities of authority, honor, ambition, and success. Working with Regulus can help amplify your inner power, increase your confidence, and guide you toward positions of influence and leadership. It is also a star of fame, making it a powerful ally in rituals aimed at recognition and achievement.

How to Work with Regulus:

1. **Authority and Leadership Ritual:** On a night when Regulus is visible, create an altar using symbols of royalty, such as a crown, lion statue, or gold candle. Light the candle and focus on Regulus, saying, "Regulus, Heart of the Lion, grant me your strength and wisdom. Help me lead with honor and shine with the light of your stars." Visualize the star's radiant energy enveloping you, filling you with a sense of dignity and confidence. Carry this energy into your daily life, particularly in situations where you need to assert authority or step into a leadership role.

2. **Fame and Recognition Spell:** Write your name on a piece of paper along with a symbol that represents your ambition (such as a crown for leadership or a star for success). Light a gold candle and place the paper under the candleholder. As you gaze at Regulus, say, "Regulus, star of honor, let my name shine with your light. Grant me the recognition I seek, as the lion's heart glows bright." Let the candle burn down safely, then keep the paper on your altar or in a special place to remind you of your intention.

3. Sirius: The Dog Star and Spiritual Guide

- **Location:** In the constellation Canis Major
- **Key Characteristics:** Spiritual awakening, intuition, guidance, prosperity
- **Mythological Background:** Sirius, known as the "Dog Star," has been revered in many cultures as a star of great spiritual significance. In ancient Egypt, it was associated with the goddess Isis and the annual flooding of the Nile, symbolizing fertility, abundance, and renewal. In esoteric traditions, Sirius is considered a portal to higher spiritual realms.
- **Magical Significance:** Sirius embodies the energies of spiritual awakening, intuition, and guidance. It is often called the "spiritual sun" and is believed to illuminate the path of the soul. Working with Sirius can help deepen your intuition, enhance spiritual growth, and attract prosperity and abundance.

How to Work with Sirius:

1. **Intuition and Spiritual Guidance Ritual:** On a night when Sirius is visible, go outside and find a quiet place to connect with its energy. Light a blue candle to represent Sirius and place a clear quartz crystal beside it. As you focus on the star, say, "Sirius, Dog Star of wisdom, open my mind to your light. Illuminate my path

with your guidance and reveal the truth in sight." Sit quietly and meditate, allowing any insights or intuitive messages to come to you. Keep the quartz crystal on your altar as a conduit for Sirius's energy, enhancing your intuition in daily life.

2. **Prosperity Spell:** For abundance and prosperity, work with Sirius during its heliacal rising (usually in late summer). Fill a small bowl with water and place silver coins or charms in it to symbolize wealth. Hold the bowl up toward Sirius, saying, "Sirius, star of abundance, bring prosperity into my life. As your light fills the night, so shall my fortune grow bright." Leave the bowl on your windowsill overnight to absorb the star's energy. The next day, pour the water into the earth as an offering, and keep the coins or charms in your prosperity area (e.g., a money altar or purse).

4. Spica: The Harvest Star

- **Location:** In the constellation Virgo
- **Key Characteristics:** Abundance, harvest, creativity, clarity, wisdom
- **Mythological Background:** Spica, the brightest star in Virgo, is associated with the goddess of the harvest and the bounties of the Earth. In mythology, it represents the ear of wheat held by Virgo, symbolizing nourishment, abundance, and the fruitfulness of hard work.
- **Magical Significance:** Spica is a star of abundance, creativity, and wisdom. It carries a nurturing energy that supports the manifestation of intentions and the harvest of one's efforts. Working with Spica can help bring clarity, enhance creative projects, and attract abundance into your life.

How to Work with Spica:

1. **Abundance Ritual:** On a night when Spica is visible, create an altar with symbols of abundance, such as wheat, grains, or coins. Light a green or gold candle to represent prosperity. As you focus on Spica, say, "Spica, star of the harvest, bring forth abundance in my life. May my work bear fruit, and my efforts be rewarded." Visualize the star's light pouring into your altar, infusing it with the energy of abundance. Keep some grains or coins on your altar as a talisman for ongoing prosperity.
2. **Creativity and Clarity Meditation:** Sit quietly and gaze at Spica in the sky or visualize it in your mind. Imagine its light shining down on you, filling your mind with clarity and creative inspiration. As you breathe in, feel this energy expanding within you, breaking through mental blocks and opening channels of creativity. Use this meditation whenever you need to gain clarity or inspiration for a project.

5. Antares: The Heart of the Scorpion

- **Location:** In the constellation Scorpius
- **Key Characteristics:** Transformation, power, intensity, spiritual insight
- **Mythological Background:** Antares, often referred to as the "Heart of the Scorpion," is known for its deep red hue and association with intensity, power, and transformation. In ancient astrology, it was considered one of the four Royal Stars, symbolizing the power to face life's challenges and embrace change.
- **Magical Significance:** Antares embodies the energies of transformation, spiritual insight, and intensity. It is a star of profound power that can help in overcoming obstacles, exploring the depths of the psyche, and embracing personal transformation.

How to Work with Antares:

1. **Transformation Ritual:** On a night when Antares is visible, create an altar using symbols of transformation, such as a snake or phoenix. Light a red or black candle to represent the star's intense energy. As you focus on Antares, say, "Antares, Heart of the Scorpion, guide me through the darkness. Transform my fear into strength, my pain into power." Visualize the star's energy surrounding you, helping you shed old layers and embrace your true self.
2. **Shadow Work Meditation:** Sit quietly and focus on Antares, allowing its red light to fill your mind. This star's energy is ideal for exploring hidden aspects of the psyche. As you meditate, ask Antares to reveal any fears, shadows, or blocks that need transformation. Allow insights to arise naturally, and use this time to acknowledge and work through these deeper aspects.

Integrating Fixed Stars into Your Star Magic Practice

Working with fixed stars involves more than simply knowing their names and meanings; it requires building a relationship with their energy over time. Here are some tips for integrating fixed stars into your regular practice:

1. **Create a Star Journal:** Keep a journal to document your experiences and rituals with different fixed stars. Record dates, intentions, and any insights or changes that occur. This practice helps you track your interactions with these celestial energies and deepen your understanding of their influence.
2. **Star Altars:** Dedicate space on your altar to the fixed stars you work with regularly. Include symbols, candles, crystals, or objects that correspond to each star's energy. Change the altar's setup depending on the star you are currently invoking, keeping it attuned to their unique vibrations.

3. **Timing Rituals:** Research the dates when specific fixed stars are most prominent (e.g., heliacal rising) and plan rituals around these times for maximum effect. The stars' positions in relation to the Moon phases can also amplify their power, allowing you to combine lunar and stellar energies in your practices.

Conclusion

Fixed stars are the ancient guardians of the night sky, each radiating a unique energy that can be harnessed in your Star Magic practices. By understanding the characteristics, mythologies, and magical associations of stars like Aldebaran, Regulus, Sirius, Spica, and Antares, you gain access to a wealth of cosmic power. These stars serve as celestial allies, guiding you toward courage, success, spiritual insight, and transformation. Whether you seek protection, abundance, clarity, or inner strength, the fixed stars are there to light your path and amplify your magic. Embrace their steadfast presence in the sky and let their energy illuminate your journey through the universe.

Chapter 9: Creating Your Star Magic Altar

In Star Magic, an altar serves as a sacred space where the celestial energies of the stars, moon, and planets can be honored, channeled, and worked with. It acts as a focal point for your intentions and rituals, providing a physical manifestation of your connection with the universe. A Star Magic altar is a powerful tool that enhances your practice by grounding stellar energy and bringing cosmic forces into your everyday life.

This chapter will guide you through the process of creating a personal altar dedicated to Star Magic. From choosing the right tools and selecting crystals to using symbols and objects that resonate with stellar energies, you will learn how to build a space that reflects your unique relationship with the cosmos. Additionally, this chapter will provide rituals to consecrate your altar, ensuring it is a place of potent and clear energy for your magical workings.

The Purpose of a Star Magic Altar

A Star Magic altar is a sacred place that helps you focus your energy and intentions while creating a direct link to the stars. It is where you can perform rituals, meditate, and connect with celestial energies. This altar serves multiple purposes:

- **Focal Point for Rituals:** It provides a space where you can perform your star-related rituals, spells, and meditations.
- **Anchor for Stellar Energy:** The altar acts as a physical anchor for cosmic energies, drawing them into your personal space.
- **Tool for Intention Setting:** By placing objects, symbols, and crystals that represent various stars, constellations, or planetary

energies, the altar becomes a powerful tool for setting and manifesting intentions.
- **Personal Reflection:** It reflects your journey in Star Magic, growing and evolving as you deepen your practice.

Your Star Magic altar can be as simple or as elaborate as you wish. The most important aspect is that it resonates with your energy and intention.

Choosing a Location for Your Star Magic Altar

Selecting the right location for your altar is crucial to create an effective and harmonious space. Here are some tips to guide you:

1. **Direction:** Traditionally, altars are set up facing a specific direction that aligns with your practice. For Star Magic, you might choose to face north, aligning with the North Star (Polaris) as a symbol of guidance and constancy. Alternatively, you could face east to welcome the rising stars and the energy of new beginnings.
2. **Space:** Select a quiet, undisturbed area where you can focus on your practice. It could be a dedicated room, a corner of your bedroom, a tabletop, or even a window ledge. Ensure it's a space where you feel comfortable and connected.
3. **Natural Light:** If possible, place your altar near a window where it can receive moonlight or starlight. This placement will enhance the altar's connection to celestial energies, particularly during significant lunar phases or celestial events.
4. **Clean and Clear:** Before setting up your altar, cleanse the space energetically. This can be done through smudging with sage, sprinkling saltwater, or using sound (such as a bell or singing bowl) to clear any stagnant or negative energies.

Tools and Items for Your Star Magic Altar

Your altar can include a variety of items that represent the stars, planets, moon phases, constellations, and cosmic energies. Each item you place on the altar adds to its magical potency and helps to ground the celestial energies into your practice. Here are some essential tools and items to consider:

1. Candles

Candles are a primary tool in Star Magic rituals. They symbolize the light of the stars and act as beacons to draw celestial energy into your space. When selecting candles for your altar, consider the following:

- **Colors:** Choose colors that correspond with the star or planetary energy you wish to work with. For example, a blue candle might represent Sirius, while a gold candle can symbolize Regulus.
- **Sizes:** Use small tea lights for daily rituals or larger pillar candles for more significant celestial events and workings.
- **Placement:** Place candles on your altar to represent stars, planets, or constellations you wish to invoke. You can arrange them in patterns that mimic the night sky, such as forming the shape of a specific constellation.

2. Crystals

Crystals act as conduits for stellar energy, each with its unique vibration that can align with different stars, planets, or celestial events. Here are some crystals commonly associated with Star Magic:

- **Clear Quartz:** Known as the "Master Healer," clear quartz amplifies energy and intention. It can be programmed to resonate with any star or celestial body.
- **Moonstone:** Closely connected to lunar energies, moonstone is ideal for working with moon phases and reflecting the nurturing energy of the stars.
- **Lapis Lazuli:** This deep blue stone is associated with cosmic wisdom, making it a powerful ally when working with stars such as Sirius and constellations like Orion.

- **Citrine:** Linked to the energy of the Sun and stars like Regulus, citrine can be used to attract success, abundance, and positivity.
- **Amethyst:** Resonating with spiritual insight and higher consciousness, amethyst is ideal for connecting with stars like Spica and celestial events like meteor showers.

Place crystals on your altar in ways that correspond with your current intentions. For example, you might create a "star grid" using quartz points arranged in the shape of a specific constellation to channel that star's energy.

3. Star and Planet Symbols

Incorporate symbols that represent stars, constellations, planets, and celestial bodies you work with:

- **Star Maps:** A small star map or image of a constellation can serve as a visual focus for drawing in specific stellar energies.
- **Astrological Symbols:** Use symbols for the Sun, Moon, and planets, either as carved stones, printed images, or metal charms.
- **Constellation Figures:** Figurines or symbols that represent constellations (e.g., a lion for Leo or a bull for Taurus) can enhance the connection to these cosmic energies.

4. Altar Cloths and Decor

The cloth and decorations on your altar set the tone for your Star Magic practice:

- **Altar Cloth:** Choose an altar cloth with a starry night sky design, celestial symbols, or colors that resonate with your intention (e.g., silver or black for the moon, blue for Sirius).
- **Decorations:** Add items like star-shaped ornaments, feathers (to represent air and the vastness of space), or small bowls of water to symbolize the cosmic ocean.

5. Candles, Incense, and Offerings

Candles and incense can invoke specific energies and aid in meditation and focus during rituals. Choose scents that correspond with the stars or energies you're working with:

- **Incense:** Frankincense, sandalwood, and myrrh are traditional resins that elevate the atmosphere of the altar, opening channels to higher realms.
- **Offerings:** Add small bowls for offerings, such as water (to honor the moon), flowers, grains, or crystals as a gift to the stars and celestial beings.

6. Divination Tools

Include divination tools that help you connect with the stars' guidance:

- **Tarot or Oracle Cards:** Choose decks that feature stars, astrology, or cosmic themes. Use them to draw cards during rituals for insight and guidance.
- **Pendulums:** A pendulum made of a star-associated crystal (like lapis lazuli) can be used for dowsing and seeking answers from the stars.

Consecrating Your Star Magic Altar

Once your altar is set up, it's essential to consecrate it to align its energy with your intentions and the celestial forces you will work with. Consecrating your altar sets the tone for it to become a sacred space for your Star Magic practice.

1. Cleansing the Space

Before consecrating, cleanse the space energetically to remove any lingering negativity. This can be done in several ways:

- **Smudging:** Burn sage, palo santo, or another cleansing herb. Wave the smoke over your altar, visualizing it purifying the area.
- **Saltwater:** Mix a small amount of sea salt with water and lightly sprinkle it around your altar, saying, "By earth and water, I cleanse this space."
- **Sound:** Ring a bell or use a singing bowl to create vibrations that disperse negative energy.

2. Calling on Celestial Energies

To consecrate your altar, you will invite the energies of specific stars, constellations, and celestial bodies to bless and empower the space.

- **Set Your Intentions:** Sit before your altar and take a few deep breaths to center yourself. Set your intentions for the altar, stating that it is a sacred space for connecting with stellar energies and performing Star Magic.
- **Light the Candles:** Light the candles on your altar, starting with one that represents a guiding star (such as the North Star or Sirius). Say, "I call upon the stars above, fill this altar with your light. May this space be a beacon of cosmic energy, guiding me on my path."
- **Invoke the Stars:** Visualize a beam of light extending from the star or constellation you are invoking, descending into the altar. For example, if you are calling upon Aldebaran, imagine a red glow surrounding the altar, filling it with the star's strength and power.

3. Consecration Ritual

Perform a consecration ritual to solidify the altar's energy. Here's a simple but powerful ritual:

- **Materials:** Gather a small dish of salt (Earth), a bowl of water (Water), a candle (Fire), and incense (Air).

- **Invoke the Elements:** Stand before the altar and say, "I call upon the elements to bless this space. By Earth (hold the salt), by Water (hold the bowl), by Fire (light the candle), and by Air (light the incense), may this altar be sacred and charged with the energy of the stars."
- **Consecrate the Tools:** Pass each item on the altar through the smoke of the incense, the flame of the candle, and sprinkle lightly with salt and water. As you do so, say, "[Item Name], I consecrate you to serve as a vessel for the energy of the stars."
- **Seal the Space:** Close your eyes and visualize the altar surrounded by a glowing sphere of light. Imagine this sphere expanding outward, forming a protective boundary that only allows in positive, cosmic energy. Say, "By the light of the stars, this altar is now consecrated. May it be a space of wisdom, guidance, and celestial power."

Maintaining Your Star Magic Altar

An altar is a living space that changes as your practice evolves. Here are some tips for maintaining and refreshing your altar:

1. **Regular Cleansing:** Cleanse the altar space periodically, especially after intense rituals or during the new moon to reset the energy.
2. **Seasonal Changes:** Update your altar to reflect celestial events, moon phases, and seasonal changes. For example, add solar symbols during the summer solstice or use a silver cloth for a full moon ritual.
3. **Daily Use:** Spend time at your altar daily, even if it's just for a moment to light a candle or meditate. This practice strengthens your connection to the celestial energies and keeps the altar charged.

Conclusion

Creating a Star Magic altar is an enriching and empowering experience that deepens your connection with the stars. By selecting meaningful items, setting up the altar with intention, and consecrating it with ritual, you establish a sacred space that serves as a gateway to the cosmos. Your altar becomes a reflection of your personal journey through the stars, evolving as you explore the vast energies of the universe. As you continue to work with your altar, you will find it becoming a wellspring of guidance, strength, and stellar magic that lights your path through the celestial mysteries.

Chapter 10: Star Magic for Manifestation

Manifestation is the art of bringing desires into reality through focused intention, energy, and action. In the realm of Star Magic, the stars act as powerful cosmic amplifiers that can enhance your ability to manifest your desires. By aligning with specific stellar energies, you can tap into the universe's rhythm to attract abundance, love, health, and success. This chapter explores how to draw down the power of the stars for manifestation, including detailed spells and rituals designed to channel stellar energy toward your goals.

The Fundamentals of Manifestation in Star Magic

In Star Magic, manifestation revolves around aligning your intentions with the specific qualities of stars, constellations, and celestial events. The stars' energy serves as a cosmic backdrop that can strengthen and guide your desires, enhancing the probability of their manifestation. Here are the key principles of manifestation in Star Magic:

1. **Intention Setting:** Clearly define what you want to manifest. The stars respond best to specific and focused intentions, so take time to articulate your desires in detail. Whether you seek love, wealth, health, or success, your intention should resonate with the star's energy you plan to work with.
2. **Stellar Alignment:** Choose the star, constellation, or celestial event that aligns with your desire. For example, work with Regulus for success and recognition, Sirius for spiritual growth, or the Pleiades for love and nurturing energy. By aligning your intention with a stellar energy that complements it, you amplify the cosmic power behind your manifestation.
3. **Ritual Timing:** Timing is crucial in Star Magic. Perform manifestation rituals when the star you're working with is visible or during an appropriate moon phase or celestial event. For example, use the waxing moon for attracting and building energy, or per-

form a ritual during a meteor shower for sudden insights and opportunities.
4. **Channeled Energy:** Drawing down star energy requires focus and visualization. As you perform your rituals, imagine the star's light pouring into your space and intention, filling it with cosmic power. This channeled energy creates a link between your desire and the vast potential of the universe.

Spells and Rituals for Manifesting with Star Magic

Here, we explore various spells and rituals designed to harness stellar energy for manifesting abundance, love, health, and success. These rituals are adaptable; feel free to modify them according to your needs and the stars that resonate with you.

1. Manifesting Abundance with Aldebaran

Aldebaran, known as the "Eye of the Bull," is a star associated with power, wealth, and success. Its strong, steady energy makes it ideal for rituals aimed at attracting abundance in all forms.

Ritual: The Eye of Prosperity
Tools Needed:

- Green candle (symbolizing abundance)
- A small bowl of salt (symbolizing the Earth's wealth)
- Citrine crystal (for prosperity)
- A coin (to represent financial success)
- A piece of paper and pen

Instructions:

1. Choose a night when Aldebaran is visible in the sky, preferably during the waxing or full moon to amplify growth.
2. Set up your altar with the green candle, bowl of salt, citrine, and coin. Write your specific abundance intention on the piece of paper (e.g., "I attract financial prosperity and stability into my life").

3. Light the green candle and focus on Aldebaran in the sky, visualizing it as a bright, red-tinged beacon of prosperity.
4. Hold the citrine in your hands and say, "Aldebaran, Eye of the Bull, I call upon your strength and abundance. Guide me to the wealth I seek. May my path be steady, and my harvest full."
5. Place the coin in the bowl of salt, followed by the paper with your intention. As you do, visualize Aldebaran's light pouring into the bowl, infusing the salt, coin, and paper with its prosperous energy.
6. Leave the bowl on your altar until the next full moon, then bury the salt in the earth as a symbol of grounding your intentions into reality. Keep the coin as a talisman for continued abundance.

2. Attracting Love with the Pleiades

The Pleiades, or the "Seven Sisters," are a cluster of stars known for their nurturing and loving energy. Working with the Pleiades is ideal for manifesting love, compassion, and deep emotional connections.

Spell: The Starry Embrace
Tools Needed:

- Pink candle (symbolizing love)
- Rose quartz crystal (for attracting love)
- A small bowl of water (symbolizing emotional flow)
- Rose petals
- A piece of pink paper and pen

Instructions:

1. Perform this ritual on a night when the Pleiades are visible, preferably during the waxing moon to attract love.
2. Set up your altar with the pink candle, bowl of water, rose quartz, and rose petals. Write your love intention on the pink paper (e.g., "I attract a loving, compassionate relationship into my life").

3. Light the pink candle and focus on the Pleiades in the sky. Imagine their soft, shimmering light descending upon you, enveloping you in warmth and comfort.
4. Hold the rose quartz in your hand and say, "Pleiades, Sisters of Love, fill my heart with your gentle light. Draw to me a love that is kind, nurturing, and true."
5. Sprinkle the rose petals into the bowl of water, followed by placing the pink paper underneath the bowl. As you do, visualize the Pleiades' energy infusing the water, petals, and paper with the essence of love.
6. Leave the bowl on your altar overnight to absorb the star energy. The next morning, use the water to wash your hands or sprinkle around your space to attract loving vibrations. Keep the rose quartz near you as a love magnet.

3. Enhancing Health with Spica

Spica, the brightest star in the constellation Virgo, is associated with health, nourishment, and well-being. Its gentle and nurturing energy makes it perfect for rituals aimed at healing and physical vitality.

Ritual: The Star of Health
Tools Needed:

- White candle (for healing)
- A small bowl of salt water (symbolizing purification)
- Amethyst crystal (for health and spiritual healing)
- A sprig of rosemary (for protection and health)
- A piece of white paper and pen

Instructions:

1. Choose a night when Spica is visible, ideally during the waxing moon to promote healing and vitality.

2. Set up your altar with the white candle, bowl of salt water, amethyst, and rosemary. Write your health intention on the white paper (e.g., "I manifest vibrant health and well-being in my body and mind").
3. Light the white candle and focus on Spica in the sky, envisioning its soft, white light as a beam of healing energy.
4. Hold the amethyst in your hand and say, "Spica, star of the harvest, bless me with your healing light. Nourish my body, mind, and spirit with vitality and strength."
5. Place the rosemary sprig in the salt water and then place the white paper underneath the bowl. As you do, visualize Spica's healing energy filling the water, rosemary, and paper.
6. Leave the bowl on your altar overnight. In the morning, use the salt water to anoint your hands, forehead, and heart, saying, "Spica, your light flows through me, bringing health and peace." Keep the amethyst on your person as a charm for continued health.

4. Manifesting Success with Regulus

Regulus, the "Heart of the Lion," is a star associated with honor, leadership, and success. Its regal energy makes it an excellent star for rituals focused on achieving personal or professional success.

Spell: The Lion's Triumph
Tools Needed:

- Gold candle (for success)
- A small dish of honey (symbolizing the sweetness of success)
- A citrine crystal (for prosperity and success)
- A piece of gold or yellow paper and pen

Instructions:

1. Perform this spell on a night when Regulus is visible, preferably during the waxing or full moon.
2. Set up your altar with the gold candle, dish of honey, and citrine. Write your success intention on the gold paper (e.g., "I manifest recognition and success in my career").
3. Light the gold candle and focus on Regulus in the sky. Imagine its golden light shining down upon you, filling you with confidence and ambition.
4. Hold the citrine crystal and say, "Regulus, Heart of the Lion, bestow upon me your strength and honor. Guide my steps to success, let my efforts be known and rewarded."
5. Dip your finger into the honey and trace a small star on the gold paper, symbolizing Regulus's energy. Visualize the star's light merging with the honey, infusing your intention with sweetness and success.
6. Leave the dish of honey on your altar for three days. Afterward, use a small amount of the honey to anoint your wrists and throat before engaging in activities related to your intention (e.g., job interviews, presentations). Keep the citrine near you as a success talisman.

Tips for Successful Star Magic Manifestation

- **Gratitude:** After performing each ritual, express gratitude to the stars and the universe for their guidance and assistance. This gratitude enhances the flow of positive energy and strengthens your connection with the cosmos.
- **Consistency:** Regularly revisit your intentions, particularly during appropriate moon phases or celestial events. Manifestation is an ongoing process that requires alignment and dedication.

- **Trust:** Trust in the power of the stars and the process of manifestation. Release any doubts or anxieties, allowing the universe to work in its own timing and manner.

Conclusion

Star Magic provides a profound way to manifest your desires by aligning them with the cosmic energies of the stars. Whether you seek abundance, love, health, or success, the stars offer an infinite reservoir of power that you can draw upon to shape your reality. By setting clear intentions, performing rituals at the right times, and channeling stellar energy into your goals, you harness the universe's rhythm to amplify your manifestation efforts. As you work with the stars in this magical process, you create a celestial partnership that not only brings your desires into being but also deepens your connection to the cosmos.

Chapter 11: Protection Through Star Magic

The stars have long been revered as celestial guardians, their distant light offering guidance, wisdom, and, most importantly, protection. In Star Magic, you can draw upon the stars' powerful energies to create barriers against negativity, ward off harmful influences, and ensure safety. By channeling specific stellar forces, you can create protective shields, talismans, and amulets that embody the stars' light, offering potent defenses in both the physical and spiritual realms.

This chapter provides an in-depth exploration of how to use star energy for protection. You will learn rituals to form protective shields around yourself, your home, and your loved ones, as well as methods for creating talismans and amulets imbued with the power of the stars. With these practices, you can invoke the ancient, steadfast guardians of the sky to watch over and safeguard your path.

The Nature of Protection in Star Magic

Protection through Star Magic involves invoking specific stars and constellations that have historically been associated with strength, vigilance, and guardianship. Stars like Aldebaran, Sirius, and Polaris possess energies that can be harnessed to shield against physical harm, psychic attacks, negative influences, and ill intentions. These celestial bodies emit a constant light, symbolizing an eternal presence that you can draw upon to establish a protective field around yourself or your space.

Protection in Star Magic is multifaceted and can be adapted to suit various situations, including:

- **Personal Protection:** Establishing a shield around your energy to ward off negativity, ill wishes, and psychic attacks.
- **Home and Space Protection:** Creating a protective barrier around your living space to keep out unwanted energies or influences.

- **Protection Talismans and Amulets:** Crafting physical objects imbued with star energy to carry or place in strategic locations as a continual source of safeguarding.

Creating Protective Shields Using Star Energy

One of the most direct methods of invoking star energy for protection is to create a shield or barrier. This shield can be constructed through visualization and ritual, calling upon the power of a specific star or constellation to form an energetic defense.

1. Aldebaran's Shield of Strength

Aldebaran, known as the "Eye of the Bull," radiates the energy of strength, courage, and protection. This ritual uses Aldebaran's power to create a shield that surrounds you, offering a formidable barrier against negativity and harm.

Ritual: Aldebaran's Protective Shield
Tools Needed:

- A red candle (representing Aldebaran's fiery energy)
- A piece of red jasper (for grounding and protection)
- A small bowl of salt (to anchor the shield to the physical realm)

Instructions:

1. Perform this ritual on a night when Aldebaran is visible, ideally during the waning moon to banish negativity.
2. Set up your altar with the red candle, red jasper, and bowl of salt. Light the candle and focus on Aldebaran in the sky, visualizing its red glow brightening and intensifying.
3. Hold the red jasper in your hands and say, "Aldebaran, Eye of the Bull, grant me your strength. Surround me with your shield, protecting me from all harm."
4. Visualize a vibrant, fiery red light emanating from Aldebaran, descending toward you and forming a protective sphere around

your body. See this light solidifying into a shield, pulsating with the strength and courage of the bull.
5. Sprinkle some salt around you in a circle, grounding the shield into the physical realm, and say, "By earth and star, this shield is formed. None shall pass, harm be warned."
6. Keep the red jasper in your pocket or wear it as a protective charm. Repeat this visualization daily to reinforce the shield, especially when feeling vulnerable or exposed to negativity.

2. Sirius's Light of Safeguarding

Sirius, the "Dog Star," is often associated with guardianship and loyalty. Its radiant, almost blinding light can be channeled to create a protective aura that repels negative energies and entities.

Ritual: Sirius's Protective Light
Tools Needed:

- A blue candle (to represent Sirius's energy)
- A piece of clear quartz (for amplifying protective energy)
- A small mirror (to reflect negativity away)

Instructions:

1. Choose a night when Sirius is visible, preferably during the full moon to maximize its protective power.
2. Set up your altar with the blue candle, clear quartz, and mirror. Light the candle and focus on Sirius, envisioning its brilliant blue-white light descending toward you.
3. Hold the clear quartz in your hand and say, "Sirius, Guardian of the Stars, surround me with your light. Reflect all harm away, shield me with your sight."
4. Visualize Sirius's light forming a sphere around you, shimmering and pulsating like a protective bubble. Place the mirror facing

outward on your altar, symbolizing the reflection and deflection of any negative energy directed toward you.
5. Keep the clear quartz near you or carry it as a talisman, allowing it to maintain the protective aura throughout your day.

Protecting Your Home with Star Magic

Your home is your sanctuary, and protecting it from unwanted energies is essential for creating a harmonious environment. In Star Magic, you can establish a celestial barrier around your living space, invoking the protective energies of stars and constellations.

3. Polaris's Star Barrier for the Home

Polaris, the North Star, is a symbol of guidance, stability, and protection. By calling upon Polaris, you can create a star barrier around your home that shields it from negative influences and harmful energies.

Ritual: Polaris's Star Barrier
Tools Needed:

- A white candle (representing Polaris's steady light)
- A bowl of saltwater (for purification)
- Four small stones (to represent the four corners of your home)
- A star map or compass (to find true north)

Instructions:

1. Choose a clear night to perform this ritual when Polaris is visible. Begin by finding true north using a compass or star map to align yourself with the North Star.
2. Set up your altar with the white candle and bowl of saltwater. Light the candle and say, "Polaris, Star of the North, I call upon your light. Guard this home, protect its walls, keep all harm from sight."

3. Dip your fingers into the saltwater and sprinkle it around the perimeter of your home, envisioning it purifying and strengthening the space.
4. Place the four stones at the four corners of your home (north, south, east, and west) to form a protective boundary. As you place each stone, visualize a beam of light connecting them, creating a star-shaped barrier around your home.
5. Once the barrier is complete, return to your altar and say, "By Polaris's light, this star barrier is formed. My home is safe, its walls are warm." Allow the candle to burn down safely, and keep the stones in place to maintain the barrier's strength.

Creating Protective Talismans and Amulets with Star Energy

Talismans and amulets are powerful objects imbued with protective star energy that you can carry with you or place in specific locations. These items act as physical vessels for the stars' light, continually radiating protection.

4. Crafting a Star Talisman

A talisman can be crafted to embody the protective energy of a specific star. Here, we'll create a talisman using the energy of Antares, known as the "Heart of the Scorpion," which is associated with vigilance, strength, and overcoming challenges.

Instructions:

1. **Choose Your Material:** Select a piece of jewelry or stone (such as obsidian or black tourmaline) to serve as your talisman. These stones naturally enhance protective energies.
2. **Consecrate the Talisman:** On a night when Antares is visible, hold the talisman in your hands and light a red candle. Focus on Antares in the sky and say, "Antares, Heart of the Scorpion, I call upon your strength. Infuse this talisman with your power, grant it the will to defend."

3. **Visualize:** Imagine a deep red light descending from Antares into the talisman, filling it with a fierce, protective energy. Picture this light radiating outward, forming a shield around the talisman.
4. **Seal the Energy:** Place the talisman on your altar and sprinkle a pinch of salt over it, saying, "By star and earth, this talisman is sealed. May it protect and guard, its power revealed."
5. **Use:** Carry the talisman with you or place it in a strategic location (e.g., your car, workspace) as a continual source of protection.

5. Crafting a Star Amulet for Home Protection

A star amulet can be hung in your home to safeguard the space from unwanted energies. This amulet draws on the energy of the Pleiades, a cluster known for its nurturing and protective qualities.

Instructions:

1. **Choose Your Amulet Base:** Select a small pouch, locket, or charm that can be filled with protective elements.
2. **Gather Elements:** Fill the amulet with items that represent the Pleiades' nurturing energy, such as lavender (for peace), sage (for cleansing), and a small piece of amethyst (for spiritual protection).
3. **Empower the Amulet:** On a night when the Pleiades are visible, hold the amulet in your hands and light a blue candle. Focus on the Pleiades and say, "Pleiades, Sisters of the Stars, fill this amulet with your grace. Guard this home with love and light, protect it through the darkest night."
4. **Visualize:** Imagine the amulet glowing with a soft, blue light, infused with the energy of the Pleiades. See this light expanding to form a protective aura that envelops your home.
5. **Placement:** Hang the amulet near the entrance of your home or in a room where protection is needed. Allow its energy to radiate throughout the space, keeping it safe and peaceful.

Maintaining Your Protective Star Magic

Protection is an ongoing process, and your star shields, talismans, and amulets may need periodic reinforcement. Here are some practices to maintain their strength:

1. **Recharge Talismans:** Place your talismans on your altar under the light of the star they were created with during significant moon phases (e.g., full moon) to recharge their energy.
2. **Renew Shields:** Repeat the shield visualization and rituals regularly, especially during challenging times or when you sense negativity around you.
3. **Cleanse Amulets:** Cleanse your amulets periodically with smoke (such as sage or palo santo) or saltwater to remove any accumulated negativity and keep their energy pure.

Conclusion

The stars offer a powerful source of protection that you can invoke through Star Magic. By aligning with stars like Aldebaran, Sirius, Polaris, and the Pleiades, you can create protective shields around yourself, your home, and your loved ones. Talismans and amulets infused with star energy serve as continual sources of safeguarding, keeping you aligned with the stars' light. Remember, the stars have watched over the Earth for millennia; their ancient energies are ready to be called upon to guard and guide you on your journey.

Chapter 12: Healing with Star Magic

The stars, ancient and timeless, are not only beacons of guidance and protection but also powerful sources of healing energy. Throughout history, the stars have been seen as cosmic centers of harmony, balance, and rejuvenation. In Star Magic, you can tap into stellar energies to facilitate healing on physical, emotional, and spiritual levels. Each star and constellation emits unique frequencies that resonate with different aspects of the human experience, allowing you to draw upon their vibrations to promote wellness and restore balance.

This chapter explores how to use stellar energy for comprehensive healing. From aligning with the frequencies of specific stars to performing rituals and meditations for physical, emotional, and spiritual well-being, you will learn various techniques to channel the stars' light for healing purposes. By consciously working with the stars, you invite their vast energies into your life, helping to nurture and support your body, mind, and spirit.

The Nature of Healing in Star Magic

Healing with Star Magic involves channeling the vibrational frequencies of stars and celestial bodies to address imbalances in the physical, emotional, and spiritual realms. Each star has its unique energy signature, which can be used to influence different aspects of health and wellness:

- **Physical Healing:** Stars like Spica and Regulus possess energies that align with physical vitality, strength, and the body's natural healing processes.
- **Emotional Healing:** The Pleiades and Antares, among others, emit nurturing and transformative frequencies that can soothe emotional wounds, release negative patterns, and encourage inner peace.

- **Spiritual Healing:** Stars such as Sirius and Alcyone (in the Pleiades cluster) are associated with spiritual growth, insight, and the alignment of the soul with higher consciousness.

The stars' light, filtered through the Earth's atmosphere, contains a spectrum of energies that can be absorbed by the body, mind, and spirit. By tuning into these frequencies and directing them with intention, you can harness the stars' healing power to bring balance and harmony into your life.

Techniques for Healing with Star Energy

The following sections outline various methods to align yourself with star frequencies for healing, including meditations, visualizations, and rituals that draw on specific stellar energies.

Physical Healing with Star Magic

Physical healing through Star Magic focuses on using the stars' stabilizing and revitalizing energies to support the body's natural healing processes. By aligning with stars that embody strength, vitality, and restoration, you can promote physical well-being and enhance recovery.

1. Healing with Spica: The Star of Harvest and Health

Spica, the brightest star in the constellation Virgo, symbolizes harvest, nourishment, and physical well-being. Its gentle yet potent energy resonates with the body's need for balance and rejuvenation.

Ritual: Spica's Healing Light
Tools Needed:

- White or green candle (representing health and healing)
- A small bowl of water (symbolizing purification)
- Clear quartz crystal (to amplify Spica's healing energy)
- A piece of paper and pen

Instructions:

1. Choose a night when Spica is visible, ideally during the waxing or full moon to amplify its healing power.
2. Set up your altar with the candle, bowl of water, and clear quartz. Write down your specific health intention on the piece of paper (e.g., "I seek healing and balance for my body").
3. Light the candle and focus on Spica in the sky, visualizing its soft, white light descending toward you.
4. Hold the quartz crystal in your hand and say, "Spica, star of the harvest, bring forth your healing light. Restore my body, balance my being, and bring health into sight."
5. Place the paper under the bowl of water and imagine Spica's light filling the bowl, charging the water with its purifying energy.
6. Dip your fingers into the water and gently anoint your forehead, heart, and hands, visualizing the star's healing light flowing through your body. Keep the quartz nearby as a continuous source of Spica's energy.

2. Solar Healing with Regulus: The Heart of the Lion

Regulus, located in the constellation Leo, is associated with strength, vitality, and the radiant power of the Sun. Its energy can be used to invigorate the body, support recovery, and instill a sense of physical confidence and resilience.

Meditation: Regulus's Solar Healing
Instructions:

1. Find a quiet place where you can sit comfortably and relax. Choose a time when Regulus is visible, such as during its peak season in late summer.
2. Close your eyes and take a few deep breaths, centering your mind and body.

3. Visualize Regulus as a radiant, golden star shining brightly in the sky. Imagine its light beaming down toward you, growing in intensity as it approaches.
4. See this golden light entering the top of your head and slowly filling your body, spreading warmth, strength, and vitality. As it flows through you, imagine it illuminating any areas of pain or imbalance, washing them away with its healing energy.
5. Continue to breathe deeply, feeling the power of Regulus invigorating every cell in your body. When you are ready, open your eyes and express gratitude for the healing you have received.

Emotional Healing with Star Magic

The stars can be powerful allies in emotional healing, helping to soothe wounds, release negative patterns, and restore inner harmony. Stars like the Pleiades and Antares resonate with the deeper emotional and transformative aspects of human experience, providing the support needed to navigate and heal emotional turbulence.

3. Emotional Release with the Pleiades: The Sisters of Love

The Pleiades, or the "Seven Sisters," are known for their nurturing and loving energy. Their light can be channeled to support emotional healing, self-love, and the release of grief or anxiety.

Ritual: Pleiades' Comforting Embrace
Tools Needed:

- Blue or pink candle (symbolizing love and emotional healing)
- Rose quartz crystal (for self-love and emotional balance)
- A small bowl of water with a few drops of lavender oil (to calm the emotions)

Instructions:

1. Perform this ritual on a night when the Pleiades are visible, preferably during the waning moon for releasing negative emotions.

2. Set up your altar with the candle, rose quartz, and bowl of water. Light the candle and focus on the Pleiades in the sky, imagining their soft, blue light descending toward you.
3. Hold the rose quartz in your hand and say, "Pleiades, sisters of the stars, embrace me with your light. Soothe my heart, calm my mind, and release all pain tonight."
4. Visualize the Pleiades' light enveloping you in a gentle, nurturing embrace. Imagine it dissolving any emotional tension or sadness within you, filling you with warmth and peace.
5. Dip your fingers into the lavender-infused water and gently touch your forehead, heart, and hands, allowing the calming energy to flow through you. Keep the rose quartz nearby as a reminder of the Pleiades' loving support.

4. Transformation with Antares: The Heart of the Scorpion

Antares, the "Heart of the Scorpion," is associated with transformation and the release of deep-seated emotions. Its energy is potent for shadow work, aiding in the exploration and healing of hidden wounds.

Meditation: Antares's Transformative Light
Instructions:

1. Choose a quiet place where you won't be disturbed. Perform this meditation on a night when Antares is visible, preferably during the waning moon.
2. Close your eyes and take deep, steady breaths, focusing your mind on the present moment.
3. Visualize Antares as a glowing red star in the sky, its light pulsating with intensity and depth. Imagine this red light descending toward you and entering your heart, filling it with warmth and power.
4. As the light spreads throughout your body, picture it illuminating the darker areas of your emotions—fear, anger, grief. Allow

these emotions to surface without judgment, acknowledging them as they come.
5. Visualize Antares's light transforming these emotions into streams of energy that flow out of you and dissipate into the universe. Feel a sense of release, lightness, and renewal.
6. When you are ready, open your eyes and express gratitude to Antares for its transformative support.

Spiritual Healing with Star Magic

Stars like Sirius and Alcyone (the brightest star in the Pleiades cluster) are associated with spiritual insight, growth, and higher consciousness. They can help align the soul with its true path, clear spiritual blockages, and promote enlightenment.

5. Spiritual Healing with Sirius: The Dog Star

Sirius, often regarded as the "Spiritual Sun," has a high vibrational frequency that supports spiritual awakening, clearing blockages, and promoting inner peace. Its light can be used to align the chakras and deepen spiritual insight.

Ritual: Sirius's Spiritual Alignment
Tools Needed:

- White or blue candle (to represent Sirius's light)
- Clear quartz crystal (to amplify spiritual energy)
- A bowl of water with sea salt (for purification)

Instructions:

1. Perform this ritual on a night when Sirius is visible, preferably during the new or full moon for heightened spiritual awareness.
2. Set up your altar with the candle, clear quartz, and saltwater. Light the candle and focus on Sirius in the sky, visualizing its bright blue-white light shining down toward you.

3. Hold the quartz crystal in your hands and say, "Sirius, star of wisdom, illuminate my soul. Clear my spirit, align my heart, make me whole."
4. Visualize Sirius's light entering the top of your head and flowing through your body, aligning and cleansing each of your chakras. See this light expanding outward, enveloping your entire aura in a protective and purifying glow.
5. Dip your fingers into the saltwater and touch your forehead, heart, and hands, sealing the spiritual healing within you. Keep the quartz on your altar as a conduit for continued spiritual growth.

6. Chakra Balancing with Alcyone: The Light of the Pleiades

Alcyone, the brightest star in the Pleiades cluster, carries an energy of illumination and spiritual harmony. It can be used to balance the chakras and promote a sense of inner peace and alignment.

Meditation: Alcyone's Chakra Healing
Instructions:

1. Find a quiet, comfortable place to sit. Close your eyes and take a few deep breaths to center yourself.
2. Visualize Alcyone as a brilliant, shining star high in the sky. Imagine its light descending toward you, becoming a beam of white light that enters the top of your head.
3. As this light flows through your body, see it passing through each of your chakras, starting at the crown and moving downward to the root. Visualize each chakra as a spinning sphere, being cleansed and balanced by Alcyone's light.
4. Spend extra time on any chakras that feel blocked or imbalanced, allowing Alcyone's energy to dissolve negativity and restore harmony.

5. When you feel complete, visualize the light expanding around you, forming a protective aura. Take a few deep breaths, and when ready, open your eyes.

Conclusion

Healing with Star Magic offers a holistic approach to wellness, addressing the physical, emotional, and spiritual aspects of being. By aligning with the frequencies of specific stars like Spica, Regulus, the Pleiades, Antares, Sirius, and Alcyone, you tap into ancient cosmic energies that support balance, transformation, and inner peace. Whether you seek to heal the body, soothe emotional wounds, or elevate your spiritual awareness, the stars stand ready to share their timeless light. As you work with stellar energies, you create a sacred partnership with the cosmos, inviting the universe's vast healing power into your life.

Chapter 13: The Magic of Shooting Stars—Making Your Wishes Come True

Shooting stars, also known as meteors, have been revered as powerful omens across cultures and ages. Their fleeting presence in the night sky evokes wonder and excitement, and they are often seen as carriers of magic and messages from the universe. In Star Magic, shooting stars represent a burst of celestial energy, a momentary opening to the universe's vast potential. The magic of these luminous trails lies in their transient nature, embodying the idea that wishes made with clarity and intent during these brief moments can be swiftly delivered to the cosmos.

This chapter delves into the mystique of shooting stars and provides detailed guidance on harnessing their ephemeral energy to make wishes, attract opportunities, and bring positive change into your life. From understanding the symbolism behind shooting stars to learning specific rituals and practices for making the most of their magic, you will discover how to turn these celestial wonders into powerful allies for manifestation.

The Symbolism and Power of Shooting Stars

A shooting star occurs when a meteoroid enters the Earth's atmosphere, burning up and creating a streak of light across the sky. In many traditions, this luminous flash is seen as a rare gift from the universe, a sign of divine presence, and a harbinger of transformation. The significance of shooting stars varies across cultures:

- **Ancient Greece:** Greeks believed that shooting stars were fallen souls or messages from the gods, representing divine intervention and an opportunity for wishes to be heard.
- **Eastern Traditions:** In some Eastern cultures, shooting stars symbolize a bridge between the earthly and heavenly realms, an ideal time to make wishes that could be carried to the stars.
- **European Folklore:** European folklore often views shooting stars as a sign of luck and a signal that one's dreams and aspirations have been acknowledged by the cosmos.

In Star Magic, shooting stars are seen as conduits of intense, focused energy. Their sudden appearance and swift departure embody the essence of change, transformation, and the fleeting yet powerful nature of opportunities. By aligning with the energy of shooting stars, you can make wishes that are carried quickly and directly into the universe's currents, accelerating the process of manifestation.

Preparing to Harness the Energy of Shooting Stars

Since shooting stars appear unexpectedly, preparing in advance to work with their energy is key to making the most of their magic. Here's how to get ready:

1. **Keep Your Intentions Clear:** Before venturing outside to gaze at the night sky, take some time to reflect on what you wish to manifest. Whether it's a personal goal, an opportunity, a desire for change, or a form of healing, clarity of intention is crucial. Write down your wishes on a piece of paper, keeping them specific and focused.
2. **Set Up Your Space:** Create a comfortable viewing area where you can relax and watch the sky. If possible, choose a location away from city lights to increase your chances of spotting shooting stars. Bring a blanket, cushions, and a notebook for jotting down thoughts or wishes during your stargazing session.
3. **Choose an Optimal Time:** Meteor showers, which occur at predictable times each year, offer the best chance to see multiple shooting stars in one night. The Perseids in August and the Geminids in December are two of the most well-known meteor showers. Planning your wish-making around these events can increase the potency of your work.

Making Wishes on a Shooting Star

When you see a shooting star, it's believed that a door to the cosmos briefly opens, allowing you to send your desires into the universe. Here's a detailed guide on how to make a wish when you spot a shooting star:

1. The Instant Wish Ritual

The classic act of wishing upon a shooting star involves quickly making a wish the moment you see the star streak across the sky. Here's how to perform this simple yet powerful ritual:

Instructions:

1. As you watch the sky, keep your mind relaxed but focused on your intentions. You may silently repeat the wish you have in mind to keep it at the forefront.
2. The moment you spot a shooting star, quickly close your eyes and silently make your wish. Visualize your desire clearly, imagining it being absorbed by the star's light as it streaks across the sky.
3. In your mind's eye, see the shooting star carrying your wish high into the heavens, where it will be received by the universe. As the light fades, affirm in your heart that your wish has been heard and is now in motion.

Tip: If you have multiple wishes, prioritize them before you start stargazing. This way, you can quickly select the most important one when the moment arises.

2. The Wish Jar Spell

If you're preparing for a known meteor shower, you can use the shooting stars' energy to charge a wish jar, a talismanic container that holds your desires and attracts opportunities over time.

Tools Needed:

- A small glass jar with a lid
- Small pieces of paper and a pen
- Herbs like bay leaves (for wishes) or rosemary (for protection)
- A small crystal, such as clear quartz, to amplify your wish

Instructions:

1. Before the meteor shower begins, prepare your wish jar by writing each of your wishes on a separate piece of paper. Fold them neatly and place them inside the jar.
2. Add a few herbs, such as bay leaves or rosemary, to enhance the energy of your wishes. Place the crystal in the jar as well, serving as a conduit for the shooting stars' energy.
3. Seal the jar with its lid and hold it in your hands. Close your eyes and focus on your intentions, visualizing them glowing with light.
4. Sit outside under the stars during the meteor shower, holding the jar in your lap. When you see a shooting star, imagine its light entering the jar, illuminating your wishes and infusing them with celestial energy.
5. Once the shower concludes, place the jar on your altar or in a safe place. Whenever you feel doubt or need to reinforce your wishes, hold the jar and reconnect with the shooting stars' energy.

Attracting Opportunities with Shooting Star Magic

Shooting stars can also be used to attract new opportunities, helping you to navigate life's changes and embrace growth. The following spell works with the dynamic energy of a shooting star to call forth opportunities into your life.

3. Opportunity Attractor Spell
Tools Needed:

- A silver candle (to represent the stars)
- A small magnet (to attract energy)
- A piece of paper and a pen

Instructions:

1. Choose a night when a meteor shower is expected, or simply go out on a clear night when shooting stars might be visible.
2. Before heading outside, write your desire for new opportunities on the piece of paper (e.g., "I attract career opportunities that align with my passions").
3. Light the silver candle and focus on its flame, envisioning it as the light of a shooting star. Say, "Stars that shoot through the sky, hear my call, to you I fly. Bring opportunities, open doors, so my life's path shines evermore."
4. Fold the paper and place the magnet inside it. Hold this bundle in your hands as you gaze at the sky, keeping your intention clear in your mind.
5. When you see a shooting star, close your eyes and imagine its light connecting with the magnet, drawing opportunities toward you like a cosmic beacon.
6. Keep the magnet-wrapped paper on your altar or carry it with you as a talisman to continually attract opportunities. Refresh this spell during subsequent meteor showers to maintain its potency.

Bringing Positive Change into Your Life

Shooting stars signify the power of change and transformation, providing a unique opportunity to set intentions for positive shifts in your life. The ritual below helps you harness their energy to break free from stagnation and welcome new beginnings.

4. The Shooting Star Change Ritual
Tools Needed:

- A white candle (symbolizing clarity and new beginnings)
- A small bowl of water (representing emotional flow)
- A stone or crystal of your choice (to ground your intention)

Instructions:

1. On the night of a meteor shower or clear night, set up your altar with the candle, bowl of water, and stone. Write down the change you wish to bring into your life (e.g., "I invite positive change and new opportunities into my life").
2. Light the white candle and focus on its flame, symbolizing the light and clarity you seek.
3. Hold the stone in your hands and close your eyes. Visualize the area of your life where you wish to see change and imagine it bathed in the light of a shooting star.
4. Sit quietly under the sky. When you see a shooting star, silently express your intention for change, feeling the stone absorbing the energy of the star.
5. Dip your fingers into the bowl of water and anoint the stone, saying, "By star and light, my change takes flight. Flow through my life, bring new delight."
6. Keep the stone on your altar or in your pocket as a reminder of the change you have set into motion. You can also place it near the entrance of your home to welcome positive energies.

Amplifying the Magic of Shooting Stars

To enhance the power of shooting star magic, you can incorporate these practices into your rituals:

- **Use Star Talismans:** Wear jewelry or carry crystals associated with stars known for bringing luck and transformation (e.g., citrine for prosperity, rose quartz for love) during meteor showers to amplify your wishes.
- **Create a Stargazing Journal:** Keep a dedicated journal for recording your wishes made on shooting stars. Note the dates, the meteor showers, and the wishes you made. Reviewing this journal

helps you track the fulfillment of your desires and deepen your relationship with star magic.
- **Practice Gratitude:** After each shooting star ritual, take a moment to express gratitude to the universe and the stars. This practice cultivates a positive mindset and aligns you with the flow of cosmic energy.

Conclusion

The magic of shooting stars lies in their fleeting brilliance, offering a brief but potent opportunity to connect with the cosmos and send your desires into the universe. By preparing in advance, setting clear intentions, and performing specific rituals, you can harness the energy of these celestial streaks to make wishes, attract opportunities, and bring about positive changes in your life. Remember, the stars are listening, and when you align your heart's desires with the shooting star's light, you create a pathway for the universe to respond. The next time you see a shooting star, seize the moment and let its magic carry your wish into the infinite sky.

Chapter 14: Star Magic and the Zodiac Signs

In astrology, the twelve zodiac signs serve as symbolic gateways to understanding human nature, personality traits, and life paths. Each sign corresponds to specific stars, constellations, and celestial energies that shape its characteristics and influence. In Star Magic, harnessing these stellar energies can enhance personal strength, balance your energy, and align your life with the cosmos. By tailoring rituals to your zodiac sign, you can create a powerful synergy between your innate qualities and the universal forces at play, amplifying the effectiveness of your magical workings.

This chapter provides an in-depth guide on how to integrate the energies of the zodiac signs into your Star Magic practice. You will learn about the unique stars and constellations associated with each zodiac sign and discover rituals tailored to enhance their strengths, address their weaknesses, and promote balance. Whether you seek to channel the bold energy of Aries or the deep intuition of Pisces, this chapter will help you align with the stellar forces that define your astrological essence.

Understanding the Zodiac in Star Magic

The zodiac is a circle of twelve 30° divisions of celestial longitude, each corresponding to one of the twelve signs. These signs are directly linked to specific constellations and stars that emit unique energies influencing personality, behavior, and potential. In Star Magic, these celestial patterns are not merely symbols; they are living energies that you can call upon to support your journey.

- **Aries (March 21 - April 19):** Linked to the constellation Aries, representing boldness and initiative.

- **Taurus (April 20 - May 20):** Associated with the constellation Taurus and stars like Aldebaran, symbolizing strength, stability, and sensuality.
- **Gemini (May 21 - June 20):** Connected to the constellation Gemini and stars Castor and Pollux, representing duality, communication, and curiosity.
- **Cancer (June 21 - July 22):** Tied to the constellation Cancer and associated with nurturing and emotional depth.
- **Leo (July 23 - August 22):** Linked to the constellation Leo and the star Regulus, symbolizing leadership, courage, and vitality.
- **Virgo (August 23 - September 22):** Associated with the constellation Virgo and the star Spica, representing purity, practicality, and healing.
- **Libra (September 23 - October 22):** Connected to the constellation Libra, embodying balance, harmony, and beauty.
- **Scorpio (October 23 - November 21):** Linked to the constellation Scorpius and the star Antares, symbolizing transformation, intensity, and mystery.
- **Sagittarius (November 22 - December 21):** Associated with the constellation Sagittarius, known for adventure, wisdom, and expansive energy.
- **Capricorn (December 22 - January 19):** Connected to the constellation Capricornus, representing ambition, discipline, and perseverance.
- **Aquarius (January 20 - February 18):** Linked to the constellation Aquarius, symbolizing innovation, independence, and visionary thinking.
- **Pisces (February 19 - March 20):** Associated with the constellation Pisces, representing intuition, spirituality, and empathy.

Tailoring Star Magic Rituals According to Your Zodiac Sign

Each zodiac sign possesses distinct strengths and vulnerabilities that can be enhanced or balanced through star-based rituals. By working with the stars and constellations linked to your sign, you can amplify your natural abilities, mitigate challenges, and foster personal growth. Below, you'll find tailored rituals for each zodiac sign, designed to align with their celestial energies.

1. Aries: Harnessing the Energy of the Ram

Stars and Constellation: Aries constellation (Hamal, Sheratan)
Key Traits: Courageous, confident, dynamic, impulsive
Ritual: The Fire of Aries
Tools Needed:

- Red candle (symbolizing Aries' fiery nature)
- A piece of carnelian or red jasper (for courage)
- A small bowl of water (to cool and balance impulsive energy)

Instructions:

1. On a Tuesday (the day ruled by Mars, Aries' planetary ruler), set up your altar with the red candle, carnelian, and bowl of water.
2. Light the candle and focus on the constellation Aries in your mind's eye, visualizing its stars glowing brightly.
3. Hold the carnelian in your hands and say, "Hamal, Sheratan, stars of Aries, grant me your courage and strength. Ignite my inner fire with boldness, yet balance my actions with wisdom."
4. Place the carnelian on your solar plexus (the energy center associated with confidence) while visualizing a glowing red light filling you with courage.
5. Dip your fingers in the water and touch your forehead, symbolizing the cooling of impulsive thoughts. Say, "As the Ram charges forth, may my actions be guided and my mind clear."

2. Taurus: Grounding with the Eye of the Bull

Stars and Constellation: Taurus constellation (Aldebaran, the Pleiades)
Key Traits: Practical, stable, patient, materialistic
Ritual: The Strength of Aldebaran
Tools Needed:

- Green candle (for growth and abundance)
- A piece of rose quartz (to soothe Taurus' need for comfort)
- A bowl of earth or soil (for grounding)

Instructions:

1. On a Friday (ruled by Venus, Taurus' planetary ruler), set up your altar with the green candle, rose quartz, and bowl of soil.
2. Light the candle and focus on Aldebaran, the "Eye of the Bull," imagining its red light radiating toward you.
3. Hold the rose quartz and say, "Aldebaran, star of Taurus, ground me in strength and serenity. Help me embrace patience, nurture growth, and find beauty in the simple things."
4. Place the rose quartz on your heart and feel the energy of Aldebaran soothing your mind, releasing tension and material concerns.
5. Touch the soil with both hands, grounding yourself, and say, "As Taurus holds steady, so shall I find balance in the gifts of the Earth."

3. Gemini: Aligning with the Twins of the Sky

Stars and Constellation: Gemini constellation (Castor and Pollux)
Key Traits: Curious, adaptable, communicative, restless
Ritual: The Wisdom of Castor and Pollux
Tools Needed:

- Yellow candle (for mental clarity and communication)
- A piece of citrine (for mental focus)
- A feather (symbolizing air, Gemini's element)

Instructions:

1. On a Wednesday (ruled by Mercury, Gemini's planetary ruler), set up your altar with the yellow candle, citrine, and feather.
2. Light the candle and visualize the twin stars, Castor and Pollux, shining brightly in the night sky.
3. Hold the citrine in your hands and say, "Castor and Pollux, stars of Gemini, open my mind to knowledge, sharpen my words with truth, and guide my curiosity with wisdom."
4. Place the citrine near your throat chakra, the center of communication, and imagine a golden light flowing from the stars into your voice.
5. Gently wave the feather through the air, clearing mental confusion, and say, "As the Twins bring harmony to duality, so may my thoughts and words flow with ease."

4. Cancer: Nurturing with the Crab's Embrace
Stars and Constellation: Cancer constellation (Acubens, Al Tarf)
Key Traits: Nurturing, intuitive, sensitive, protective
Ritual: The Waters of Cancer
Tools Needed:

- Silver or blue candle (representing the Moon, Cancer's ruler)
- A moonstone crystal (for emotional balance)
- A bowl of saltwater (to represent the ocean's nurturing energy)

Instructions:

1. On a Monday (ruled by the Moon, Cancer's planetary ruler), set up your altar with the candle, moonstone, and saltwater.
2. Light the candle and visualize the stars of Cancer glowing softly, like a gentle tide under the moonlight.
3. Hold the moonstone and say, "Acubens, Al Tarf, stars of Cancer, fill my heart with your nurturing light. Help me embrace my emotions and protect my inner peace."
4. Place the moonstone on your heart and visualize a soothing, silver light flowing through you, calming and balancing your emotional waves.
5. Dip your fingers in the saltwater and touch your forehead, heart, and hands, saying, "As the Crab holds close, so shall I find strength in my nurturing nature."

5. Leo: Radiating with the Lion's Heart

Stars and Constellation: Leo constellation (Regulus, Algieba)
Key Traits: Confident, generous, dramatic, self-assured
Ritual: The Light of Regulus
Tools Needed:

- Gold candle (for vitality and self-expression)
- A piece of tiger's eye (for courage and self-esteem)
- A small mirror (to reflect Leo's radiant energy)

Instructions:

1. On a Sunday (ruled by the Sun, Leo's planetary ruler), set up your altar with the candle, tiger's eye, and mirror.
2. Light the candle and focus on Regulus, the "Heart of the Lion," visualizing its golden light enveloping you.
3. Hold the tiger's eye in your hand and say, "Regulus, star of Leo, fill me with your light. Grant me courage, confidence, and the power to shine my truth."
4. Look into the mirror and see yourself surrounded by a brilliant, golden aura. Affirm your inner strength by saying, "As the Lion roars, so shall I stand proud in my light."
5. Keep the tiger's eye near you to continually channel Regulus's energy.

6. Virgo: Balancing with the Maiden's Wisdom

Stars and Constellation: Virgo constellation (Spica, Vindemiatrix)
Key Traits: Practical, analytical, health-conscious, modest
Ritual: The Harvest of Spica
Tools Needed:

- Green or white candle (symbolizing healing and purity)
- A piece of amethyst (for spiritual clarity and balance)
- A bundle of dried herbs (such as lavender or rosemary for calming)

Instructions:

1. On a Wednesday, set up your altar with the candle, amethyst, and herbs.
2. Light the candle and focus on Spica, the brightest star in Virgo, visualizing its soft, white light surrounding you.
3. Hold the amethyst in your hands and say, "Spica, star of Virgo, align me with your wisdom. Let me nurture my mind, body, and spirit with grace and harmony."
4. Place the amethyst near your solar plexus and imagine Spica's energy flowing through your body, clearing tension and promoting inner balance.
5. Wave the bundle of herbs through the candle flame, saying, "As the Maiden tends the harvest, so shall I tend to myself with care and clarity."

7. Libra: Harmonizing with the Scales

Stars and Constellation: Libra constellation (Zubenelgenubi, Zubeneschamali)
Key Traits: Diplomatic, harmonious, graceful, indecisive
Ritual: The Balance of Libra
Tools Needed:

- Pink or white candle (for harmony and peace)
- A piece of rose quartz (to promote love and balance)
- A small scale or two stones of equal size (to symbolize Libra's need for balance)

Instructions:

1. On a **Friday** (ruled by Venus, Libra's planetary ruler), set up your altar with the candle, rose quartz, and scale or stones.
2. Light the candle and focus on the stars of **Libra**, imagining their soft light shining down, bringing balance and harmony to your space.
3. Hold the rose quartz in your hands and say, "Zubenelgenubi, Zubeneschamali, stars of Libra, grant me your sense of harmony. May your light balance my mind, body, and spirit, and guide me in my relationships."
4. Place the rose quartz near your heart, visualizing its calming energy radiating throughout your being, soothing indecisiveness and bringing clarity.
5. Use the scale or stones as a symbol. If using a scale, place an object on each side to signify the balance you seek in life. If using stones, hold one in each hand, imagining yourself as the center of equilibrium.
6. Close by saying, "As Libra holds the scales, so shall I find balance in love, thought, and action."

8. Scorpio: Transmuting with the Scorpion's Intensity

Stars and Constellation: Scorpius constellation (Antares, Shaula)
Key Traits: Intense, transformative, passionate, secretive
Ritual: The Shadow of Antares
Tools Needed:

- Black or dark red candle (for transformation and mystery)
- A piece of obsidian or smoky quartz (for grounding and protection)
- A small bowl of salt (to absorb negativity)

Instructions:

1. On a **Tuesday** (ruled by Mars, co-ruler of Scorpio), arrange your altar with the candle, obsidian, and bowl of salt.
2. Light the candle and visualize **Antares**, the heart of the Scorpion, glowing red in the night sky, radiating transformative energy.
3. Hold the obsidian in your hands and say, "Antares, star of Scorpius, guide me through the shadows. Help me embrace transformation, release what no longer serves, and rise renewed."
4. Place the obsidian on your root chakra (at the base of the spine), visualizing its grounding energy anchoring you as the intensity of Scorpio fills your being.
5. Dip your fingers into the bowl of salt, symbolizing the absorption of negative energy, and say, "As the Scorpion sheds its skin, so shall I release my burdens, transforming them into strength."
6. Close the ritual by visualizing yourself surrounded by Antares' protective energy, ready to face and transform any challenges.

9. Sagittarius: Seeking with the Archer's Aim

Stars and Constellation: Sagittarius constellation (Kaus Australis, Nunki)
Key Traits: Adventurous, philosophical, optimistic, blunt
Ritual: The Arrow of Sagittarius
Tools Needed:

- Purple or blue candle (for wisdom and spiritual exploration)
- A piece of lapis lazuli (for insight and truth)
- An arrow or feather (symbolizing the Archer's aim)

Instructions:

1. On a **Thursday** (ruled by Jupiter, Sagittarius' planetary ruler), set up your altar with the candle, lapis lazuli, and arrow or feather.
2. Light the candle and visualize the stars of **Sagittarius**, glowing with a vibrant energy that calls forth adventure and wisdom.
3. Hold the lapis lazuli and say, "Kaus Australis, Nunki, stars of Sagittarius, guide my path with your wisdom. Grant me the courage to seek truth and the strength to journey boldly into the unknown."
4. Place the lapis lazuli on your third eye chakra (center of the forehead) to open your mind to new possibilities and insights.
5. Take the arrow or feather and hold it steady, imagining it as a symbol of your aim and focus. Visualize your goals as a target and see the arrow flying straight and true toward it.
6. Say, "As the Archer seeks the stars, so shall I seek my truth with clarity and purpose."

10. Capricorn: Climbing with the Sea-Goat's Determination

Stars and Constellation: Capricornus constellation (Dabih, Algedi)
Key Traits: Ambitious, disciplined, practical, reserved
Ritual: The Ascent of Capricorn
Tools Needed:

- Green or black candle (for grounding and growth)
- A piece of tiger's eye (for focus and perseverance)
- A small stone or crystal (to represent the mountain)

Instructions:

1. On a **Saturday** (ruled by Saturn, Capricorn's planetary ruler), arrange your altar with the candle, tiger's eye, and stone.
2. Light the candle and focus on the stars of **Capricornus**, visualizing them as a steady and guiding light on your path to success.
3. Hold the tiger's eye and say, "Dabih, Algedi, stars of Capricorn, grant me your strength and perseverance. Help me climb the mountain of my ambitions with patience and resolve."
4. Place the tiger's eye near your root chakra to ground your energy and draw strength from the earth.
5. Take the stone and hold it in your hands, imagining it as the peak of your goal. Visualize yourself climbing steadily, each step bringing you closer to the top.
6. Close by saying, "As the Sea-Goat ascends, so shall I reach my goals with steady determination."

11. Aquarius: Innovating with the Water Bearer

Stars and Constellation: Aquarius constellation (Sadalsuud, Sadalmelik)
Key Traits: Innovative, independent, humanitarian, unpredictable
Ritual: The Waters of Innovation
Tools Needed:

- Silver or electric blue candle (for originality and visionary thinking)
- A piece of amethyst (for clarity and inspiration)
- A bowl of water (to represent Aquarius' fluid and free nature)

Instructions:

1. On a **Saturday** (co-ruled by Saturn and Uranus, Aquarius' planetary rulers), set up your altar with the candle, amethyst, and bowl of water.
2. Light the candle and visualize **Sadalsuud** and **Sadalmelik**, stars of Aquarius, shining brightly, sending waves of innovative energy into your space.
3. Hold the amethyst and say, "Sadalsuud, Sadalmelik, stars of Aquarius, inspire my mind with your boundless creativity. Let

me think freely, explore new ideas, and break through limitations."
4. Place the amethyst on your crown chakra (top of the head) to open your mind to cosmic inspiration and guidance.
5. Gently swirl your fingers through the bowl of water, representing the flow of new ideas, and say, "As the Water Bearer pours forth, so shall I pour forth new visions into the world."
6. Close the ritual by envisioning a stream of silver light flowing through you, carrying the energy of innovation and freedom.

12. **Pisces: Dreaming with the Fish**

Stars and Constellation: Pisces constellation (Alrescha, Fum al Samakah)
Key Traits: Intuitive, compassionate, dreamy, sensitive
Ritual: The Dream Waters of Pisces
Tools Needed:

- Sea green or lavender candle (for intuition and healing)
- A piece of aquamarine (for emotional clarity)
- A bowl of moon-charged water (to enhance Pisces' intuitive energy)

Instructions:

1. On a **Thursday** (ruled by Jupiter, co-ruler of Pisces with Neptune), arrange your altar with the candle, aquamarine, and moon water.
2. Light the candle and visualize the stars of **Pisces**, shining softly, guiding you into a state of calm reflection and intuition.
3. Hold the aquamarine and say, "Alrescha, Fum al Samakah, stars of Pisces, fill me with your depth and compassion. Let my dreams and intuition flow as freely as the waters of the universe."

4. Place the aquamarine on your heart chakra to deepen your emotional connection and understanding.
5. Dip your fingers into the moon water and anoint your third eye and heart, symbolizing the merging of intuition and emotion.
6. Close by saying, "As the Fish swims through the cosmic sea, so shall I swim through the depths of my dreams and inner truth."

Conclusion: Aligning with Your Zodiac Sign in Star Magic

Working with the stars and constellations associated with your zodiac sign in Star Magic rituals helps you align more deeply with your innate qualities. By invoking these celestial energies, you enhance your strengths, balance your weaknesses, and open pathways for personal growth. Each ritual provided in this chapter is tailored to resonate with the unique attributes of each sign, allowing you to channel the starry forces that define your astrological essence. As you incorporate these rituals into your practice, you'll find that your connection to the cosmos deepens, empowering you to live in harmony with the universe's rhythms.

Conclusion

Each zodiac sign carries a unique set of traits and energies influenced by its corresponding stars and constellations. By tailoring your Star Magic rituals to align with your sign's celestial characteristics, you can enhance your natural strengths, balance your energies, and foster personal growth. Whether you are channeling the courage of Aries, the nurturing nature of Cancer, or the spiritual wisdom of Pisces, the stars offer their light to guide and empower you on your journey. Embrace the celestial rhythm of your zodiac sign and let the magic of the stars harmonize your life with the cosmos.

Chapter 15: The Science of Star Energy

Stars have fascinated humanity for millennia, not just for their beauty but for the profound influence they exert on our world. While stars are central to countless myths, legends, and magical practices, their true power lies in their physical nature. In Star Magic, the energy of stars is believed to influence life on Earth, drive cosmic rhythms, and empower magical workings. By exploring the scientific principles behind stars and their energy, we can gain a deeper understanding of how these celestial bodies impact the universe and how their mystical properties might be grounded in real, observable phenomena.

This chapter delves into the science of star energy, covering how stars form, how they emit energy, and the ways this energy travels through space to affect Earth and its inhabitants. Understanding the physical processes behind stars allows us to build a bridge between the mystical aspects of Star Magic and the realities of astrophysics, providing a scientific framework for the practices we explore.

What Are Stars? The Basics of Stellar Physics

Stars are immense, luminous spheres of plasma held together by gravity. They are primarily composed of hydrogen and helium, the two lightest elements in the universe. Through nuclear fusion in their cores, stars produce and emit vast amounts of energy in the form of light and heat, which radiates outwards into space. This energy sustains life on planets, influences planetary atmospheres, and even drives the cycles of ecosystems on Earth.

Key Components of Stars:

1. **Core:** The core is the central region of a star, where nuclear fusion occurs. In the intense heat and pressure of the core, hydrogen atoms combine to form helium, releasing enormous amounts of energy. This energy then travels outward, ultimately reaching the star's surface and radiating into space as light.

2. **Radiative and Convective Zones:** Surrounding the core are the radiative and convective zones, where energy is transported outwards through radiation and convection currents.
3. **Photosphere:** The photosphere is the visible surface of the star, from which light and heat radiate into space.
4. **Corona:** Beyond the photosphere lies the corona, a layer of extremely hot, diffuse plasma that extends far into space.

How Stars Emit Energy

Stars emit energy in various forms, primarily as electromagnetic radiation, including visible light, infrared radiation, ultraviolet light, X-rays, and gamma rays. This energy influences everything in its path, shaping cosmic environments and potentially affecting the subtle energies associated with Star Magic.

1. Nuclear Fusion: The Powerhouse of Stars

The primary process powering stars is nuclear fusion. In the core of a star, temperatures soar to millions of degrees, causing hydrogen atoms to collide and fuse into helium. This fusion process releases a tremendous amount of energy in the form of light and heat. The equation describing this energy release is encapsulated in Einstein's famous equation:

$E = mc^2$

- **E** represents energy,
- **m** is the mass of the hydrogen atoms involved in fusion,
- **c** is the speed of light.

This equation illustrates how even a small amount of mass can produce a vast amount of energy, explaining the immense and enduring luminosity of stars.

2. Electromagnetic Radiation: The Star's Light

The energy produced in the star's core travels outward, eventually reaching the surface and escaping as electromagnetic radiation. Stars emit a wide spectrum of electromagnetic waves, including:

- **Visible Light:** The light we see when we look at stars in the night sky. This light carries the unique energy signature of each star, depending on its composition, temperature, and age.
- **Infrared Radiation:** Though invisible to the naked eye, infrared radiation warms planetary surfaces and influences atmospheric conditions.
- **Ultraviolet Light:** High-energy radiation that can affect living organisms. Ultraviolet light from stars plays a role in shaping planetary atmospheres and can trigger chemical reactions essential for life.
- **X-rays and Gamma Rays:** Emitted by high-energy processes in stars, particularly those undergoing explosive events like supernovae. These rays can influence the dynamics of interstellar space and impact planetary systems over time.

The Influence of Star Energy on Earth

While the Sun is the most significant star for life on Earth, other stars also exert influence through their electromagnetic emissions, gravitational forces, and cosmic interactions. Here's how star energy can affect Earth and potentially explain the mystical effects described in Star Magic.

1. Solar Radiation: The Sun's Life-Giving Energy

The Sun, our closest star, radiates energy that sustains life on Earth. Its light drives photosynthesis, powers weather systems, and regulates the planet's climate. Solar radiation also affects the human body and psyche, influencing circadian rhythms, mood, and health.

- **Sunspots and Solar Flares:** Periodic increases in solar activity, such as sunspots and solar flares, release bursts of electromagnetic radiation that can impact Earth's magnetic field. These solar events can disrupt communication systems, affect weather patterns, and even correlate with fluctuations in human emotions and behaviors, supporting the idea that star energy can directly influence life on Earth.

2. Starlight: Subtle Energies and Biological Rhythms

Beyond the Sun, the light emitted by distant stars reaches Earth, albeit much more faintly. While the direct physical impact of distant starlight on Earth is limited due to its vast travel distance, researchers have found that even minimal changes in light exposure can influence biological processes.

- **Circadian Rhythms:** The human body is attuned to the daily cycle of light and darkness. Starlight, especially during moonlit nights, can subtly affect these rhythms, influencing sleep patterns and mood. In Star Magic, this connection supports the idea that certain stellar energies, when invoked intentionally, can align with our internal cycles to promote well-being.

3. Cosmic Rays: Star Energy in the Atmosphere

Stars, especially those undergoing supernova explosions, emit high-energy particles known as cosmic rays. When these cosmic rays reach Earth, they interact with the atmosphere, creating secondary particles that can penetrate the planet's surface. Though the effects of cosmic rays on living organisms are not fully understood, studies suggest they may influence cloud formation, climate patterns, and even genetic mutations over long periods.

In Star Magic, cosmic rays can be seen as a tangible manifestation of star energy interacting with Earth's atmosphere. They represent the stars' ability to impact life on a microscopic level, potentially affecting the energetic and physical aspects of our environment.

Star Energy and Human Perception

The human body is composed of elements forged in stars—carbon, oxygen, nitrogen, and others formed during stellar nucleosynthesis. This cosmic origin has led some researchers and mystics to propose that humans have an intrinsic resonance with stellar energy. Our natural affinity for the stars may explain why stargazing evokes a sense of wonder, peace, and connection.

1. Biophotons: Light Within the Human Body

Biophotons are weak emissions of light produced by living organisms, including the human body. This phenomenon suggests that cells communicate using light, emitting low-level electromagnetic radiation. Although biophotons are not directly related to starlight, the concept of the body producing and interacting with light provides a potential link to how we might resonate with star energy.

In the context of Star Magic, the idea of biophotons supports the practice of visualizing star light entering the body during rituals and meditations, aligning our own inner light with the celestial energies.

2. The Pineal Gland: A Celestial Connection

The pineal gland, located in the brain, is sensitive to light and regulates sleep-wake cycles through the production of melatonin. Some mystics and scientists believe that the pineal gland is linked to spiritual experiences, often referred to as the "third eye."

- **Starlight and the Pineal Gland:** Exposure to natural light, including starlight, influences the pineal gland's activity. In Star Magic, the pineal gland may act as a receptor for subtle stellar energies, enhancing intuition, meditation, and spiritual perception. This could explain why rituals performed under specific stars or moon phases feel particularly potent and transformative.

The Mystical Aspects of Star Energy in Magic

While science explains the physical properties and effects of star energy, the mystical aspects of Star Magic emerge from the interplay between cosmic forces and human consciousness. When you invoke the power of stars during rituals, you are tapping into their light, frequencies, and archetypal symbolism, aligning your intentions with the grand orchestration of the cosmos.

1. Resonance and Intentionality: Directing Star Energy

In physics, resonance occurs when an object vibrates in response to a matching frequency. Similarly, in Star Magic, focusing your mind on a specific star or constellation allows your energy to resonate with that celestial body's vibration. This resonance amplifies your intentions, creating a direct channel for stellar energy to influence your life.

- **Visualization:** The practice of visualizing star light entering the body or filling a space during rituals creates a mental resonance with the star's energy. The more you connect with the star's unique characteristics, the stronger the resonance becomes, enhancing the effectiveness of your magical workings.

2. Archetypes of Stars and Constellations: Symbolic Power

Each star and constellation carries archetypal meanings—Leo as the lion, Virgo as the maiden, Orion as the hunter. These symbols are encoded with powerful psychological and spiritual associations. When you work with these symbols in Star Magic, you are not only invoking physical energy but also tapping into the collective unconscious and the deeper layers of the psyche.

- **Star-Based Talismans:** Creating talismans associated with specific stars uses symbolic resonance to channel their energy. For example, a talisman bearing the symbol of Sirius may draw on its associations with guidance and higher knowledge, influencing the subconscious mind to align with these qualities.

Conclusion: Bridging Science and Star Magic

The science of star energy reveals that stars are not just distant points of light, but dynamic, energetic forces that shape the cosmos and influence life on Earth. Through nuclear fusion, electromagnetic radiation, cosmic rays, and light interactions, stars emit energy that can be detected, measured, and even felt on a subtle level. By understanding these scientific principles, we can ground the mystical practices of Star Magic in a framework that recognizes the stars' vast influence on the universe.

The interplay between the physical properties of star energy and the mystical aspects of intention, resonance, and archetypal symbolism allows for a more holistic understanding of Star Magic. As you harness the energy of stars in your rituals, you are not only invoking ancient cosmic forces but also aligning with the fundamental processes of the universe, creating a powerful synergy between science and magic. By deepening your knowledge of the stars' scientific properties, you enhance your practice, grounding your magic in the timeless dance of light and energy that defines the cosmos.

Chapter 16: Planetary Magic and Star Magic

In the grand tapestry of the cosmos, stars and planets share a dynamic relationship that has been studied and revered for centuries. While stars are ancient beacons of cosmic energy, planets move among them, influencing astrological and magical practices. The interplay between stars and planets creates a vast network of energies that affect all aspects of life. In Star Magic, understanding the influence of planetary energies alongside the fixed stars allows for a more comprehensive approach to working with celestial forces. By combining planetary magic with star magic, you can amplify your rituals, align with cosmic rhythms, and tap into specific energies for your intentions.

This chapter explores the intricate relationship between planets and stars, highlighting how to weave planetary magic into your star-based practices. We will delve into the correspondences and magical significance of each planet, offering insights into how planetary energies can be invoked and harmonized with star energy in your magical workings.

The Relationship Between Stars and Planets

Stars and planets have a symbiotic relationship in the cosmos. Stars like our Sun provide light, warmth, and the gravitational anchor around which planets orbit. In astrology, planets are viewed as "wanderers" among the fixed stars, influencing events, emotions, and energies on Earth. Each planet carries distinct characteristics and rules over different aspects of life, such as communication, love, ambition, and spirituality.

- **Stars:** Stars are fixed celestial bodies that serve as sources of light, energy, and cosmic guidance. They represent archetypal forces and eternal principles.
- **Planets:** Planets, including the Sun and Moon, are wandering celestial bodies that move through the zodiac, interacting with the energy of stars. They symbolize dynamic forces and the flow of change, influencing the practical aspects of our daily lives.

In Star Magic, incorporating planetary magic involves aligning planetary energies with the fixed stars' more stable vibrations. For example, invoking Venus during a ritual with the Pleiades can enhance love and beauty, while calling upon Mars with Aldebaran amplifies courage and strength. Understanding the magical correspondences of each planet allows you to create harmonious rituals that blend the influences of stars and planets, magnifying their impact.

Planetary Correspondences and Their Magical Significance

Each planet has its unique set of correspondences, energies, and rulerships. By incorporating these planetary influences into Star Magic, you can tailor your rituals to target specific aspects of life. Below is an overview of each planet, its characteristics, and how it can be integrated into star-based practices.

1. Sun: Vitality, Ego, and Success
Symbol: ☉
Day: Sunday
Color: Gold, Yellow
Associated Star: Regulus (in the constellation Leo)
Magical Significance: The Sun represents life force, vitality, personal power, and success. It embodies the core of your identity, your sense of self, and how you express your will in the world. In Star Magic, the Sun's energy can be used to boost confidence, enhance personal power, and attract success and recognition.

Incorporating Sun Energy in Star Magic:

- Perform rituals with Regulus, the "Heart of the Lion," on Sundays to align with the Sun's energy for confidence and success.
- Light a gold candle during a solar ritual and visualize the Sun's light combining with the star's energy to empower your intentions.

Ritual:

- **The Radiance of Regulus and the Sun:** On a Sunday, light a gold candle and focus on Regulus in the sky. Visualize the Sun's radiant energy merging with Regulus, filling you with strength and courage. Say, "Regulus and Sun, stars of power, grant me the strength to shine this hour."

2. Moon: Emotions, Intuition, and Nurturing
Symbol: ☽
Day: Monday
Color: Silver, White
Associated Stars: The Pleiades (in the constellation Taurus), Sirius (in Canis Major)
Magical Significance: The Moon governs emotions, intuition, and the subconscious mind. Its cyclical nature reflects the waxing and waning of energy, making it an essential influence in magic. In Star Magic, the Moon's energy enhances rituals related to healing, nurturing, dreams, and emotional balance.

Incorporating Moon Energy in Star Magic:

- Work with the Pleiades or Sirius on Monday nights to enhance intuitive and emotional aspects of your practice.
- Use moonstone or silver items during rituals to channel lunar energy, especially when working with stars known for their nurturing qualities.

Ritual:

- **Lunar Blessings with the Pleiades:** On a Monday, place a silver candle on your altar. Focus on the Pleiades cluster and visualize their soft blue light merging with the Moon's energy. Say,

"Pleiades and Moon, grant me your light, guide my dreams and nurture my night."

3. Mercury: Communication, Intellect, and Travel
Symbol: ⟡
Day: Wednesday
Color: Yellow, Light Blue
Associated Stars: Castor and Pollux (in the constellation Gemini)
Magical Significance: Mercury rules communication, intellect, learning, and travel. It represents the mind's agility, adaptability, and the ability to convey thoughts clearly. In Star Magic, Mercury's energy can be harnessed for rituals involving study, eloquence, negotiation, and quick decision-making.

Incorporating Mercury Energy in Star Magic:

- Perform star rituals with Castor and Pollux on Wednesdays to enhance communication, learning, and intellectual pursuits.
- Include symbols like quills or scrolls to represent Mercury's influence during rituals.

Ritual:

- **Words of the Twins:** On a Wednesday, light a yellow candle and focus on the stars Castor and Pollux. Imagine Mercury's swift energy enhancing their light, filling you with clarity and eloquence. Say, "Castor, Pollux, and Mercury bright, grant me the words, the knowledge, the light."

4. Venus: Love, Beauty, and Harmony

Symbol: ♀
Day: Friday
Color: Green, Pink
Associated Stars: Aldebaran (in the constellation Taurus), Spica (in Virgo)
Magical Significance: Venus governs love, beauty, harmony, and attraction. It symbolizes the principles of pleasure, aesthetic appreciation, and the power of relationships. In Star Magic, Venus's energy enhances spells related to love, romance, artistic expression, and abundance.

Incorporating Venus Energy in Star Magic:

- Combine Venus's influence with stars like Aldebaran or Spica during Friday rituals to draw love, harmony, and abundance into your life.
- Use rose petals, copper items, or green candles to symbolize Venus during star magic workings.

Ritual:

- **Aldebaran's Heart of Love:** On a Friday, light a green candle and place rose petals on your altar. Visualize Aldebaran's light merging with Venus's aura, creating a sphere of loving energy around you. Say, "Aldebaran and Venus, stars aligned, bring love, beauty, and joy divine."

5. Mars: Action, Courage, and Conflict

Symbol: ♂
Day: Tuesday
Color: Red, Scarlet
Associated Stars: Aldebaran (in Taurus), Antares (in Scorpius)
Magical Significance: Mars rules action, courage, aggression, and conflict. It embodies the warrior spirit and the drive to overcome obstacles. In Star Magic, Mars's energy can be used for rituals that require assertiveness, protection, and the initiation of new projects.

Incorporating Mars Energy in Star Magic:

- Perform rituals with Antares or Aldebaran on Tuesdays to invoke the warrior energy needed for courage, strength, or overcoming challenges.
- Use iron or weapons as symbols of Mars's energy on your altar.

Ritual:

- **Antares' Shield of Courage:** On a Tuesday, light a red candle and focus on Antares in the sky. Visualize Mars's fiery energy blending with the star's light to form a protective shield around you. Say, "Antares and Mars, warriors bright, grant me the strength to stand and fight."

6. Jupiter: Expansion, Luck, and Wisdom

Symbol: ♃
Day: Thursday
Color: Royal Blue, Purple
Associated Stars: Spica (in Virgo), Alcyone (in the Pleiades)
Magical Significance: Jupiter is the planet of expansion, luck, prosperity, and wisdom. It encourages growth, generosity, and the pursuit of higher knowledge. In Star Magic, Jupiter's influence can be harnessed for rituals related to abundance, success, spiritual growth, and good fortune.

Incorporating Jupiter Energy in Star Magic:

- Work with Spica or Alcyone on Thursdays to attract prosperity, knowledge, and personal growth.
- Use symbols like keys or coins to represent Jupiter during star rituals.

Ritual:

- **Spica's Abundant Harvest:** On a Thursday, light a purple candle and place a small key on your altar. Visualize Spica's light merging with Jupiter's energy, creating a flow of abundance. Say, "Spica and Jupiter, stars of grace, bring fortune, wisdom, and blessings in place."

7. Saturn: Structure, Discipline, and Karma
Symbol: ♄
Day: Saturday
Color: Black, Dark Blue
Associated Stars: Algenubi (in Leo), Deneb Algedi (in Capricorn)
Magical Significance: Saturn governs structure, discipline, karma, and boundaries. It embodies the principles of time, endurance, and the lessons learned through challenges. In Star Magic, Saturn's energy can be used to enforce boundaries, break negative patterns, and build lasting foundations.

Incorporating Saturn Energy in Star Magic:

- Invoke the energy of Algenubi or Deneb Algedi on Saturdays to enhance discipline, protection, and boundary-setting.
- Include items like rings or chains to symbolize Saturn's influence in your rituals.

Ritual:

- **Deneb Algedi's Boundary Shield:** On a Saturday, light a black candle and visualize Deneb Algedi's light merging with Saturn's energy to form a protective boundary around you. Say, "Deneb Algedi and Saturn wise, strengthen my borders, open my eyes."

8. Uranus: Innovation, Rebellion, and Change
Symbol: ⟡
Day: Wednesday (alternative)
Color: Electric Blue, Turquoise
Associated Stars: Zeta Tauri (in Taurus)
Magical Significance: Uranus is the planet of innovation, rebellion, sudden change, and the unexpected. It represents the force of creativity, freedom, and the breaking of old patterns. In Star Magic, Uranus's energy can be harnessed for spells that involve transformation, originality, and breaking free from restrictions.

Incorporating Uranus Energy in Star Magic:

- Combine Uranus's influence with stars like Zeta Tauri for rituals that promote personal liberation, creativity, and transformative change.
- Use symbols like lightning bolts or circles to represent Uranus's radical energy.

Ritual:

- **Zeta Tauri's Spark of Change:** Light a turquoise candle and focus on Zeta Tauri. Visualize its energy merging with Uranus's electric power, filling you with inspiration and courage to embrace change. Say, "Zeta Tauri and Uranus bright, spark my path, illuminate the night."

9. Neptune: Illusion, Dreams, and Spirituality
Symbol: ⟡
Day: Thursday
Color: Sea Green, Purple
Associated Stars: Fomalhaut (in the constellation Pisces Austrinus)
Magical Significance: Neptune governs dreams, intuition, spirituality,

illusion, and the deep subconscious. Its energy is connected to mystical experiences, spiritual insights, and the exploration of the unseen realms. In Star Magic, Neptune's influence helps enhance psychic abilities, deepen meditation practices, and connect with the spiritual aspects of the universe. Working with stars like **Fomalhaut** amplifies Neptune's energy, offering clarity amidst confusion and a direct connection to higher wisdom.

Incorporating Neptune Energy in Star Magic:

- Perform rituals on **Thursdays**, using sea green or purple candles to evoke Neptune's mysterious energy.
- Invoke **Fomalhaut** during meditation to enhance your intuition, connect with your inner dreams, and explore the spiritual realms.
- Work with water elements, such as bowls of moon-charged water, to channel Neptune's fluid, transformative power in your rituals.

Ritual: The Illumination of Fomalhaut and Neptune

- **Tools Needed:** Sea green or purple candle, a piece of aquamarine, a bowl of moon-charged water.
- **Instructions:**
    1. Perform this ritual on a **Thursday** during Neptune's hour to access its mystical energy.
    2. Light the sea green candle and place the bowl of moon-charged water on the altar to symbolize Neptune's fluid, dreamlike nature.
    3. Hold the aquamarine in your hands and focus on **Fomalhaut**, visualizing it glowing brightly in the night sky. Imagine Neptune's energy merging with Fomalhaut's starry light, creating a swirling vortex of dreamlike energy around you.
    4. Say, "Fomalhaut, guardian of the mystical, and Neptune, keeper of dreams, open my mind to the infinite. Guide my

intuition, deepen my vision, and reveal what lies beneath the surface."

5. Dip your fingers into the moon-charged water and anoint your third eye (center of the forehead), feeling the flow of Neptune's energy washing over you, enhancing your psychic awareness and spiritual insight.

When to Use: This ritual is ideal for enhancing intuition, exploring dreams, deepening meditation, or when seeking clarity in situations clouded by illusion or confusion.

10. Pluto: Transformation, Power, and Rebirth
Symbol: ⯓
Day: Tuesday
Color: Black, Dark Red
Associated Stars: Antares (in the constellation Scorpius)
Magical Significance: Pluto embodies transformation, power, intensity, and rebirth. It governs the processes of death and renewal, helping us confront our shadows and emerge stronger. In Star Magic, Pluto's energy facilitates deep personal transformations, the release of old patterns, and the empowerment to face challenges head-on. Combining Pluto's energy with stars like **Antares** amplifies its transformative power, assisting in shadow work and profound change.

Incorporating Pluto Energy in Star Magic:

- Perform rituals on **Tuesdays** to align with Pluto's transformative force, using black or dark red candles to symbolize its intense energy.
- Work with **Antares**, the heart of the Scorpion, to harness the full depth of Pluto's power for rituals involving transformation, release, and personal empowerment.
- Use symbols of death and rebirth, such as skulls or phoenix feathers, to anchor Pluto's energy during your rituals.

Ritual: The Transformation of Antares and Pluto

- **Tools Needed:** Black candle, a piece of obsidian, a small bowl of salt.
- **Instructions:**
    1. Perform this ritual on a **Tuesday** during Pluto's hour to connect with its transformative energy.
    2. Light the black candle, representing the darkness and power of Pluto. Place the bowl of salt on the altar as a symbol of purification and release.
    3. Hold the obsidian in your hands and visualize **Antares**, glowing deep red in the night sky. Imagine Pluto's energy merging with Antares' light, creating a powerful aura of transformation around you.
    4. Say, "Antares, star of shadows, and Pluto, lord of transformation, I call upon your power to guide me through the darkness. Help me release what no longer serves and rebirth myself in strength."
    5. Place the obsidian near your root chakra, feeling the grounding and purifying energy flowing through you. Dip your fingers into the salt and sprinkle a small amount over the candle flame, symbolizing the release of old patterns and the birth of new strength within you.

When to Use: This ritual is perfect for times when you need to undergo deep personal change, release unhealthy habits, face your shadow self, or seek empowerment during challenging transitions.

By understanding and incorporating Neptune and Pluto's energies into your Star Magic practices, you can work with some of the most profound forces in the cosmos. Neptune opens pathways to intuition, dreams, and spiritual insight, while Pluto guides you through the depths of transformation, helping you emerge renewed and empowered. Combining these planetary energies with the corresponding stars like **Fomalhaut** and **Antares** adds layers of potency to your rituals, allowing you to tap into the universe's infinite power for growth, healing, and change.

Conclusion

The planets and stars form a complex and interwoven system of cosmic energies that influence life, magic, and the universe's natural rhythms. By incorporating planetary magic into your Star Magic practice, you align with the dynamic forces that drive change, growth, and transformation. Each planet offers a unique set of correspondences and magical influences that can be harnessed in conjunction with specific stars to enhance the potency of your rituals. By understanding the relationship between planets and stars, you can create powerful, nuanced magical workings that resonate deeply with the celestial forces guiding the cosmos.

Chapter 17: Star Magic for Love and Relationships

Love, one of the most powerful forces in the universe, has long been associated with the stars. From ancient myths to modern-day astrology, the stars have been seen as guardians of love, guiding the fate of lovers, illuminating the path to finding true connection, and enhancing emotional bonds. In Star Magic, you can harness the energy of specific stars and constellations to attract love, deepen relationships, and strengthen bonds. This chapter explores how to use star energy to influence love and relationships, with detailed rituals to invite romance, enhance emotional intimacy, and nurture existing connections.

Stars like Aldebaran, the Pleiades, and Spica radiate specific vibrations that resonate with love, beauty, harmony, and loyalty. By aligning with these celestial energies, you can channel their influence into your love life, amplifying your intentions and creating an atmosphere of warmth, compassion, and passion. Whether you seek to attract a new partner, bring harmony into an existing relationship, or deepen emotional bonds, the stars offer their light and power to help guide your heart.

Understanding the Stars in Love Magic

The stars have always held a special place in matters of love and relationships. Ancient civilizations named constellations and stars after gods and goddesses of love, beauty, and desire, believing that these celestial bodies could influence human emotions and romantic destinies. In Star Magic, each star emits a specific frequency that corresponds to different aspects of love and intimacy. Some stars are associated with passion, others with loyalty, and still others with nurturing and compassion.

Key Stars in Love Magic:

- **Aldebaran (in Taurus):** Symbolizes strength, passion, and sensuality. Ideal for enhancing physical attraction and intimacy.

- **The Pleiades (in Taurus):** Associated with emotional nurturing, deep connections, and romance. Useful for creating a bond that is both comforting and passionate.
- **Spica (in Virgo):** Represents beauty, harmony, and the purity of love. Perfect for fostering grace, trust, and balance in relationships.
- **Sirius (in Canis Major):** Known as the "Dog Star," it embodies loyalty, devotion, and spiritual connection. Enhances long-term commitment and unconditional love.

By invoking the energy of these stars, you can tailor your magical workings to meet your specific desires and needs in love. The following sections outline how to work with these stars, offering rituals designed to attract love, enhance emotional intimacy, and strengthen relationships.

Rituals for Attracting Love

Attracting love involves opening your heart and aligning your energy with the cosmic vibrations that resonate with romance and connection. Stars like Aldebaran and the Pleiades can assist in drawing love into your life, amplifying your personal magnetism, and creating an aura of attraction around you.

1. Aldebaran's Flame of Attraction

Aldebaran, known as the "Eye of the Bull," radiates a powerful and passionate energy that can ignite attraction and stir the flames of desire. This ritual uses Aldebaran's fiery essence to enhance your personal allure and draw love into your life.

Tools Needed:

- Red candle (symbolizing passion)
- A piece of rose quartz (for love and attraction)
- A bowl of water with rose petals (to represent romantic energy)
- A piece of red cloth

Instructions:

1. Choose a night when Aldebaran is visible in the sky, preferably during a waxing or full moon to enhance attraction.
2. Set up your altar with the red candle, rose quartz, bowl of water, and red cloth. Light the candle and focus on Aldebaran in the sky, visualizing its fiery red light shining down upon you.
3. Hold the rose quartz in your hands and say, "Aldebaran, Eye of the Bull, ignite my heart with your passionate flame. Draw love to me with your strength and power."
4. Visualize Aldebaran's light forming a glowing, red aura around you, filling you with confidence, warmth, and magnetic allure.
5. Dip your fingers into the water and sprinkle it around you, saying, "By the stars' light, love shall come. My heart is open; my will is done."
6. Wrap the rose quartz in the red cloth and carry it with you as a talisman of attraction.

Tips for Enhanced Results: Perform this ritual during a Friday, the day associated with Venus, to further strengthen its power in attracting love.

2. The Pleiades' Call for Romantic Connection

The Pleiades, a cluster of stars in the constellation Taurus, are associated with nurturing, emotional warmth, and romantic allure. This ritual calls upon the energy of the Pleiades to create an inviting aura that draws romantic prospects into your life.

Tools Needed:

- Pink candle (symbolizing romance and emotional connection)
- A piece of amethyst (for emotional clarity)
- A small bottle of rose oil (to anoint the body)
- A white or silver cloth

Instructions:

1. Choose a night when the Pleiades are visible, preferably during the waxing moon.
2. Set up your altar with the pink candle, amethyst, rose oil, and white cloth. Light the candle and focus on the Pleiades, imagining their soft, blue light descending upon you.
3. Hold the amethyst and say, "Pleiades, stars of love and grace, open my heart to your embrace. Draw to me the love I seek, a bond that's strong, yet tender and meek."
4. Visualize the Pleiades' light surrounding you in a soft pink glow, enhancing your charm and inviting romantic possibilities.
5. Anoint your pulse points (wrists, neck, heart) with the rose oil, saying, "By the stars' tender light, I call love to my sight."
6. Wrap the amethyst in the silver cloth and place it under your pillow to invite dreams of love and guidance.

Rituals for Enhancing Relationships

Enhancing an existing relationship requires nurturing the bond between partners, deepening emotional intimacy, and fostering harmony. Stars like Spica and Sirius offer energies that can bring balance, beauty, and loyalty to relationships, helping partners connect on deeper levels.

3. Spica's Harmony of Love

Spica, the brightest star in the constellation Virgo, is associated with beauty, harmony, and balance. This ritual harnesses Spica's energy to bring grace and understanding into your relationship, promoting a balanced and loving connection.

Tools Needed:

- White or green candle (for harmony and purity)
- A piece of green aventurine (for emotional healing and harmony)
- A small dish of honey (to symbolize sweetness)

Instructions:

1. Perform this ritual on a Friday night when Spica is visible, preferably during the waxing or full moon.
2. Set up your altar with the candle, aventurine, and honey. Light the candle and focus on Spica in the sky, visualizing its gentle, white light descending into the room.
3. Hold the aventurine and say, "Spica, star of grace and light, bless our love with harmony bright. Let our hearts beat as one, in peace and joy, our love begun."
4. Dip your fingers into the honey and touch it to your heart, then to your partner's (or imagine doing so if they're not physically present). Visualize Spica's light wrapping around both of you, weaving a harmonious bond.
5. Place the aventurine in a central place in your home as a reminder of the star's energy supporting your relationship.

4. Sirius's Bond of Loyalty

Sirius, the "Dog Star," represents loyalty, commitment, and deep spiritual connections. This ritual strengthens the bond between partners, fostering devotion and trust.

Tools Needed:

- Blue candle (for loyalty and devotion)
- A piece of lapis lazuli (for communication and spiritual connection)
- Two small pieces of string or ribbon (to symbolize the bond)

Instructions:

1. Choose a night when Sirius is visible in the sky, ideally during the full moon to enhance its power of commitment.

2. Set up your altar with the blue candle, lapis lazuli, and ribbons. Light the candle and focus on Sirius, imagining its bright blue light enveloping you and your partner.
3. Hold the lapis lazuli and say, "Sirius, star of loyalty true, bless our bond, make it anew. With love and trust, our hearts entwine, in light and truth, our spirits shine."
4. Take the two ribbons and tie them together into a simple knot, visualizing the connection between you and your partner growing stronger with each loop.
5. Keep the lapis lazuli in a shared space, such as the bedroom or living room, as a talisman of your bond. Store the knotted ribbons in a safe place as a symbol of your unity.

Rituals for Strengthening Emotional Bonds

Deepening emotional intimacy in a relationship requires opening hearts, fostering empathy, and maintaining a safe space for vulnerability. The Pleiades and Sirius are stars that emit nurturing and loving energy, perfect for rituals aimed at enhancing emotional bonds.

5. The Pleiades' Heart Connection

This ritual uses the nurturing energy of the Pleiades to foster emotional intimacy and understanding between partners. It is ideal for couples who wish to deepen their emotional connection and share their innermost feelings.

Tools Needed:

- Pink or white candle (for emotional warmth)
- Two rose quartz crystals (one for each partner)
- A small bowl of water with rose petals

Instructions:

1. Choose a night when the Pleiades are visible, preferably during the waxing moon.

2. Set up your altar with the candle, rose quartz crystals, and bowl of water. Light the candle and focus on the Pleiades, visualizing their soft light filling the room.
3. Each partner holds a rose quartz crystal in their hands. Say together, "Pleiades, stars of tender care, open our hearts, our love to share. Let our bond grow deep and true, with trust and warmth, we start anew."
4. Visualize the Pleiades' light forming a bridge between your hearts, carrying love, understanding, and empathy.
5. Dip your fingers into the water and touch your partner's forehead, then your own, symbolizing emotional clarity and openness.
6. Keep the rose quartz crystals near each other in a central place in your home to maintain the bond of emotional warmth.

Conclusion

The stars have guided lovers and shaped romantic destinies for millennia, and through Star Magic, you can call upon their timeless energy to influence your love life. By aligning with the energies of stars like Aldebaran, the Pleiades, Spica, and Sirius, you can attract love, deepen emotional intimacy, and strengthen the bonds in your relationships. Whether you seek to ignite passion, foster harmony, or create a nurturing connection, the stars are ready to lend their light, enhancing your heart's desires with their celestial magic. Embrace the power of Star Magic in your love life and let the stars illuminate your path to deeper, more fulfilling relationships.

Chapter 18: Connecting with Your Star Guardians

Throughout history, various cultures and spiritual traditions have spoken of celestial beings, star guardians, and cosmic guides who watch over humanity from the stars. These ethereal entities, often referred to as "star guardians" or "star beings," are believed to possess ancient wisdom, profound insight, and a deep connection to the universe's mysteries. In Star Magic, connecting with your star guardians can provide guidance, protection, and transformative knowledge. By establishing a relationship with these celestial beings, you open a gateway to the cosmos, allowing you to draw upon their power and insight to navigate life's challenges and spiritual growth.

This chapter delves into the concept of star guardians, exploring their characteristics, origins, and roles in human spiritual practices. It will guide you through various methods to connect with these guardians, including meditative journeys, invocations, and ritual practices designed to foster a deeper bond with these celestial protectors. By learning how to communicate with your star guardians, you can receive messages of wisdom, guidance, and support, helping you align with the cosmic forces that shape your destiny.

Who Are Star Guardians?

Star guardians are celestial beings believed to inhabit or originate from the stars, constellations, and other cosmic realms. They are often seen as intermediaries between the divine and the human, possessing knowledge that transcends time and space. Different cultures and spiritual traditions have described these guardians in various forms:

- **Angelic Beings:** In some esoteric traditions, star guardians are viewed as higher-dimensional angelic beings associated with specific stars or constellations. Archangels like Michael, Gabriel, and Raphael are often linked with celestial bodies, believed to serve as guardians of cosmic knowledge and protection.

- **Star Spirits:** Indigenous cultures, such as the Native American and Aboriginal Australian peoples, speak of star spirits or star ancestors who serve as guides and protectors. These spirits are seen as wise and loving beings, offering guidance through dreams, visions, and rituals.
- **Extraterrestrial Beings:** In modern metaphysical thought, star guardians are sometimes perceived as advanced extraterrestrial beings from distant star systems like Sirius, the Pleiades, and Orion. These star beings are thought to be spiritually evolved, aiding humanity's evolution by transmitting wisdom and healing energy.

Regardless of their form, star guardians are considered benevolent forces, attuned to the cosmic order and capable of assisting those who seek to connect with them. By establishing a relationship with your star guardians, you can access their wisdom, receive protection, and gain insights that help align your spiritual path with the universe's rhythm.

Preparing to Connect with Your Star Guardians

Connecting with your star guardians requires an open heart, a quiet mind, and a willingness to receive guidance from beyond the physical realm. Here are some preparatory steps to help you create the right environment for establishing a connection:

1. **Set Your Intention:** Before attempting to contact your star guardians, set a clear intention. What do you seek from this connection? Whether you desire guidance, protection, healing, or spiritual growth, having a focused intention helps create a receptive channel for communication.
2. **Create a Sacred Space:** Prepare a quiet, comfortable space where you can meditate and perform rituals without distractions. Consider setting up a small altar with items associated with the stars, such as crystals (e.g., selenite, amethyst), star-shaped symbols, candles, and star charts.

3. **Cleanse Your Energy:** Cleanse yourself and your space to remove any lingering negative energy. You can do this by burning sage, palo santo, or using sound tools like a singing bowl or bell.
4. **Practice Centering Techniques:** Meditative breathing, grounding exercises, and visualization can help quiet the mind and open your consciousness to higher vibrations. Spend a few moments centering yourself before beginning the connection process.

Methods to Connect with Your Star Guardians

There are several ways to connect with your star guardians, ranging from meditative practices to ritual invocations. Choose the method that resonates most with you or combine multiple techniques to deepen your connection.

1. Star Meditation: Journey to the Stars

Star meditation is a guided visualization practice designed to take you on an astral journey to meet your star guardians. This technique uses relaxation, deep breathing, and imagery to elevate your consciousness to the star realms.

Instructions:

1. **Find a Comfortable Position:** Sit or lie down in a comfortable position. Close your eyes and take a few deep breaths, inhaling peace and exhaling tension. Let your body and mind relax completely.
2. **Visualize a Star Gateway:** In your mind's eye, visualize a brilliant star shining above you. This star serves as a gateway to the cosmic realm. As you focus on its light, imagine it growing larger, forming a shimmering portal that invites you to enter.
3. **Travel to the Stars:** Envision yourself stepping through the star portal, feeling a sense of lightness as you are gently transported through the cosmos. Stars, constellations, and nebulae surround you as you journey deeper into the star realm.

4. **Meet Your Star Guardians:** As you travel, you begin to sense a presence—your star guardians. They may appear as glowing figures, ethereal beings of light, or take on forms that resonate with your personal beliefs. Allow the guardians to reveal themselves to you in their unique way.
5. **Receive Guidance:** When you encounter your guardians, greet them and express your intention to connect. You may ask them for guidance, insight, or simply to share their wisdom with you. Remain open to whatever form the communication takes—words, images, feelings, or symbols.
6. **Return and Ground:** When you feel the encounter is complete, thank your star guardians and begin to visualize yourself traveling back through the star portal. As you return to your physical surroundings, take a few deep breaths to ground yourself and gently open your eyes.

Journaling: After the meditation, write down any messages, symbols, or impressions you received. Keeping a star guardian journal helps you track your experiences and develop a deeper connection over time.

2. Ritual Invocation: Calling Upon the Star Guardians

Invoking your star guardians through ritual is a powerful way to create a sacred space for communication and to invite their protective and guiding energies into your life.

Tools Needed:

- White or blue candle (representing star energy)
- Incense (such as frankincense or sandalwood)
- A star-shaped object or star chart
- A piece of clear quartz (to amplify energy)

Instructions:

1. **Create Your Sacred Space:** Set up your altar with the candle, incense, star object, and quartz. Light the candle and incense, focusing on the star object as a representation of your connection to the cosmos.
2. **Open a Circle:** Stand before your altar and take a few deep breaths. Visualize a circle of light forming around you, creating a protective barrier.
3. **Invoke the Guardians:** Hold the quartz in your hands and say, "Guardians of the stars, beings of cosmic light, I call upon you to join me this night. Guide me with wisdom, protect me with grace, from the realms of the stars, fill this space."
4. **Listen and Feel:** Close your eyes and become aware of the energy in the room. You may feel a change in temperature, a tingling sensation, or a deep sense of calm. These are signs that your star guardians are present.
5. **Ask for Guidance:** Speak your intention or question aloud, or communicate it mentally. Then, remain silent and open, allowing the guardians to communicate in their own way.
6. **Close the Ritual:** When you feel the connection is complete, thank your star guardians and say, "I thank you, guardians of the stars, for your presence and guidance. May your light continue to shine upon my path." Visualize the circle of light dissolving and extinguish the candle.

3. Dreamwork with Star Guardians

Star guardians often communicate through dreams, providing guidance, insights, and messages when the conscious mind is at rest. By setting the intention to connect with your guardians before sleep, you can invite their presence into your dream state.

Instructions:

1. **Prepare for Sleep:** Before going to bed, cleanse your energy with a brief meditation or use a cleansing tool like a selenite wand.
2. **Create a Star Talisman:** Place a small star-shaped object, piece of moonstone, or clear quartz under your pillow. This serves as a conduit for star guardian energy.
3. **Set Your Intention:** As you lie in bed, say aloud or mentally, "Star guardians, I invite you into my dreams tonight. Share your wisdom and guidance with me in the realm of sleep."
4. **Keep a Dream Journal:** Upon waking, immediately write down any dreams, symbols, or feelings you remember. Over time, you may notice recurring themes or messages that your star guardians are conveying.

Strengthening Your Connection with Star Guardians

Building a strong relationship with your star guardians requires patience, openness, and regular practice. Here are some tips to deepen your bond:

- **Regular Meditation:** Incorporate star meditation into your routine, allowing time for encounters with your guardians. The more frequently you visit the star realms in meditation, the more familiar you become with your guardians' presence.
- **Star Altar:** Create a permanent star altar in your home where you can place symbols, crystals, and objects associated with your star guardians. Use this space for meditation, ritual work, and to leave offerings of gratitude.

- **Offerings:** Leave small offerings of herbs, flowers, or water on your star altar to honor your guardians. Offerings symbolize respect and appreciation, strengthening the energetic link between you and the celestial beings.

Signs of Connection and Messages from Star Guardians

Your star guardians may communicate through various signs and synchronicities. Common signs include:

- **Dream Symbols:** Recurring symbols, stars, constellations, or celestial themes in your dreams.
- **Intuitive Nudges:** Strong gut feelings or inner voices guiding you toward certain decisions or actions.
- **Celestial Events:** Increased sightings of shooting stars, unusual star patterns, or feeling an intense connection during celestial events like meteor showers or eclipses.
- **Subtle Energies:** Sensations of warmth, tingling, or a calming presence during meditation or ritual work.

Conclusion

Connecting with your star guardians opens a doorway to the universe's ancient wisdom and loving guidance. These celestial beings, whether seen as angelic forces, star spirits, or cosmic guides, offer support, protection, and insight, helping you navigate your spiritual path with clarity and strength. By practicing meditative journeys, ritual invocations, and dreamwork, you can foster a deep and lasting relationship with your star guardians. As you build this connection, you will find yourself more attuned to the cosmic energies around you, empowered by the guardians' light and wisdom to align your life with the stars.

Chapter 19: Dreaming with the Stars—Astral Travel and Lucid Dreaming

The stars have long been seen as gateways to other realms, bridges between the physical world and the vast expanse of the universe. Cultures throughout history have linked stars with the dream world, believing that during sleep, the soul can journey through the cosmos to connect with higher realms, receive wisdom, and explore the mysteries of existence. In Star Magic, dreaming serves as a profound tool for astral travel and lucid dreaming, allowing the seeker to use the stars as guides in their nightly adventures. This chapter explores how to harness star energy to enhance your dreams, practice astral travel, and master lucid dreaming, along with tips for dream recall and interpretation.

The Connection Between Stars and Dreams

The dream world has always been associated with the stars and the night sky. Many ancient cultures believed that dreams were messages from the gods, the spirits, or the stars themselves. For example, in ancient Greek mythology, the goddess Nyx, personifying the night, was said to control dreams and provide guidance through the stars. Similarly, some Native American traditions hold that the stars are the souls of ancestors watching over dreamers and imparting wisdom.

In the context of Star Magic, dreams are considered gateways to the astral plane, a realm where the soul can explore without the limitations of the physical body. By aligning with the energy of specific stars, you can influence your dream state, enhance your ability to lucid dream, and travel astrally to other dimensions. Stars like Alcyone in the Pleiades, Sirius, and Antares are known to radiate energies that support astral journeys, intuitive insights, and dream recall.

Preparing for Dream Work with the Stars

To work with star energy during dreaming, preparation is key. By setting your intention, creating a conducive sleeping environment, and using specific rituals, you can enhance your ability to experience lucid dreams and astral travel.

1. **Set Your Dream Intention:** Before you sleep, set a clear intention for your dream work. Do you wish to connect with a specific star, receive guidance, travel to a particular astral realm, or experience a lucid dream? Write down your intention in a dream journal to solidify your focus.

2. **Create a Dream Altar:** Set up a small dream altar near your bed to help you align with star energy. Include star-related objects like crystals (e.g., moonstone, labradorite), a star chart, candles, and herbs such as mugwort or lavender to promote restful sleep and enhance dreams.

3. **Cleanse Your Energy:** Cleanse yourself and your sleeping space before bed using sage, palo santo, or selenite to remove negative energies that could interfere with your dream work. A clear and balanced energetic state is crucial for successful dream exploration.

Working with Star Magic for Astral Travel

Astral travel, or astral projection, is the practice of consciously separating the astral body from the physical body to explore other dimensions or realms. In Star Magic, the stars serve as beacons or guideposts that you can follow during your astral journeys. Stars like Sirius, the Pleiades, and Antares are considered particularly powerful for aiding astral travel.

1. Astral Travel to the Stars: The Pleiadian Journey

The Pleiades, a star cluster in the constellation Taurus, is known for its mystical and nurturing energy. Working with the Pleiades during astral travel can offer profound insights, spiritual healing, and a sense of cosmic connection.

Tools Needed:

- A piece of moonstone or labradorite (to enhance psychic abilities)
- A blue or silver candle (to represent star energy)
- A star chart or image of the Pleiades cluster

Instructions:

1. **Prepare Your Space:** Before going to bed, light the blue or silver candle on your dream altar and place the moonstone or labradorite nearby. Focus on the image of the Pleiades, allowing its energy to fill the room.
2. **Set Your Intention:** Hold the crystal in your hands and say, "Pleiades, stars of wisdom and light, guide my soul this dream-filled night. I seek to journey through your space, to learn, to heal, to find my place."
3. **Astral Travel Visualization:** Lie down comfortably, close your eyes, and take a few deep breaths. Visualize yourself surrounded by a sphere of white light that serves as a protective bubble. Imagine this sphere rising up and leaving your physical body, traveling through the starry sky.
4. **Connect with the Pleiades:** As you travel, focus on the Pleiades cluster, visualizing it growing brighter and drawing you closer. Feel its gentle, nurturing energy enveloping you as you enter its realm. Allow your astral body to explore this starry domain, paying attention to any symbols, messages, or experiences you encounter.
5. **Return and Ground:** When you feel ready to return, visualize your astral body descending back to your physical form, re-entering your body, and grounding into the Earth. Take a few deep breaths before opening your eyes.

Tips: Keep a dream journal by your bed to record any impressions, messages, or experiences upon waking. The more you practice, the more vivid and controlled your astral journeys will become.

Enhancing Lucid Dreaming with Star Magic

Lucid dreaming is the ability to become consciously aware that you are dreaming and to exert some level of control over the dream's direction. Certain stars, such as Sirius and Antares, are associated with enhancing awareness and clarity, making them ideal for promoting lucid dreaming.

2. Lucid Dreaming with Sirius: The Dog Star's Clarity

Sirius, the brightest star in the night sky, is known for its powerful energy and association with higher awareness. Working with Sirius can help you achieve clarity and focus within your dreams, facilitating the lucid dreaming process.

Tools Needed:

- A piece of clear quartz (to amplify clarity)
- A blue candle (to represent Sirius)
- Mugwort tea (to enhance dream vividness)

Instructions:

1. **Nighttime Ritual:** Before bed, prepare a cup of mugwort tea and place it on your dream altar. Light the blue candle and hold the clear quartz in your hands.
2. **Invoke Sirius:** Close your eyes and visualize Sirius shining brightly in the night sky. As you focus on its light, say, "Sirius, star of clarity and sight, guide me in my dreams tonight. I seek awareness, lucid and clear, to explore my dreams without fear."
3. **Drink the Tea:** Sip the mugwort tea slowly, imagining it filling your body with the star's energy, enhancing your dream state.
4. **Dream Affirmation:** Lie down in bed and repeat to yourself, "Tonight, I will realize I am dreaming. I will be conscious within my dream."
5. **Dream Anchors:** Choose a simple "dream anchor" to use in your dreams, such as looking at your hands or checking the time. During the day, practice this action while saying, "Am I dreaming?" This practice will carry over into your dream state, triggering lucidity when you see your anchor in the dream.

Tips for Lucid Dreaming:

- **Reality Checks:** Perform regular reality checks throughout the day to train your mind to recognize dream states. This habit increases your chances of becoming lucid while dreaming.
- **Dream Journaling:** Keep a detailed dream journal to record your dreams upon waking. Writing down your dreams reinforces your connection to the dream world and helps identify recurring themes and symbols that may trigger lucidity.

Using Star Magic for Dream Recall and Interpretation

Dream recall is essential for working with dreams and understanding the messages they contain. Stars like Alcyone (in the Pleiades) and Antares are known for enhancing intuition and memory, making them valuable allies for dream recall and interpretation.

3. Dream Recall with Alcyone: The Pleiades' Memory Keeper

Alcyone, the brightest star in the Pleiades, carries a deep, intuitive energy that can aid in dream recall and understanding the symbolic language of dreams.

Tools Needed:

- A piece of amethyst (to enhance intuition)
- A purple or indigo candle (to represent psychic awareness)
- A dream journal and pen

Instructions:

1. **Nighttime Preparation:** Light the purple candle on your dream altar and hold the amethyst in your hands.
2. **Invoke Alcyone:** Focus on Alcyone in the Pleiades and say, "Alcyone, keeper of dreams, shine your light on my sleep. I seek to remember the messages I receive, to understand and interpret with clarity deep."

3. **Place the Amethyst:** Place the amethyst under your pillow or on your nightstand to enhance dream recall.
4. **Dream Recall Affirmation:** As you lie down to sleep, repeat the affirmation, "When I wake, I will remember my dreams."
5. **Morning Journal:** Upon waking, immediately write down any dreams, symbols, feelings, or messages you remember. Do this before moving or thinking about your day to capture the dream's essence.

4. Dream Interpretation with Star Guidance

After recalling your dreams, interpreting them is the next step to uncovering their messages. Star Magic emphasizes the use of stars as guides in this process, providing clarity and insight.

Instructions:

1. **Review Symbols:** After writing down your dream, identify any symbols, colors, or recurring themes. Consider how these elements may relate to your life and the intention you set before sleep.
2. **Seek Star Insights:** Meditate on a specific star, such as Sirius for clarity or Antares for transformation, and ask for guidance in interpreting your dream. You may receive impressions, feelings, or insights that clarify the dream's meaning.
3. **Consult Star-Based Tools:** Use star charts, astrology, or tarot cards associated with star imagery to explore the dream's significance further. The symbols in your dream may correspond to specific celestial energies, offering deeper layers of understanding.

Tips for Enhancing Dream Work

- **Use Essential Oils:** Incorporate essential oils like lavender, clary sage, or frankincense into your bedtime routine to promote relaxation and enhance dream vividness.

- **Lunar Phases:** Pay attention to the moon phases when working with dreams. The waxing moon is ideal for setting dream intentions, while the full moon enhances dream clarity and recall.
- **Create a Dream Pouch:** Make a small pouch filled with herbs like mugwort, chamomile, and lavender, along with crystals like amethyst or moonstone. Place the pouch under your pillow to support restful sleep and dream recall.

Conclusion

Dreaming with the stars opens a doorway to the universe's vast realms, allowing you to explore the depths of your subconscious, travel through the cosmos, and receive messages from the divine. By harnessing the energy of stars like the Pleiades, Sirius, and Alcyone, you can enhance your ability to experience astral travel and lucid dreaming, gaining insights that guide your spiritual journey. Through setting intentions, practicing visualization, and recording your experiences, you cultivate a deeper relationship with the dream world and the stars that guide it. Let the stars illuminate your dreams, offering their ancient wisdom as you journey through the night's celestial embrace.

Chapter 20: Stellar Divination—Reading the Stars for Guidance

Throughout human history, the stars have been regarded as cosmic oracles, revealing secrets about the universe, the future, and the nature of reality. Ancient civilizations turned to the stars for guidance, believing that the celestial patterns and movements influenced life on Earth. Stellar divination, also known as "astromancy" or "star reading," is a practice that involves interpreting the positions, patterns, and energies of the stars to gain insights into the past, present, and potential future. In Star Magic, stellar divination provides a means to connect with the cosmos, align with its rhythms, and receive guidance on life's journey.

This chapter delves into the art of stellar divination, offering detailed methods for reading star patterns, interpreting celestial movements, and using the energy of specific stars to gain insights. By learning how to interpret the night sky and the cosmic dance of stars, you can uncover hidden truths, make informed decisions, and navigate the future with confidence and clarity.

Understanding Stellar Divination

Stellar divination is a form of astrology that focuses on the stars and constellations rather than just the planets. While traditional astrology emphasizes the zodiac signs and planetary movements, stellar divination goes deeper, exploring the influence of fixed stars, star clusters, and their dynamic relationships. By observing the positions of stars in relation to the Earth and the movements of celestial bodies, stellar diviners can glean valuable information about personal and collective experiences, potential outcomes, and spiritual lessons.

In stellar divination, the positions and alignments of stars and constellations are seen as cosmic messages. The stars act as a celestial map, reflecting the energies present in your life and providing guidance on how to navigate challenges, embrace opportunities, and align with your higher purpose.

Tools for Stellar Divination

Before you begin practicing stellar divination, it is helpful to gather the following tools to aid in your readings:

1. **Star Charts and Celestial Maps:** A star chart or celestial map is essential for locating stars, constellations, and celestial events in the night sky. These tools provide a visual representation of the stars' positions relative to Earth at any given time.
2. **Telescopes or Binoculars:** While not mandatory, using a telescope or binoculars can enhance your star-gazing experience, allowing you to view celestial bodies in greater detail.
3. **Astrological Software:** Many modern diviners use astrological software that includes detailed information about fixed stars, star clusters, and celestial events, simplifying the process of locating and interpreting star positions.
4. **Notebook or Journal:** Keep a dedicated journal to record your observations, interpretations, and the insights gained from your stellar readings.
5. **Crystals and Altar Items:** Including crystals like clear quartz, amethyst, or selenite on your altar can help amplify your divination work and connect you with celestial energies.

Interpreting Star Patterns for Divination

The stars form patterns in the sky that have been named and studied for thousands of years. These patterns, known as constellations, are believed to carry specific energies, archetypes, and symbolic meanings. In stellar divination, interpreting these star patterns can provide insights into various aspects of your life, such as love, career, health, and spiritual growth.

1. **Constellation Divination: Reading Star Patterns**

Each constellation represents a unique set of qualities, lessons, and influences. By observing the positions and interactions of constellations in the night sky, you can receive messages related to specific life situations or questions.
Instructions:

1. **Identify the Constellation:** Choose a clear night and locate a constellation that draws your attention. Use your star chart or celestial map to identify the constellation and the fixed stars within it. For example, if you notice the constellation Orion, you might focus on stars like Betelgeuse or Rigel.
2. **Contemplate Its Meaning:** Reflect on the symbolic meaning of the constellation. For instance, Orion represents strength, bravery, and the pursuit of goals. Its appearance in the sky may suggest that now is a time for courage and assertive action in your life.
3. **Observe Interactions:** Pay attention to the nearby stars and constellations. Are they aligning, separating, or crossing paths? These interactions can provide additional layers of meaning. For example, if you see Orion near the Pleiades, it may indicate a time to blend strength with nurturing energy.
4. **Interpret the Message:** Use your intuition to interpret the constellation's message in relation to your current life situation. Consider how the qualities of the constellation apply to your question or concern. Write down your insights in your journal for later reflection.

Example Interpretation:
If you see the constellation Leo high in the sky, it may signal a period of self-expression, confidence, and leadership. If Leo aligns with the star

Regulus, known as the "Heart of the Lion," the message may be to embrace your power and lead with integrity.

Celestial Movements and Divination

In addition to fixed stars and constellations, the movements of celestial bodies, such as the Moon, planets, and asteroids, in relation to stars provide vital information for stellar divination. These movements create dynamic changes in the sky's energy, influencing personal experiences and potential outcomes.

2. Lunar Phases and Star Interaction

The Moon's phases play a crucial role in stellar divination, as they amplify or modify the energies of the stars they pass. For example, a full moon in proximity to the star Antares in the constellation Scorpius may indicate a time of intense emotions, transformation, and revealing hidden truths.

Instructions:

1. **Track the Lunar Phase:** Begin by noting the current lunar phase. Is it a waxing crescent, full moon, or waning gibbous? The Moon's phase will influence the interpretation of the star it interacts with.
2. **Identify the Star or Constellation:** Use a star chart to find the stars near the Moon's position. Pay attention to significant stars or constellations that the Moon may be approaching or moving away from.
3. **Interpret the Energy:** Consider the symbolic meaning of the star or constellation in relation to the Moon's phase. For instance, if the full moon is near the star Aldebaran, associated with strength and passion, it may signal a culmination of efforts and the need to assert your desires boldly.
4. **Record Your Observations:** Write down your observations and interpretations, noting how the interaction of the Moon and stars reflects your current life circumstances or offers guidance for future decisions.

Example Interpretation:

If the new moon is near the Pleiades cluster, it might signify a time for setting intentions related to nurturing, emotional healing, and building connections. The new moon's energy of beginnings combined with the Pleiades' influence could encourage you to focus on personal growth and relationship harmony.

3. Planetary Alignments with Stars

Planetary alignments, also known as "conjunctions," occur when planets pass close to specific stars. These alignments create powerful energetic dynamics that can significantly impact divination outcomes.

Instructions:

1. **Find Planetary Alignments:** Use an astrological software or a celestial map to locate current planetary alignments with stars. For example, you may notice Venus aligning with the star Spica in the constellation Virgo.
2. **Consider Planetary Influence:** Reflect on the nature of the planet involved in the alignment. Venus governs love, beauty, and harmony, so its conjunction with Spica (associated with purity and grace) suggests themes of love, relationship harmony, and the pursuit of beauty.
3. **Determine the Message:** Interpret the alignment based on the planet and star's combined energies. If Venus aligns with Spica, it might indicate a favorable time for love spells, beauty rituals, or resolving conflicts in relationships.
4. **Use Divinatory Tools:** Incorporate tarot cards, runes, or pendulums during the planetary alignment to ask specific questions. The energy of the alignment can enhance the accuracy and depth of your divinatory insights.

Example Interpretation:

If Mars aligns with the star Regulus, the "Heart of the Lion," it could signify a period of assertiveness, courage, and taking bold actions. However, it may also warn of potential conflicts and the need to balance assertiveness with compassion.

Using Star-Based Oracles for Divination

In addition to observing the night sky, star-based oracles such as tarot decks featuring star imagery, astrology cards, or star runes can be used to channel stellar energy during divination practices. These tools provide a tangible way to connect with star wisdom and translate celestial messages into practical guidance.

4. Star Oracle Reading

Tools Needed:

- A star-themed oracle deck or astrology cards
- A star map or chart for reference

Instructions:

1. **Set Your Intention:** Before shuffling the cards, set a clear intention or ask a specific question. For example, "What guidance do the stars have for me regarding my career?"
2. **Draw the Cards:** Shuffle the deck while focusing on your question. Draw three cards and lay them out in front of you.
3. **Interpret the Cards:** Refer to the symbols, stars, and celestial elements on the cards to interpret their meaning. Cross-reference the imagery with your star map to deepen your understanding. For instance, if you draw a card representing Sirius, consider its associations with clarity, spiritual insight, and loyalty.
4. **Synthesize the Message:** Combine the meanings of the cards to form a cohesive message. Record the reading in your journal, noting how the star-based symbols align with your situation.

Tips for Effective Stellar Divination

1. **Regular Sky Observations:** Spend time regularly observing the night sky. Becoming familiar with the stars, constellations, and celestial movements enhances your intuitive connection and sharpens your divination skills.
2. **Keep a Star Diary:** Maintain a diary where you record star positions, lunar phases, planetary alignments, and your interpretations. Reviewing your diary can reveal patterns and improve your ability to read the stars over time.
3. **Incorporate Meditation:** Practice star meditations to deepen your connection with specific stars or constellations. This practice opens your mind to receiving more profound insights during divination.

Conclusion

Stellar divination is an ancient and profound art that taps into the wisdom of the stars to provide guidance and insights into life's mysteries. By learning to interpret star patterns, celestial movements, and planetary alignments, you can unlock messages from the cosmos that illuminate your path and empower you to make informed decisions. Whether you seek answers about love, career, health, or spiritual growth, the stars are ever-present, offering their light to guide you. As you cultivate your practice of stellar divination, you will find that the night sky becomes a living oracle, reflecting the rhythms of the universe and the flow of your own life. Embrace the stars as your cosmic guides, and let their timeless wisdom shine upon your journey.

Chapter 21: Star Magic for Personal Growth

Personal growth is a journey of transformation, one that requires inner reflection, clarity, confidence, and a willingness to embrace change. The stars, with their ancient wisdom and cosmic energy, can be powerful allies in this process, offering guidance, strength, and illumination along the way. In Star Magic, the celestial bodies serve as mirrors to our inner landscape, helping us identify areas for self-improvement and providing the energy needed to pursue our goals and aspirations.

This chapter explores how to harness the power of the stars for personal growth, with a focus on building confidence, gaining clarity, and fostering motivation. You will find rituals and techniques designed to align your energy with the stars' empowering vibrations, allowing you to tap into their guidance for self-transformation.

Understanding Star Magic and Personal Growth

Star Magic is based on the principle that the stars radiate energy and emit vibrations that can influence our thoughts, emotions, and actions. Each star and constellation carries unique characteristics, symbolizing various aspects of human experience. By connecting with the stars, we can draw upon their energies to enhance our own strengths, overcome weaknesses, and align with the universe's flow.

- **Confidence:** Certain stars, such as Regulus and Aldebaran, exude an energy of courage, self-assurance, and strength. Working with these stars can bolster your inner confidence, helping you to face challenges with a bold heart.
- **Clarity:** Stars like Sirius and Alcyone (in the Pleiades) are associated with wisdom, insight, and spiritual vision. Their light can clear mental fog, providing a clearer perspective on life's complexities.

- **Motivation:** Stars and constellations linked to dynamic energy, such as Betelgeuse in Orion, can spark motivation, drive, and the determination needed to pursue personal growth.

Preparing for Personal Growth Rituals with Star Magic

To begin your journey of personal growth through Star Magic, it is important to create an environment conducive to reflection, intention-setting, and energetic work. Follow these steps to prepare:

1. **Set Your Intention:** Clarify what aspect of personal growth you wish to focus on. Do you want to build self-confidence, gain clarity on a situation, or boost your motivation to achieve a goal? Write your intention in a journal, as this will be central to your star magic practices.
2. **Create a Sacred Space:** Choose a quiet place where you can perform rituals and meditate without interruption. Set up an altar with items that resonate with your intention, such as crystals, candles, star maps, or symbols of the stars you will work with.
3. **Cleanse Your Space:** Cleanse your space using incense, sage, or a selenite wand to remove any stagnant or negative energy. This helps create a clear, receptive environment for star energy.

Rituals for Building Confidence

Confidence is the foundation of personal growth. It empowers you to take action, embrace change, and stand firm in your beliefs and decisions. Stars like Regulus, the "Heart of the Lion" in the constellation Leo, and Aldebaran, the "Eye of the Bull" in Taurus, radiate an energy of strength, assertiveness, and self-assurance.

1. Regulus' Empowerment Ritual

Regulus is associated with courage, leadership, and self-expression. This ritual harnesses Regulus' energy to build inner confidence and help you radiate self-assuredness.

Tools Needed:

- Gold or yellow candle (symbolizing the Sun and confidence)
- A piece of tiger's eye (for courage and inner strength)
- A small mirror (to reflect self-image)
- A star chart showing the constellation Leo and Regulus

Instructions:

1. **Create Your Space:** Light the candle and place the tiger's eye and mirror on your altar. Lay out the star chart with the constellation Leo and focus on the star Regulus.
2. **Set Your Intention:** Hold the tiger's eye in your hands and close your eyes. Say, "Regulus, Heart of the Lion, grant me your courage and strength. Help me shine with confidence, like your brilliant light."
3. **Visualize:** Visualize a golden light emanating from Regulus in the sky, growing brighter and descending toward you. Imagine this light entering your body, filling you with warmth, strength, and self-assurance.
4. **Mirror Affirmation:** Look into the mirror and, while still holding the tiger's eye, say aloud, "I am confident. I am strong. I am worthy of success and respect." Repeat this affirmation three times, feeling Regulus' energy amplifying your words.
5. **Closing:** Blow out the candle and keep the tiger's eye on your altar as a reminder of Regulus' empowering energy. Perform this ritual whenever you need a confidence boost.

Tips: Perform this ritual on a Sunday, the day associated with the Sun, to further enhance its confidence-building power.

2. Aldebaran's Shield of Inner Strength

Aldebaran, the bright star in Taurus, symbolizes strength, resilience, and unwavering determination. This ritual connects you with Aldebaran's steadfast energy, helping you build confidence that remains firm even in the face of challenges.

Tools Needed:

- Red or orange candle (for strength and determination)
- A piece of hematite (to ground and fortify)
- A bowl of saltwater (to symbolize resilience)

Instructions:

1. **Prepare Your Altar:** Light the candle and place the hematite and bowl of saltwater on your altar. Focus on Aldebaran in the sky or on a star chart.
2. **Invoke Aldebaran:** Hold the hematite in your hands and say, "Aldebaran, Eye of the Bull, fill me with your strength and resilience. Help me stand firm, confident, and unshaken."
3. **Visualize:** Close your eyes and imagine Aldebaran's red-orange light radiating toward you, forming a protective shield around your body. Feel its energy strengthening your resolve and grounding your confidence.
4. **Saltwater Anointment:** Dip your fingers into the saltwater and touch your forehead, heart, and wrists, saying, "By Aldebaran's light, I am strong, I am bold, I am unbreakable."
5. **Closing:** Keep the hematite with you during the day as a reminder of Aldebaran's protective and confident energy.

Tips: Repeat this ritual whenever you need to reinforce your inner strength, especially before facing difficult situations.

Rituals for Gaining Clarity

Clarity is crucial for personal growth, as it helps you see the truth of situations, understand your emotions, and make informed decisions. Stars like Sirius, the "Dog Star," and Alcyone in the Pleiades are associated with spiritual insight, wisdom, and mental clarity.

3. Sirius' Light of Insight

Sirius is known for its association with higher knowledge, intuition, and spiritual clarity. This ritual connects you with Sirius' bright, clear light to enhance mental clarity and provide insights into your life path.

Tools Needed:

- Blue or white candle (to symbolize clarity and purity)
- A piece of clear quartz (to amplify mental focus)
- A small bowl of water (to reflect and clarify)

Instructions:

1. **Prepare Your Space:** Light the candle and place the clear quartz and bowl of water on your altar. Focus on Sirius, either in the sky or on a star map.
2. **Invoke Sirius:** Hold the clear quartz in your hands and say, "Sirius, star of wisdom and light, shine your clarity upon me. Clear my mind, sharpen my sight, and reveal the truths I need to see."
3. **Visualization:** Close your eyes and visualize a brilliant, blue-white light shining from Sirius, illuminating your mind and washing away confusion or mental fog. Imagine this light entering your forehead, filling your mind with its clear, crisp energy.
4. **Water Reflection:** Look into the bowl of water and focus on your reflection. As you gaze, ask, "What do I need to see clearly in my life?" Remain open to any thoughts, feelings, or images that arise.
5. **Closing:** Blow out the candle and place the clear quartz under your pillow to promote clarity during your dreams.

Tips: Perform this ritual during the waxing moon to enhance its power of illumination and insight.

4. Alcyone's Truth-Seeking Meditation

Alcyone, the brightest star in the Pleiades, is associated with spiritual wisdom and inner vision. This meditation helps you connect with Alcyone's energy to gain deeper clarity and understanding of your life.

Tools Needed:

- Purple candle (for intuition and inner wisdom)
- Amethyst crystal (to enhance spiritual insight)

Instructions:

1. **Set Up Your Space:** Light the purple candle and hold the amethyst in your hands. Sit comfortably and close your eyes.
2. **Visualize Alcyone:** In your mind's eye, picture the Pleiades cluster shining in the night sky, focusing on Alcyone's bright light. Imagine this light expanding and enveloping you in a sphere of calm, clear energy.
3. **Meditate:** Breathe deeply and slowly, focusing on the light surrounding you. Silently ask, "Alcyone, what truths do I need to see? Show me the path to clarity and understanding."
4. **Listen and Observe:** Remain in a state of quiet contemplation, allowing thoughts, feelings, or images to emerge. Trust that Alcyone's light is illuminating the truths you seek.
5. **Closing:** When you feel ready, open your eyes and write down any insights or impressions in your journal. Keep the amethyst on your altar as a symbol of Alcyone's guidance.

Rituals for Boosting Motivation

Motivation fuels personal growth, giving you the energy and determination to pursue your goals. Stars associated with dynamic energy, such as Betelgeuse in Orion, emit vibrations that can spark motivation and drive.

5. Betelgeuse's Fire of Determination

Betelgeuse, the red supergiant in Orion, represents strength, action, and the will to forge ahead. This ritual draws upon Betelgeuse's fiery energy to boost your motivation and propel you toward your goals.

Tools Needed:

- Red or orange candle (for energy and determination)
- A piece of carnelian or garnet (for motivation and action)
- A piece of paper and a pen

Instructions:

1. **Set Your Space:** Light the candle and hold the carnelian or garnet in your hands. Sit before your altar and focus on Betelgeuse.
2. **Set Your Intention:** On the piece of paper, write down a specific goal or area where you seek increased motivation.
3. **Invoke Betelgeuse:** Say, "Betelgeuse, star of fire and might, ignite my spirit and fuel my drive. Help me take action, bold and swift, and move forward with purpose and strength."
4. **Visualize:** Visualize a powerful red light radiating from Betelgeuse, filling you with energy, passion, and determination. See this light surrounding your written goal, empowering it with the force of your intention.
5. **Affirmation:** While holding the stone, say, "I am motivated. I am driven. I am unstoppable in achieving my goals." Repeat this affirmation three times.
6. **Closing:** Fold the paper and place it under the candle. Keep the stone with you as a source of motivation.

Tips: Perform this ritual on a Tuesday, the day ruled by Mars, to enhance its motivating energy.

Conclusion

The stars hold an ancient and boundless power that, when harnessed, can significantly impact your journey of personal growth. By working with stars like Regulus, Aldebaran, Sirius, and Betelgeuse, you can draw upon their specific energies to build confidence, gain clarity, and fuel your motivation. These rituals and meditations serve as tools to connect you with the cosmic forces that align with your higher purpose, empowering you to pursue self-improvement with a sense of guidance, strength, and determination. As you incorporate Star Magic into your personal growth practices, you will find that the stars not only light up the night sky but also illuminate the path to your own transformation.

Chapter 22: Star Magic in Ritual Circles

Star Magic, while often practiced individually, can become even more powerful and transformative when incorporated into group rituals and coven circles. The collective energy of a group aligned with the stars creates a vibrant synergy, allowing participants to harness stellar energies more profoundly. In ritual circles, practitioners can channel star power to amplify their intentions, enhance group harmony, and deepen spiritual connections. This chapter explores how to incorporate Star Magic into group rituals, offering tips for leading stellar-based ceremonies and aligning a collective's energy with the cosmos.

The Power of Group Rituals in Star Magic

Group rituals serve as a way to unify intentions, amplify energy, and create a sacred space where participants can work with cosmic forces together. When multiple individuals come together with a shared focus, the energy generated is exponentially stronger, providing a more potent channel for stellar energies to flow. This collaborative atmosphere not only enhances each participant's personal connection to the stars but also helps to balance and align the group's collective vibration with cosmic rhythms.

Benefits of Incorporating Star Magic in Ritual Circles:

1. **Amplification of Intent:** A group's combined intention, directed toward a star or constellation, increases the ritual's power, making it easier to manifest desired outcomes.
2. **Shared Guidance:** Each member may receive different insights and messages from the stars, creating a more comprehensive understanding of the energies at play.

3. **Collective Support:** The ritual circle provides emotional and spiritual support, helping each participant deepen their connection to the cosmos.

Preparing for a Stellar Ritual Circle

Before performing a group ritual centered around Star Magic, preparation is crucial. The facilitator or ritual leader should set the tone, establish a clear intention, and ensure the participants are aligned with the star energies being invoked.

1. **Select a Cosmic Focus: Choose a specific star, constellation, or celestial event to center the ritual. Consider the group's intention—are you seeking clarity from Sirius, courage from Regulus, or healing from the Pleiades? Use an ephemeris or astrological software to determine the best time for the ritual based on the star's visibility and alignment.**

2. **Plan the Ritual Structure: Decide on the elements and flow of the ritual, including opening the circle, invoking the stars, conducting activities (such as meditation, chanting, or energy work), and closing the circle. Prepare any tools, symbols, or offerings needed to represent the star energies involved.**

3. **Gather Ritual Tools: For stellar rituals, consider including:**

- **Star Maps:** To locate and focus on specific stars during the ritual.
- **Crystals:** Stones like clear quartz, labradorite, and selenite amplify star energies.
- **Candles:** Use candles in colors associated with the star's energy (e.g., blue for Sirius, gold for Regulus).
- **Incense:** Frankincense, sandalwood, or other cosmic-scented incenses to invoke celestial vibrations.
- **Drums or Bells:** To raise energy and facilitate meditation or trance states.

4. **Set Up the Space:** Create a sacred space where the group can gather in a circle. If outdoors, choose a location with an open view of the night sky. If indoors, arrange the space to represent the cosmos, using star charts, celestial symbols, and candles to create an atmosphere conducive to star magic.

Aligning Group Energy with the Stars

To effectively channel star energy, it is essential to align the group's collective energy with the cosmic forces being invoked. This involves grounding, centering, and synchronizing the participants' focus.

1. Grounding and Centering: The Star Anchor

Before beginning the main ritual, guide the group through a grounding exercise to connect with the Earth and a centering practice to align with the stars. This process, known as "star anchoring," helps each participant become a conduit for star energy.

Instructions:

1. **Grounding:** Instruct participants to close their eyes, take deep breaths, and visualize roots growing from their feet into the Earth. This grounding connects their energy to the Earth, creating a stable foundation for the star energy to flow.
2. **Centering:** Once grounded, ask everyone to focus on their solar plexus (the energy center associated with personal power) and imagine a sphere of white light expanding outward. This sphere represents their inner star, aligning them with the cosmos.
3. **Star Connection:** As a group, visualize a beam of light extending upward from the crown of each person's head, reaching into the night sky. Picture these beams connecting to the specific star or constellation chosen for the ritual. Feel the group's energy merging with the star's light, creating a shared, unified connection.

Conducting Star Magic Rituals in Circles

Once the group is aligned with the star energy, the main ritual can begin. This section provides detailed examples of stellar rituals that can be performed in a group setting, emphasizing collaboration and collective intention.

2. Invoking the Star: The Constellation Circle Ritual

This ritual focuses on invoking a constellation, such as Orion or the Pleiades, to draw its qualities into the circle. The group collectively calls upon the constellation to receive guidance, strength, and inspiration.

Tools Needed:

- Candles representing the stars of the constellation (e.g., 3 candles for Orion's Belt)
- Star map showing the constellation
- Crystals associated with the constellation's energy (e.g., moonstone for the Pleiades, carnelian for Orion)

Instructions:

1. **Form the Circle:** Arrange participants in a circle, with the candles placed at the circle's center to represent the constellation.
2. **Open the Circle:** The ritual leader opens the circle by walking clockwise around the group, carrying a lit candle to signify the star's light. As the leader moves, they may chant or recite a blessing invoking the cosmos.
3. **Invoke the Constellation:** After the circle is opened, the leader calls upon the chosen constellation. For example:
"Orion, hunter of the sky, we call to you. Lend us your strength, your courage, and your sight. Shine upon us with your celestial power and guide our spirits this night."
4. **Candle Lighting:** Participants take turns lighting the candles representing the constellation's stars. As each candle is lit, the group collectively chants the name of the star (e.g., "Alnilam, Alnitak, Mintaka" for Orion's Belt).
5. **Meditation and Sharing:** Guide the group into a meditation to connect with the constellation's energy. Afterward, participants

can share any insights, feelings, or messages they received during the meditation.
6. **Closing:** The leader walks counterclockwise around the circle, thanking the constellation and extinguishing the central candle. The group then grounds themselves by visualizing their roots returning to the Earth.

3. Stellar Healing Circle: The Pleiades Nurturing Ritual

This ritual uses the nurturing and healing energy of the Pleiades to promote emotional and spiritual well-being within the group. Participants work together to channel the cluster's energy for collective and individual healing.

Tools Needed:

- Blue or silver candles (to represent the Pleiades)
- A bowl of water with floating flowers (to symbolize nurturing energy)
- Moonstone or rose quartz crystals for each participant

Instructions:

1. **Circle Formation:** Arrange the group in a circle around the bowl of water, placing the candles in a smaller circle around the bowl.
2. **Open the Circle:** The leader opens the circle by lighting the candles, saying, "We open this circle to the Pleiades, stars of grace and nurture. Bring your healing light into our circle and into our hearts."
3. **Invocation of the Pleiades:** The leader continues, "Pleiades, sisters of the sky, lend us your nurturing touch. Bring healing to our minds, hearts, and spirits. We open ourselves to your celestial embrace."

4. **Energy Sharing:** Ask participants to hold their moonstone or rose quartz and focus on the Pleiades. Guide them to visualize a soft blue light radiating from the star cluster, filling the circle and each person with its calming, healing energy.
5. **Group Healing Chant:** Lead the group in a chant to enhance the energy, such as, "Pleiades, stars so bright, heal us in your gentle light." Repeat the chant several times, allowing the energy to build.
6. **Release and Grounding:** After the chant, instruct participants to place their crystals around the bowl, symbolizing the release of any burdens into the nurturing water. Close the circle by thanking the Pleiades and extinguishing the candles.

Tips for Leading Stellar-Based Ritual Circles

1. **Set the Ritual Tone:** Begin each ritual by setting a clear intention and focusing the group's energy on the star or constellation being invoked. This focus strengthens the connection and amplifies the ritual's effects.
2. **Encourage Participation:** Invite each participant to take an active role, such as lighting candles, chanting, or sharing insights. Engaging everyone helps to unify the group's energy and deepen the ritual experience.
3. **Be Mindful of Timing:** Choose ritual times that align with celestial events, such as star alignments, moon phases, or specific constellations' visibility. Timing enhances the ritual's potency and aligns it with natural cosmic rhythms.
4. **Use Visualization:** Guide the group through visualizations of stars, star patterns, or beams of light to create a strong mental and spiritual link to the stars.
5. **Close with Grounding:** Always end rituals with a grounding exercise to help participants return to their physical selves and anchor the energy they have received.

Conclusion

Incorporating Star Magic into group rituals and coven circles can greatly enhance the power and transformative potential of your practices. By aligning the collective energy with specific stars, constellations, and celestial events, the group becomes a unified channel for the cosmos, capable of amplifying intentions, receiving guidance, and fostering deep spiritual connections. Whether invoking the strength of Orion, the nurturing light of the Pleiades, or the insight of Sirius, group rituals offer a unique opportunity to explore the mysteries of the stars together. As you lead or participate in stellar rituals, you will discover that the circle not only reflects the cosmic unity of the universe but also becomes a microcosm of the stars, radiating light, power, and wisdom.

Chapter 23: The Cosmic Web—Connecting with the Universe

The stars are not isolated points of light scattered across the night sky; they are part of an intricate, interconnected cosmic web that encompasses the entire universe. This web is composed of the forces, energies, and vibrations that permeate all of existence, connecting every star, planet, celestial body, and living being in a vast, dynamic network. In Star Magic, tapping into this cosmic web enables you to access universal wisdom, synchronize your energy with the cosmos, and align yourself with the universe's rhythms. By recognizing your place within this cosmic structure, you can draw upon its power to enhance your life, facilitate personal growth, and explore deeper spiritual dimensions.

In this chapter, we explore the concept of the cosmic web and how the stars, along with other celestial bodies, form an intricate network of energy that connects all things. You will learn techniques to tap into this universal web, synchronize your energy with the cosmos, and access the wisdom it holds. From meditative practices to rituals and star-based visualization exercises, this chapter guides you on how to align with the cosmic web and draw upon its limitless knowledge and power.

Understanding the Cosmic Web

The cosmic web is the universe's vast, interconnected structure, comprising dark matter, galaxies, stars, planets, and other celestial bodies. Scientists have observed that galaxies are arranged in a vast network of filaments, creating a web-like pattern that spans the entire cosmos. This physical web of galaxies is mirrored by the metaphysical web of energies that connects every star, planet, and living being. In spiritual traditions, this cosmic web is often seen as the universe's lifeblood, through which energy, information, and wisdom flow.

- **The Web as a Source of Universal Wisdom:** The cosmic web holds the universe's collective knowledge, embodying the cycles, patterns, and rhythms that govern all things. By connecting to this web, you can access insights into your life's path, find your place within the universe, and receive guidance on navigating life's challenges.

- **Synchronizing Your Energy:** Tapping into the cosmic web allows you to align your own energy with the universe's flow, creating a sense of harmony, balance, and purpose. This synchronization helps you move in tune with cosmic cycles, enhancing your ability to manifest desires, heal, and grow spiritually.

Preparing to Connect with the Cosmic Web

Connecting with the cosmic web requires an open heart, a quiet mind, and a willingness to embrace the universe's infinite possibilities. To begin this process, create a sacred space and prepare yourself for this deeper connection with the cosmos.

1. Set Your Intention: Before you attempt to connect with the cosmic web, set a clear intention. Are you seeking universal wisdom, emotional balance, or a deeper understanding of your life's purpose? Writing down your intention in a journal can help you stay focused during your practice.

2. Create a Cosmic Altar: Set up a space dedicated to cosmic connection. Include star charts, celestial symbols, crystals (such as amethyst, clear quartz, or labradorite), candles, and representations of stars or constellations. This altar serves as an anchor point for your energy and a focal point during your meditative practices.

3. Cleanse and Ground: Use incense, sage, or a cleansing crystal like selenite to clear any stagnant energy from your space and aura. Ground yourself by visualizing roots growing from your feet into the Earth, providing a stable base for your cosmic journey.

Techniques for Tapping into the Cosmic Web

There are several ways to connect with the cosmic web and access its wisdom. From meditation to rituals and visualization exercises, these techniques help you attune to the universe's vibrations and harmonize your energy with the stars.

1. Cosmic Web Meditation: Journey to the Universal Mind

This meditation practice is designed to guide you into the cosmic web, where you can experience the interconnectedness of all things and access the wisdom of the universe.

Tools Needed:

- A piece of clear quartz or selenite (to enhance connection)
- White or silver candle (to symbolize the universe's light)
- A quiet space where you can sit undisturbed

Instructions:

1. **Create Your Space:** Light the candle and hold the clear quartz or selenite in your hands. Sit comfortably in front of your cosmic altar, close your eyes, and take several deep breaths.
2. **Grounding and Centering:** Visualize roots growing from your feet, connecting you to the Earth. As you breathe, imagine a white light expanding from your heart, enveloping you in a protective sphere of energy.
3. **Visualize the Cosmic Web:** In your mind's eye, picture yourself floating in the vast expanse of space. Around you, the stars, galaxies, and nebulae form a glowing, web-like network that extends in all directions. Each filament pulses with light, connecting the stars in a shimmering web of energy.
4. **Connecting with the Web:** Imagine a beam of light extending from your heart to the cosmic web. As your light merges with the

web, feel the energy and information flow into you, filling you with a sense of peace, unity, and understanding.
5. **Receiving Universal Wisdom:** Ask the universe a question or focus on an area of your life where you seek guidance. Remain open and listen to the impressions, thoughts, or sensations that arise. Trust that the cosmic web is providing you with the insights you need.
6. **Returning:** When you are ready to end the meditation, slowly retract your beam of light from the web and focus on your breath. Feel your feet connected to the Earth, grounding you. Open your eyes and take a few moments to reflect on your experience.

Tips: Keep a journal nearby to write down any insights or messages received during the meditation. Over time, you may notice recurring themes or patterns that provide deeper understanding.

2. The Cosmic Cord Ritual: Synchronizing Your Energy with the Stars

This ritual uses visualization and energy work to synchronize your personal energy with the stars and the cosmic web. By creating an energetic cord that links you to the universe, you can enhance your ability to manifest, heal, and align with the cosmic flow.

Tools Needed:

- Blue or purple candle (to represent cosmic energy)
- A piece of labradorite or amethyst (to aid in spiritual connection)
- A silver or white cord or ribbon

Instructions:

1. **Set Up Your Space:** Light the candle and place the labradorite or amethyst on your altar. Hold the silver or white cord in your hands and sit comfortably.

2. **Grounding:** Close your eyes and take deep breaths. Visualize roots extending from your feet into the Earth, anchoring you.
3. **Cosmic Cord Creation:** Hold the cord in your hands and visualize it glowing with a silver-white light. Imagine one end of the cord attaching to your heart, while the other extends outward into space, seeking a star or a point in the cosmic web.
4. **Connect with the Universe:** See the cord weaving itself into the cosmic web, creating a direct link between you and the stars. Feel the energy flowing through the cord, synchronizing your heartbeat with the rhythm of the universe.
5. **Intention Setting:** Speak your intention aloud: "I am connected to the cosmic web. My energy is aligned with the universe, flowing with its wisdom, light, and guidance. I move in harmony with the stars."
6. **Energy Synchronization:** Visualize the energy from the stars flowing through the cord into your heart, spreading throughout your body, filling you with a sense of unity and balance. Allow this energy to dissolve any blockages or stagnant energy, creating a harmonious flow within you.
7. **Closing:** When you feel the connection is complete, gently wrap the cord and place it on your altar as a symbol of your link to the cosmic web.

Tips: Perform this ritual during significant celestial events, such as full moons, equinoxes, or star alignments, to enhance its effects.

3. Stellar Visualization: Drawing Down Universal Energy

This visualization technique allows you to draw energy from specific stars or constellations within the cosmic web to enhance various aspects of your life, such as clarity, courage, or healing.

Instructions:

1. **Choose a Star:** Select a star or constellation that embodies the energy you wish to work with. For example, if you seek wisdom, choose Sirius; for healing, the Pleiades; for courage, Regulus.
2. **Create Your Space:** Light a candle that corresponds to the star's energy (e.g., blue for Sirius) and sit comfortably. Hold a crystal associated with the star's energy, such as selenite for Sirius.
3. **Visualize the Star:** Close your eyes and picture the star shining brightly in the night sky. See its light radiating outward, connecting to the cosmic web's filaments.
4. **Draw Down the Energy:** Visualize a beam of light extending from the star to you. As the light reaches you, feel it entering your body, filling you with the star's energy. Imagine this light spreading throughout your body, enhancing the aspect you wish to improve (e.g., filling your mind with clarity, your heart with courage).
5. **Synchronize and Ground:** As the star's energy flows through you, synchronize your breath with the universe's rhythm. Inhale the star's light, exhale any negativity or resistance. When you are ready, ground yourself by focusing on your breath and feeling the connection between you and the Earth.

Tips: Practice this visualization regularly to strengthen your connection with the cosmic web and the stars' energy.

The Wisdom of the Cosmic Web

The cosmic web not only connects all things but also holds the universe's accumulated wisdom. This wisdom can manifest as insights, synchronicities, and a deeper understanding of your life's purpose and the patterns that shape your experiences. When you synchronize with the cosmic web, you become more attuned to these subtle messages, allowing you to make decisions that align with the universe's flow.

- **Synchronicities:** As you deepen your connection with the cosmic web, you may notice an increase in synchronicities—meaningful coincidences that guide you toward your goals or reveal hidden truths.
- **Universal Rhythm:** By tuning into the cosmic web, you become more aware of the universe's natural rhythms, such as planetary cycles, lunar phases, and celestial events. This awareness allows you to plan your actions in harmony with cosmic timing, enhancing their effectiveness.

Tips for Enhancing Your Cosmic Connection

1. **Practice Regularly:** Consistent meditation, visualization, and rituals help strengthen your connection to the cosmic web, making it easier to access its wisdom and energy.
2. **Observe Celestial Events:** Pay attention to celestial events, such as meteor showers, eclipses, and star alignments. These events can serve as powerful gateways for connecting with the cosmic web and enhancing your energy work.
3. **Keep a Cosmic Journal:** Document your experiences, insights, and any messages received during your practices. Over time, you may notice patterns that reveal a deeper understanding of your place within the cosmic web.

Conclusion

The cosmic web is the universe's vast network of interconnected energy, through which wisdom, guidance, and cosmic rhythms flow. By tapping into this web, you can align your energy with the stars, access universal knowledge, and move in harmony with the cosmos. Through meditation, rituals, and visualization exercises, you can deepen your connection to this intricate web, drawing upon its power to enhance your personal growth, spiritual journey, and understanding of the universe's mysteries. Embrace the cosmic web as both a source of guidance and a reminder of your place in the infinite dance of stars, planets, and energies that shape all existence. As you weave your own light into the cosmic web, you become a part of its ever-expanding brilliance, embodying the universe's wisdom, strength, and beauty.

Chapter 24: Star Magic for Protection Against Dark Energies

The stars have long been seen as symbols of light, guidance, and purity, standing against the darkness of the vast, unknown cosmos. In various cultures and spiritual traditions, stars are revered as powerful guardians that can repel negative energies, dark entities, and unwanted influences. By harnessing the protective energy of the stars, you can create a barrier of light that shields you from harm, cleanses your surroundings, and preserves your inner peace. Star Magic offers unique techniques and rituals that draw on the stars' ancient power to ward off dark forces and protect your energy.

This chapter explores how to use the protective energies of specific stars, constellations, and celestial bodies to shield yourself from negativity. From rituals invoking star energy to creating star-based talismans, you will learn how to use stellar power as a spiritual shield. By working with the stars, you can create a lasting aura of protection around you, banishing dark entities and ensuring that only positive, high-vibration energies can enter your space.

The Protective Power of the Stars

The stars, with their constant light and eternal presence, have long been regarded as symbols of hope and strength in the face of darkness. Many stars and constellations are associated with protective qualities:

- **Aldebaran:** Known as the "Eye of the Bull" in Taurus, Aldebaran embodies strength, resilience, and unwavering protection. It serves as a guardian star that shields against negative influences.
- **Antares:** The bright, red star in the heart of Scorpius is linked with courage and spiritual defense, offering protection against malevolent forces and psychic attacks.
- **Sirius:** Often called the "Dog Star," Sirius symbolizes loyalty, guardianship, and purification. It can cleanse spaces of dark energies and provide a protective shield for spiritual seekers.

- **The Pleiades:** This star cluster is associated with nurturing, healing, and emotional protection, creating a sphere of safety and comfort around those who invoke its energy.

By aligning with the protective energies of these stars, you can create an energetic shield that not only repels negativity but also fortifies your spirit and inner light.

Preparing for Stellar Protection Rituals

Before performing protection rituals using Star Magic, it is crucial to prepare yourself and your space to ensure a clear and focused connection with the stars.

1. Set Your Intention: Clearly define what you are seeking protection from. Are you shielding yourself from negative thoughts, psychic attacks, dark entities, or harmful environments? Write down your intention in a journal to reinforce your focus during the ritual.

2. Create a Protective Space: Set up a sacred space where you will perform your rituals. Include items associated with protective stars, such as crystals (e.g., obsidian, black tourmaline, clear quartz), candles, star charts, and protective symbols. Cleanse the space with sage, palo santo, or selenite to clear away any lingering negative energy.

3. Ground and Center: Ground yourself by visualizing roots growing from your feet into the Earth, anchoring you. Then, center your energy by focusing on your heart and imagining a sphere of white light expanding around you. This light forms the foundation of your protective shield.

Rituals for Stellar Protection

The following rituals harness the energy of specific stars to create powerful protective shields. These practices can be performed when you feel the need for added protection or regularly to maintain a safe and positive environment.

1. Aldebaran's Shield of Strength

Aldebaran, known for its strength and resilience, can serve as a guardian against negativity and dark forces. This ritual draws on Aldebaran's energy to create a powerful protective shield around you.

Tools Needed:

- Red or orange candle (to represent Aldebaran's fiery energy)
- A piece of obsidian or black tourmaline (for grounding and protection)
- A bowl of saltwater (to symbolize cleansing)
- A star chart showing the constellation Taurus and Aldebaran

Instructions:

1. **Create Your Space:** Light the candle and place the obsidian or black tourmaline and the bowl of saltwater on your altar. Lay out the star chart with Taurus and focus on Aldebaran.
2. **Set Your Intention:** Hold the obsidian in your hands and say, "Aldebaran, Eye of the Bull, grant me your strength and unwavering shield. Protect me from all that is dark, harmful, and untrue."
3. **Visualize the Shield:** Close your eyes and visualize Aldebaran's fiery, red-orange light expanding from the sky and enveloping you in a sphere of light. See this light forming a protective barrier around you, impenetrable to negative energies.
4. **Water Cleansing:** Dip your fingers into the saltwater and sprinkle it around your body, saying, "By Aldebaran's light and the pu-

rifying waters, I cleanse and protect my energy. No darkness shall enter, only light shall remain."

5. **Affirmation:** Repeat the following affirmation three times: "I am protected. I am strong. The light of Aldebaran shields me from all harm."
6. **Closing:** Blow out the candle and keep the obsidian near you as a protective talisman.

Tips: Perform this ritual during the waxing moon to enhance the building of your protective shield.

2. Antares' Fire of Defense

Antares, the bright red star in Scorpius, embodies courage and spiritual defense. This ritual invokes Antares' fiery energy to protect against psychic attacks and dark entities.

Tools Needed:

- Red candle (symbolizing Antares' fiery nature)
- A piece of hematite or smoky quartz (to ground and deflect negative energy)
- A star chart showing the constellation Scorpius and Antares

Instructions:

1. **Set Up Your Space:** Light the red candle and place the hematite on your altar. Focus on the star chart, locating Antares within Scorpius.
2. **Invoke Antares:** Hold the hematite in your hands and say, "Antares, heart of the Scorpion, ignite your fire of protection. Burn away all that is harmful, shield me from the darkness that seeks to harm."
3. **Visualize the Fire:** Visualize a bright red flame emanating from Antares, forming a circle of fire around you. This flame does not

burn you but instead creates a protective barrier that repels any negative energy or dark forces.
4. **Shield Strengthening:** Imagine the flame growing stronger, surrounding you in an unbreakable shield. Feel the heat and power of Antares filling you with courage and strength.
5. **Affirmation:** Say aloud, "I am protected by the fire of Antares. No darkness may cross this sacred flame."
6. **Closing:** Blow out the candle and place the hematite on your altar or carry it with you as a protective stone.

Tips: Repeat this ritual during times of heightened stress or when you feel particularly vulnerable to psychic attacks.

Creating Star-Based Talismans for Protection

In addition to rituals, you can create talismans infused with star energy to carry protection with you wherever you go. These talismans serve as constant reminders of the stars' protective light and can be worn or placed in your home.

3. Sirius Protection Talisman

Sirius, the "Dog Star," is known for its purifying and protective properties. This talisman ritual calls upon Sirius to create a shield against negative energies.

Tools Needed:

- A small piece of silver jewelry (ring, pendant, etc.) or a small pouch
- A piece of selenite or clear quartz
- Blue or white candle
- Incense (frankincense or sandalwood)

Instructions:

1. **Prepare the Talisman:** Light the candle and the incense. Place the silver jewelry or pouch on your altar along with the selenite.

2. **Invoke Sirius:** Hold the selenite in your hands and focus on Sirius. Say, "Sirius, guardian of purity and light, bless this talisman with your protective energy. May it ward off darkness and cleanse all negativity."
3. **Infuse the Talisman:** Pass the silver jewelry or pouch through the incense smoke, visualizing a blue-white light from Sirius descending into the talisman. See this light radiating outward, creating a shield around the item.
4. **Affirmation:** Say aloud, "By the light of Sirius, this talisman is my shield. Darkness shall not touch me; I am protected and guided by the stars."
5. **Wearing the Talisman:** Wear the jewelry or carry the pouch with you as a protective charm. Whenever you feel threatened, hold the talisman and visualize the light of Sirius surrounding you.

Tips: Cleanse and recharge the talisman regularly by placing it in moonlight or passing it through incense smoke.

The Pleiadian Shield: A Protective Circle Ritual

The Pleiades star cluster is known for its nurturing and healing energy, which can be used to create a protective circle for emotional and spiritual safety. This ritual is ideal for cleansing your environment and establishing a sphere of protective energy.

Tools Needed:

- Seven small candles (to represent the seven sisters of the Pleiades)
- A bowl of water (to symbolize emotional protection)
- Moonstone or rose quartz

Instructions:

1. **Set Up the Circle:** Arrange the candles in a circle around the bowl of water. Place the moonstone or rose quartz inside the bowl.
2. **Light the Candles:** Light each candle, saying the name of one of the Pleiades sisters with each lighting: "Maia, Electra, Taygete, Alcyone, Celaeno, Sterope, Merope."
3. **Invoke the Pleiades:** Stand in the center of the circle and say, "Pleiades, stars of nurturing light, I call upon your shield of protection. Surround this space with your gentle embrace, ward off all negativity, and bring peace to this place."
4. **Visualize the Shield:** Imagine the stars of the Pleiades shining down, forming a dome of light around you. Feel this light cleansing your aura and creating a protective barrier.
5. **Affirmation:** Repeat, "I am safe within the stars' embrace. Darkness cannot enter; only love and light remain."
6. **Closing:** Extinguish the candles in the order they were lit, thanking each of the Pleiades sisters for their protection.

Tips: Perform this ritual whenever you need to cleanse your environment and establish a safe, protective space.

Maintaining Stellar Protection

Protection is an ongoing process that involves regular maintenance of your energetic boundaries. Here are some tips to maintain the stellar shield you create:

- **Daily Shielding:** Visualize a sphere of light from your chosen star surrounding you each morning, reinforcing your protective barrier.
- **Regular Cleansing:** Cleanse your space and talismans regularly using sage, incense, or moonlight to remove any accumulated negative energy.
- **Affirmations:** Incorporate protective affirmations into your daily routine to keep your energy aligned with the stars' light.

Conclusion

The stars, with their eternal light and cosmic power, offer a formidable defense against dark energies, negative influences, and psychic attacks. By invoking stars like Aldebaran, Antares, Sirius, and the Pleiades, you can create a powerful shield of light around yourself, your home, and your loved ones. Whether through ritual, talisman creation, or visualization, the protective energies of the stars serve as a guardian force, ensuring that you remain enveloped in light, strength, and positivity. Embrace the stars as your celestial protectors, and let their brilliance keep darkness at bay as you walk confidently on your spiritual path.

Chapter 25: Empowering Yourself with Star Magic

The stars, with their vast energy and timeless wisdom, have the power to illuminate our paths, boost our inner strength, and amplify our personal power. By connecting with the cosmic forces of specific stars or celestial events, we can harness their energies to empower ourselves, finding courage, self-belief, and a deeper sense of purpose. Star Magic offers various methods to tap into these celestial powers, providing rituals and practices that help you align with the universe's flow and amplify your personal energy. In this chapter, we explore how to empower yourself through Star Magic, using star-centered rituals, visualizations, and ceremonies to activate and strengthen your inner power.

The Concept of Empowerment in Star Magic

Empowerment in Star Magic involves drawing on the energy of stars, constellations, and cosmic events to awaken and magnify your inherent strengths. Each star emits specific vibrations that correspond to certain qualities, such as confidence, determination, clarity, and resilience. By connecting with these stars and their energies, you can attune to their frequency, using them as cosmic amplifiers for your own power.

Stars for Empowerment:

- **Regulus:** Known as the "Heart of the Lion," Regulus embodies strength, courage, and leadership. Connecting with this star can bolster your confidence and help you step into your power.
- **Vega:** Located in the constellation Lyra, Vega radiates a sense of harmony, creativity, and inspiration, empowering you to express your unique gifts.
- **Altair:** A star in the constellation Aquila, Altair represents swift action, boldness, and the power to overcome obstacles.
- **Betelgeuse:** The red supergiant in Orion symbolizes strength, resilience, and the fiery drive to pursue your goals with passion.

Celestial Events for Empowerment:

- **Full Moons:** The full moon is a time of heightened energy and illumination, ideal for rituals aimed at amplifying your personal power.
- **Solar Eclipses:** A solar eclipse represents transformation and renewal, offering a powerful moment to reclaim and empower your inner self.
- **Meteor Showers:** Meteor showers carry the energy of rapid change and new opportunities, allowing you to seize the moment and harness the power of the stars.

Preparing for Empowerment Rituals with Star Magic

Empowerment through Star Magic requires focus, intention, and a clear connection with the energies you wish to invoke. To prepare for empowerment rituals, create an environment conducive to spiritual work and attune your mind and spirit to receive stellar energy.

1. Set Your Intention: Before beginning any empowerment ritual, define your intention. Are you seeking to boost your self-confidence, embrace your creativity, or gain the strength to pursue a particular goal? Write your intention in a journal to clarify and solidify your focus.

2. Create a Cosmic Altar: Set up an altar dedicated to the star you wish to work with. Include star charts, crystals (such as citrine for confidence, carnelian for action, or clear quartz for amplification), candles, and other symbols associated with empowerment.

3. Cleanse Your Space: Use incense, sage, or a selenite wand to cleanse your space, removing any negative or stagnant energy that could interfere with the ritual.

Rituals for Personal Empowerment with the Stars

The following rituals harness the energy of specific stars and celestial events to help you tap into your inner power, amplify your strengths, and embody your highest potential.

1. Regulus' Ritual of Strength and Confidence

Regulus, the "Heart of the Lion" in the constellation Leo, embodies courage, strength, and leadership. This ritual draws upon Regulus' fiery energy to empower you, helping you embrace your self-worth and inner strength.

Tools Needed:

- Gold or yellow candle (to represent the power and strength of Regulus)
- A piece of citrine or tiger's eye (for confidence and courage)
- A mirror (to reflect self-empowerment)
- A star chart showing the constellation Leo and Regulus

Instructions:

1. **Create Your Space:** Light the candle and place the citrine or tiger's eye and the mirror on your altar. Lay out the star chart with Leo and focus on Regulus.
2. **Invoke Regulus:** Hold the citrine in your hands and say, "Regulus, Heart of the Lion, shine your strength upon me. Fill me with courage, confidence, and the power to lead my life with boldness."
3. **Visualize:** Close your eyes and visualize a golden light radiating from Regulus in the sky, descending toward you. See this light enveloping your body, filling every cell with its warmth, strength, and courage.
4. **Mirror Affirmation:** Look into the mirror and, while holding the citrine, say aloud, "I am powerful. I am confident. I shine with the strength of the stars." Repeat this affirmation three times, feeling the energy of Regulus amplifying your words.

5. **Closing:** Blow out the candle and keep the citrine with you as a talisman of strength. Carry it as a reminder of Regulus' empowering energy whenever you need a boost of confidence.

Tips: Perform this ritual on a Sunday, the day ruled by the Sun, to align with solar energy, enhancing the ritual's effectiveness.

2. Vega's Harmony of Self-Expression

Vega, the brightest star in the constellation Lyra, resonates with harmony, creativity, and inspiration. This ritual connects you with Vega's energy to empower your self-expression, helping you share your unique gifts with the world.

Tools Needed:

- Blue or silver candle (to represent Vega's energy)
- A piece of sodalite or lapis lazuli (for clear communication and self-expression)
- A journal and pen

Instructions:

1. **Set Your Space:** Light the candle and place the sodalite on your altar. Hold the journal and pen nearby.
2. **Invoke Vega:** Hold the sodalite in your hands and say, "Vega, star of harmony and inspiration, empower my voice, my creativity, and my truth. Help me express my unique light with confidence and grace."
3. **Visualize:** Imagine Vega's blue-white light descending from the sky, entering your throat and heart centers. Feel this light expanding, clearing any blocks to your self-expression, and filling you with inspiration and clarity.
4. **Free Writing:** Open your journal and write freely for a few minutes, letting your thoughts, feelings, and ideas flow without judg-

ment. This exercise helps to tap into Vega's empowering energy of self-expression.
5. **Affirmation:** After writing, say, "I am a vessel of creativity. I express my truth with confidence and harmony."
6. **Closing:** Extinguish the candle and keep the sodalite with you whenever you need to express yourself confidently.

Tips: Use this ritual before public speaking, creative projects, or any situation where you need to express yourself clearly and confidently.

3. Altair's Ritual of Bold Action

Altair, the bright star in the constellation Aquila, symbolizes swift action, boldness, and the power to overcome obstacles. This ritual connects you with Altair's energy, helping you take decisive action toward your goals.

Tools Needed:

- Red or orange candle (to represent Altair's boldness)
- A piece of carnelian or garnet (to enhance motivation and courage)
- A small piece of paper and a pen

Instructions:

1. **Set Your Space:** Light the candle and place the carnelian on your altar. Hold the paper and pen in your hands.
2. **Invoke Altair:** Hold the carnelian and say, "Altair, star of the bold and the swift, grant me your power to act with courage and decisiveness. Help me move forward fearlessly toward my goals."
3. **Visualize:** Imagine a red-orange light emanating from Altair, filling you with energy, motivation, and a sense of purpose. Feel this light coursing through your veins, igniting your drive to take action.

4. **Set Your Intention:** On the piece of paper, write down a goal or action you want to take but have been hesitant about. Hold the paper over the candle's flame (without burning it) and say, "By the power of Altair, I embrace action. I am bold. I am unstoppable."
5. **Closing:** Blow out the candle and keep the carnelian with you as a motivator. Place the paper on your altar as a reminder of your commitment to take bold steps.

Tips: Perform this ritual during a waxing moon to align with the energy of growth and forward momentum.

Empowering Yourself During Celestial Events

Celestial events like full moons, solar eclipses, and meteor showers are powerful moments for empowerment. These events intensify stellar energy, offering an ideal opportunity to amplify your personal power.

4. Full Moon Empowerment Ritual

The full moon is a time of peak energy and illumination, making it perfect for empowerment rituals that activate and amplify your strengths.

Tools Needed:

- A silver or white candle (to represent the full moon's light)
- Clear quartz crystal (to amplify energy)
- A bowl of water (to symbolize the moon's reflection)

Instructions:

1. **Set Up Your Space:** Light the candle and place the clear quartz near the bowl of water on your altar.
2. **Moonlight Invocation:** Sit comfortably and gaze at the water's surface. Imagine the moonlight shining down, filling the bowl and the space around you with its luminous energy.

3. **Empowerment Visualization:** Hold the clear quartz and close your eyes. Visualize the moon's light entering your body, filling you with its powerful, radiant energy. See this light expanding, amplifying your strengths, and washing away any self-doubt or fear.
4. **Affirmation:** Say aloud, "By the light of the full moon, I am empowered. My strengths are magnified, my purpose is clear, and my spirit shines brightly."
5. **Closing:** Blow out the candle and keep the clear quartz on your altar to continue absorbing the moon's empowering energy.

Tips: Repeat this ritual every full moon to maintain and amplify your personal empowerment.

Tips for Enhancing Empowerment with Star Magic

1. **Daily Affirmations:** Incorporate star-based affirmations into your daily routine. For example, "I shine with the strength of Regulus" or "Vega's light inspires my creativity."
2. **Wear Star Talismans:** Create or wear talismans infused with the energy of stars associated with empowerment, such as a pendant charged under Regulus' light.
3. **Visualize Star Light:** When you need an instant boost of empowerment, close your eyes and visualize the light of your chosen star filling your body, strengthening your aura, and amplifying your power.

Conclusion

Empowerment through Star Magic is about recognizing and amplifying your inner strength by connecting with the potent energies of the stars and celestial events. Whether invoking the courage of Regulus, the creative inspiration of Vega, or the boldness of Altair, these stellar forces act as cosmic amplifiers, helping you to step confidently into your power and express your highest potential. By practicing the rituals and techniques in this chapter, you can draw on the stars' brilliance to light up your inner world, overcome obstacles, and pursue your dreams with unshakeable confidence. As you empower yourself with Star Magic, you become a beacon of cosmic light, shining brightly in the universe and manifesting your destiny.

Chapter 26: Star Magic in Meditation and Visualization

Meditation and visualization are powerful tools for connecting with the cosmic energies of the stars and harnessing their influence in your life. When you incorporate Star Magic into these practices, you tap into the stars' ancient wisdom, align your energy with the cosmos, and deepen your inner awareness. The light, power, and vibrations of the stars can amplify the benefits of meditation, helping you find clarity, peace, empowerment, and insight. In this chapter, we will explore how to use stellar energy to enhance meditation and visualization, offering guided meditations and exercises that align you with the stars' power.

The Role of Stars in Meditation and Visualization

The stars have been used as focal points in spiritual practices for centuries. Their steady light and timeless presence serve as reminders of the vastness of the universe and our connection to it. In meditation, the stars can:

- **Provide Clarity:** The stars' light symbolizes illumination, helping to clear the mind and enhance mental focus.
- **Offer Healing:** The gentle energy of stars like those in the Pleiades can create a soothing and nurturing space for emotional and spiritual healing.
- **Facilitate Guidance:** By connecting with specific stars or constellations during meditation, you can receive insights and messages from the universe, guiding you in your journey.
- **Amplify Intention:** Using stellar energy in visualization exercises can intensify your intentions, helping you manifest desires, overcome challenges, and cultivate inner peace.

Preparing for Star Magic Meditation and Visualization

Before beginning any star-centered meditation or visualization practice, it's important to create a conducive environment and prepare your mind to receive stellar energy.

1. **Set Up a Star Altar:** Prepare a meditation space that includes items associated with stars, such as crystals (clear quartz, moonstone, selenite), candles, star charts, or symbols of specific constellations. This altar serves as an anchor for your energy and a focal point during your practices.

2. **Choose Your Star Focus:** Decide which star, constellation, or celestial body you wish to connect with in your meditation. Different stars resonate with different energies; for example, Sirius is associated with clarity and spiritual insight, while Betelgeuse embodies strength and resilience.

3. **Cleanse the Space:** Cleanse your meditation space with sage, palo santo, or a selenite wand to remove negative or stagnant energy, creating a clear and receptive environment for your practice.

4. **Ground Yourself:** Grounding is crucial before working with stellar energy. Visualize roots growing from your feet into the Earth, anchoring you. This grounding helps stabilize your energy and prepare you to receive cosmic vibrations.

Guided Star Magic Meditations

The following guided meditations focus on connecting with specific stars or star clusters to enhance your inner strength, intuition, healing, and overall sense of harmony. Each meditation is designed to align your energy with the cosmic forces, drawing down stellar light to illuminate your inner landscape.

1. Sirius Clarity Meditation

Sirius, the "Dog Star," is one of the brightest stars in the night sky and is known for its association with wisdom, clarity, and spiritual insight. This meditation uses the energy of Sirius to clear mental fog, enhance intuition, and provide spiritual guidance.

Tools Needed:

- Blue or white candle (to represent Sirius)
- A piece of clear quartz or selenite (for clarity and amplification)

Instructions:

1. **Prepare Your Space:** Light the candle and place the clear quartz or selenite on your altar. Sit comfortably in front of the altar, close your eyes, and take several deep breaths to relax your body.
2. **Grounding:** Visualize roots extending from your feet into the Earth, anchoring your energy.
3. **Connecting with Sirius:** In your mind's eye, picture the night sky. Focus on Sirius, the brightest star shining brilliantly above you. Visualize a beam of blue-white light descending from Sirius, enveloping you in its glow.
4. **Drawing in the Light:** Imagine this light entering your body through the crown of your head, flowing down through your entire body. As the light moves, it clears away mental fog, negative thoughts, and emotional blockages. Feel its clarity washing over you, filling you with insight and calm.
5. **Receive Guidance:** In the silence and stillness, ask Sirius for guidance on a question or issue you are facing. Remain open and listen for any impressions, thoughts, or sensations that arise. Trust that Sirius' wisdom is illuminating your path.
6. **Returning:** When you are ready, visualize the light slowly retracting back to Sirius. Focus on your breath, feeling your feet on the ground. Open your eyes and take a few moments to reflect on your experience.

Tips: Write down any insights or feelings you received during the meditation in a journal. Over time, these reflections can reveal deeper layers of wisdom.

2. Pleiadian Healing Meditation

The Pleiades star cluster, often called the Seven Sisters, is known for its nurturing, soothing, and healing energy. This meditation guides you in connecting with the Pleiades to promote emotional healing and spiritual harmony.

Tools Needed:

- Seven small candles (to represent the stars of the Pleiades)
- A piece of moonstone or rose quartz (for emotional healing)

Instructions:

1. **Set Up Your Space:** Arrange the seven candles in a circle around your meditation space. Light the candles and place the moonstone or rose quartz in the center.
2. **Visualizing the Pleiades:** Close your eyes and imagine the night sky. See the Pleiades cluster, a group of seven stars glowing softly with a blue-white light. Focus on this light, feeling its gentle, nurturing energy.
3. **Drawing in Healing Energy:** Visualize beams of light extending from each of the Pleiades stars, converging and descending toward you. See this light forming a cocoon around your body, filling you with a sense of comfort, peace, and healing.
4. **Healing the Heart:** As you breathe, imagine the light moving to your heart center, releasing any emotional pain, stress, or sadness. Feel the light expanding within your heart, creating a space of warmth and unconditional love.
5. **Affirmation:** In the silence, mentally repeat the affirmation: "I am healed. I am whole. The light of the Pleiades nurtures and protects me."
6. **Closing:** When you are ready, visualize the light gently withdrawing back to the Pleiades. Open your eyes and blow out the candles, thanking the Pleiades for their healing energy.

Tips: Perform this meditation during the waxing or full moon to enhance its healing power.

3. Betelgeuse Empowerment Meditation

Betelgeuse, the red supergiant in the constellation Orion, embodies strength, resilience, and fiery determination. This meditation connects you with Betelgeuse's empowering energy, helping you ignite your inner fire and overcome challenges.

Tools Needed:

- Red or orange candle (to symbolize Betelgeuse's energy)
- A piece of carnelian or garnet (for strength and courage)

Instructions:

1. **Create Your Space:** Light the candle and place the carnelian or garnet on your altar. Sit comfortably, close your eyes, and take several deep breaths.
2. **Visualizing Betelgeuse:** In your mind's eye, picture the constellation Orion. Focus on Betelgeuse, the bright red star shining with a warm, intense glow. Visualize its red-orange light expanding and descending toward you.
3. **Igniting Inner Fire:** See this light entering your solar plexus (the area just above your navel), filling you with warmth and power. Feel this fiery energy spreading throughout your body, awakening your inner strength and determination.
4. **Empowerment Affirmation:** While feeling the energy of Betelgeuse within you, repeat the affirmation: "I am powerful. I am courageous. The fire of Betelgeuse burns within me, lighting my path."
5. **Focus on Empowerment:** Take a moment to focus on a challenge you wish to overcome or a goal you want to achieve. Visualize yourself succeeding, fueled by Betelgeuse's empowering light.

6. **Returning:** When you feel ready, visualize the light slowly retracting back to Betelgeuse. Ground yourself by focusing on your breath and the connection between your body and the Earth.

Tips: Use this meditation whenever you need a boost of courage, especially before confronting difficult situations or pursuing important goals.

Star Visualization Exercises for Daily Alignment

In addition to guided meditations, visualization exercises can help you regularly align your energy with the stars. These exercises are simple yet powerful ways to bring stellar energy into your daily life.

4. Morning Star Alignment

Start your day by visualizing a beam of light from your chosen star entering your crown and filling your body with its energy. This exercise sets a positive tone for the day, aligning you with the star's vibration.

Instructions:

1. **Choose a Star:** Select a star that resonates with the energy you need for the day. For example, choose Sirius for clarity or Vega for creativity.
2. **Visualize the Light:** Close your eyes and imagine the star shining brightly above you. Visualize a beam of light descending from the star into your crown, filling your body with its energy.
3. **Set Your Intention:** As the light fills you, set an intention for the day. For example, "I align with the clarity of Sirius. Today, my mind is clear, and my thoughts are focused."
4. **Affirmation:** Repeat your intention three times, feeling the star's energy amplifying it.

5. Star Gazing Meditation

This simple exercise involves gazing at the night sky to connect with the stars and align your energy with the cosmos.

Instructions:

1. **Find a Quiet Spot:** Go outside on a clear night and find a quiet spot where you can comfortably sit or lie down.
2. **Gaze at the Stars:** Look up at the sky and choose a star that draws your attention. Focus on this star, noticing its brightness, color, and position in the sky.
3. **Connect with the Light:** As you gaze at the star, imagine its light traveling through space and reaching you. Feel this light entering your body, filling you with a sense of calm, peace, and connection to the universe.
4. **Breathe:** Breathe deeply, synchronizing your breath with the twinkling of the star. With each inhale, draw in the star's energy; with each exhale, release any tension or negativity.
5. **Closing:** When you are ready, close your eyes and take a moment to thank the star for its presence and light.

Tips: Perform this exercise regularly to deepen your connection with the stars and maintain an alignment with their energy.

Conclusion

Star Magic in meditation and visualization offers a profound way to align with the cosmos, amplify your inner power, and receive cosmic guidance. By incorporating the energy of stars like Sirius, the Pleiades, and Betelgeuse into your practices, you tap into ancient celestial forces that support clarity, healing, empowerment, and harmony. Whether through guided meditations or simple visualizations, these techniques help you attune to the stars' light, filling your spirit with their wisdom and power. As you practice Star Magic in meditation, you will find that the stars not only illuminate the night sky but also shine within you, guiding you on your journey of self-discovery, inner strength, and spiritual growth.

Chapter 27: The Magic of the Milky Way—Channeling Galactic Energy

The Milky Way, our home galaxy, stretches across the night sky as a luminous river of stars, embodying the vastness and mystery of the cosmos. In the realm of Star Magic, the Milky Way is a potent symbol of infinite potential, interconnectedness, and cosmic power. It represents not just individual stars, but the synergy of billions of celestial bodies working together in harmony. By learning how to channel the energy of the Milky Way, you can access a source of profound power for large-scale manifestations and personal transformations. This chapter explores the magic of the Milky Way, guiding you through rituals, visualizations, and practices that tap into the galaxy's energy to facilitate deep spiritual change and bring about your most ambitious desires.

The Symbolism and Power of the Milky Way

The Milky Way has been a source of awe and inspiration for countless cultures throughout history. Many ancient civilizations viewed the Milky Way as a celestial pathway, a bridge to the divine, or a cosmic river that connects all life. Its shimmering arc across the sky is often seen as a reminder of our place in the universe and the limitless potential that exists within and around us.

In Star Magic, the Milky Way is regarded as:

- **A Symbol of Unity:** The Milky Way is a collection of billions of stars, nebulae, and cosmic dust, working in unison to create a magnificent, harmonious structure. It reminds us that we, too, are part of a greater whole, interconnected with the universe.
- **A Source of Galactic Power:** The sheer scale and energy of the Milky Way offer an immense source of power that can be channeled for personal transformation, spiritual growth, and the manifestation of large-scale intentions.

- **A Gateway to Higher Consciousness:** The Milky Way serves as a bridge to higher realms of consciousness, guiding us to explore the deeper mysteries of the cosmos and the self.

Preparing for Galactic Energy Work

To channel the energy of the Milky Way effectively, it is crucial to prepare your mind, body, and environment to receive and align with such vast cosmic forces. Here's how to get started:

1. Set Up a Galactic Altar: Create a sacred space dedicated to the Milky Way. Include star maps, images of the galaxy, and crystals associated with cosmic energy, such as selenite, amethyst, and labradorite. Arrange candles, incense, and symbols that represent vastness, unity, and infinite potential.

2. Choose Your Focus: Decide on the purpose of your galactic energy work. Are you seeking to manifest a large-scale goal, undergo a deep personal transformation, or connect with the universe's wisdom? Write down your intention to help focus your practice.

3. Cleanse and Ground: Before channeling galactic energy, cleanse your space using sage, palo santo, or sound tools like a singing bowl. Ground yourself by visualizing roots growing from your feet into the Earth. This grounding is vital for maintaining balance when working with such expansive energy.

Channeling the Energy of the Milky Way

The following techniques and rituals guide you in connecting with the Milky Way's energy, drawing upon its power for manifestation, transformation, and cosmic insight. These practices involve visualization, ritual work, and meditative exercises designed to align you with the galaxy's vast energy and potential.

1. **Milky Way Alignment Meditation**

This meditation helps you connect with the Milky Way, aligning your energy with the galaxy's flow to access its transformative power. It is ideal for those seeking to gain a broader perspective, expand their consciousness, and tap into the universe's potential.

Tools Needed:

- Silver or white candle (to represent the Milky Way)
- A piece of labradorite or clear quartz (to facilitate cosmic connection)

Instructions:

1. **Prepare Your Space:** Light the candle and place the labradorite or clear quartz on your altar. Sit comfortably and close your eyes, taking several deep breaths to relax and center yourself.
2. **Grounding:** Visualize roots extending from your feet into the Earth, anchoring you.
3. **Visualizing the Milky Way:** In your mind's eye, imagine the night sky. See the Milky Way as a glowing river of stars, stretching across the sky in a brilliant arc. Focus on the light and the swirling patterns of stars, nebulae, and cosmic dust.
4. **Aligning with Galactic Energy:** Visualize a beam of light extending from your heart center to the Milky Way. As the light connects with the galaxy, feel its energy flowing back down into your heart, filling you with a sense of unity, peace, and infinite potential.
5. **Expanding Consciousness:** Allow the energy of the Milky Way to expand within you, illuminating your mind and spirit. Imagine this energy dissolving any limitations, doubts, or fears, leaving you open and receptive to the galaxy's vast wisdom.

6. **Receiving Guidance:** In the stillness, ask the Milky Way for guidance on your path or a specific question. Remain open and listen to any impressions, thoughts, or sensations that arise.
7. **Returning:** When you are ready, slowly retract your beam of light from the Milky Way, bringing your awareness back to your physical body. Open your eyes and take a few moments to reflect on your experience.

Tips: Perform this meditation during the new moon or when the Milky Way is visible in the sky to enhance its effects.

2. Galactic Manifestation Ritual

The Milky Way, with its immense energy, can be harnessed for large-scale manifestations. This ritual helps you channel the galaxy's power to manifest a significant goal or desire, aligning it with the universe's flow.

Tools Needed:

- Silver, gold, or purple candle (to represent galactic energy)
- A piece of amethyst or clear quartz (for amplifying intention)
- A small piece of paper and a pen

Instructions:

1. **Create Your Space:** Light the candle and place the amethyst on your altar. Sit comfortably in front of your altar, close your eyes, and take deep breaths to relax.
2. **Set Your Intention:** On the piece of paper, write down your intention or goal. Focus on a large-scale manifestation, such as career success, spiritual growth, or profound transformation.
3. **Visualize the Milky Way:** Close your eyes and visualize the Milky Way stretching across the sky, radiating with light and energy. Imagine this energy swirling and gathering into a powerful vortex above you.

4. **Channel the Energy:** Hold the paper with your written intention in your hands. Visualize the galactic vortex sending a beam of light into your heart, filling you with its immense power. See this light flowing from your heart into the paper, infusing your intention with the Milky Way's energy.
5. **Speak Your Intention:** Say aloud, "By the power of the Milky Way, I align with the universe's vast potential. My intention is manifesting with the galaxy's infinite energy. So it is."
6. **Release and Burn:** Light the paper using the candle's flame and place it in a fireproof dish to burn. As the paper burns, visualize your intention being released into the cosmos, carried by the Milky Way's flow to manifest in your life.
7. **Closing:** Extinguish the candle and keep the amethyst on your altar as a reminder of your connection to the Milky Way's power.

Tips: Perform this ritual during a new moon or celestial events like meteor showers to amplify its potency.

3. Galactic Energy Clearing Visualization

The Milky Way's energy can also be used to cleanse and clear blockages, both within yourself and your surroundings. This visualization exercise helps you channel galactic light to purify your energy field, promoting balance and harmony.

Tools Needed:

- White candle (to represent the purifying light of the Milky Way)
- A piece of selenite or clear quartz (for cleansing)

Instructions:

1. **Set Up Your Space:** Light the candle and place the selenite on your altar. Sit comfortably, close your eyes, and take deep breaths to relax.

2. **Visualizing the Milky Way:** In your mind's eye, see the Milky Way as a swirling river of light, glowing with silvery-white energy. Focus on the galaxy's movement, feeling its vast and purifying presence.
3. **Channeling the Light:** Visualize a beam of light extending from the Milky Way, descending toward you. As the light reaches you, imagine it enveloping your entire body, swirling around you in a cleansing spiral.
4. **Cleansing:** See the galactic light moving through your body, dissolving any blockages, negativity, or stagnant energy. Feel it clearing your mind, heart, and spirit, leaving you refreshed and balanced.
5. **Expanding the Cleansing:** If you wish to clear your space, imagine the light expanding outward from your body, filling the room with its purifying glow. See the light sweeping through every corner, washing away any negative or lingering energy.
6. **Closing:** When you feel cleansed, visualize the light retracting back to the Milky Way. Open your eyes and take a deep breath, feeling the balance and harmony within you.

Tips: Use this visualization exercise regularly to maintain a clear and balanced energy field.

Working with Celestial Events in the Milky Way

Certain celestial events, such as meteor showers, eclipses, and solstices, carry enhanced galactic energy, providing powerful moments to connect with the Milky Way and amplify your star magic practices.

4. Meteor Shower Connection

Meteor showers are periods when Earth passes through the debris left by comets, resulting in a celestial display of shooting stars. These showers carry the Milky Way's transformative energy, making them ideal for setting intentions, releasing the old, and welcoming the new.

Instructions:

1. **Find a Quiet Spot:** During a meteor shower, find a quiet place outside where you can watch the sky.
2. **Gaze and Connect:** As you watch the meteors, imagine each shooting star as a spark of the Milky Way's energy. Visualize the light of the meteors entering your body, filling you with the galaxy's transformative power.
3. **Set an Intention:** While observing the meteor shower, set an intention for transformation or change. Whisper your intention to the stars, asking the Milky Way to guide and support you in your journey.
4. **Receive the Energy:** Close your eyes and feel the energy of the meteors flowing through you, creating shifts and opening new pathways in your life.

Tips: Use this exercise to mark the beginning of a new phase or to support transitions in your life.

Conclusion

The Milky Way, as a symbol of vast cosmic potential and unity, offers a powerful source of energy for large-scale manifestations, deep spiritual transformations, and personal empowerment. By channeling the galaxy's energy through meditation, rituals, and visualization exercises, you align yourself with the infinite flow of the universe, tapping into its wisdom and strength. Whether you seek to manifest significant goals, clear energetic blockages, or expand your consciousness, the Milky Way serves as a cosmic ally, guiding and supporting your journey. Embrace the magic of the Milky Way, and let its river of stars illuminate your path, reminding you of the boundless power that lies within the galaxy—and within yourself.

Chapter 28: Star Magic and Time Travel—Tapping into Celestial Timelines

The stars, ancient and timeless, have witnessed the unfolding of the universe for billions of years. Their light carries the echoes of distant pasts, the potential of future possibilities, and the mysteries of alternate dimensions. In the practice of Star Magic, the stars serve as gateways to different timelines and dimensions, allowing us to explore past lives, glimpse future potentials, and access other realms of existence. By tapping into the energy of specific stars, constellations, and celestial events, you can use the concept of star-based time travel to gain insights, heal past traumas, and align with your highest potential. This chapter delves into the mystical art of star-based time travel, offering techniques, rituals, and guided visualizations to journey through time and space.

Understanding Star-Based Time Travel

The idea of time travel in Star Magic is less about physically moving through time and more about using stellar energy to access different timelines, dimensions, and states of consciousness. Stars are ancient cosmic entities; their light carries the imprints of the universe's history and the vibrations of countless potential futures. By aligning with the stars' energy, you can traverse these celestial timelines, exploring your past lives, gaining glimpses of future possibilities, and even connecting with alternate realities.

Key Aspects of Star-Based Time Travel:

- **Past Life Exploration:** Stars act as beacons of memory, guiding you to the energetic imprints of your past lives. By connecting with certain stars, you can access insights into your soul's journey, learn from past experiences, and heal unresolved traumas.
- **Future Glimpses:** The stars also embody the universe's potentiality. By focusing on particular stars or celestial events, you can receive glimpses of future possibilities, helping you align your choices with your desired outcomes.

- **Alternate Dimensions:** Some stars, especially those with a mystical reputation like Sirius or the Pleiades, are believed to act as portals to alternate dimensions or parallel universes. Through star-based meditation and visualization, you can explore these realms and gain a broader perspective on reality.

Preparing for Stellar Time Travel

Before engaging in star-based time travel, it is crucial to prepare yourself and your environment to facilitate safe and focused exploration of celestial timelines.

1. Create a Timeless Altar: Designate a sacred space for your time travel practices. Include items such as star maps, symbols of infinity, crystals (like amethyst for spiritual insight, labradorite for protection, and clear quartz for amplification), candles, and items that represent both the past (old coins, relics) and the future (new objects, technology symbols).

2. Choose Your Focus: Decide which aspect of time travel you wish to explore. Are you seeking to delve into past lives, glimpse future possibilities, or explore alternate dimensions? Having a clear intention will help guide your journey.

3. Cleanse and Protect: Use sage, palo santo, or selenite to cleanse your space, ensuring it is free from negative or stagnant energy. Additionally, ground yourself by visualizing roots extending from your feet into the Earth. This grounding provides stability as you navigate different timelines.

Techniques for Star-Based Time Travel

The following techniques and rituals allow you to harness the energy of the stars to journey through time. These practices involve guided visualizations, meditations, and rituals that connect you with specific stars and celestial timelines, providing insights and wisdom from past, future, and alternate dimensions.

1. Sirius Past Life Meditation

Sirius, the brightest star in the night sky, is often associated with spiritual insight, higher consciousness, and the ability to access ancient wisdom. This meditation guides you to connect with Sirius to explore your past lives, uncover hidden memories, and gain insights into your soul's journey.

Tools Needed:

- Blue or white candle (to represent Sirius)
- A piece of amethyst or moonstone (to enhance spiritual vision)

Instructions:

1. **Prepare Your Space:** Light the candle and place the amethyst on your altar. Sit comfortably, close your eyes, and take several deep breaths to relax and center yourself.
2. **Grounding:** Visualize roots growing from your feet into the Earth, anchoring you.
3. **Connecting with Sirius:** In your mind's eye, imagine the night sky. See Sirius shining brilliantly above you, radiating a bright blue-white light. Visualize this light forming a beam that descends toward you, enveloping your body.
4. **Journey to the Past:** As you breathe in the light of Sirius, set your intention to explore a past life. Mentally say, "Sirius, star of wisdom and memory, guide me to the timeline I need to see. Reveal to me the past that carries lessons for my present."

5. **Visualization:** Imagine a door of starlight appearing in front of you. When you feel ready, step through this door, allowing Sirius' energy to guide you into a past life. Observe your surroundings: notice any impressions, emotions, people, or events that come to you. Do not force the experience; let the visions flow naturally.
6. **Receiving Insights:** Spend a few moments exploring this past timeline. Ask any questions you have and remain open to the answers. You may not receive words, but images, sensations, or feelings that convey the messages you seek.
7. **Returning:** When you are ready, visualize yourself stepping back through the door of starlight, returning to the present. Slowly withdraw the light of Sirius, grounding yourself by focusing on your breath and the connection between your body and the Earth.
8. **Reflect:** Open your eyes and take a moment to write down any insights or memories you received during the meditation.

Tips: Perform this meditation during a new moon or when Sirius is visible in the sky to enhance its effects.

2. Future Glimpse Ritual with Vega

Vega, a bright star in the constellation Lyra, is associated with harmony, inspiration, and cosmic vision. This ritual uses Vega's energy to glimpse possible future timelines, helping you align your actions with your highest potential.

Tools Needed:

- Silver or white candle (to symbolize Vega's energy)
- A piece of clear quartz or labradorite (to amplify vision)
- A piece of paper and a pen

Instructions:

1. **Set Up Your Space:** Light the candle and place the clear quartz on your altar. Sit comfortably, close your eyes, and take deep breaths to center yourself.
2. **Set Your Intention:** On the piece of paper, write down a specific question or situation for which you seek a glimpse of the future. Fold the paper and hold it in your hands.
3. **Visualizing Vega:** In your mind's eye, see Vega shining brightly in the night sky. Visualize a beam of silvery light extending from Vega to your third eye (the space between your eyebrows), filling you with its visionary energy.
4. **Accessing Future Timelines:** Mentally say, "Vega, star of vision and possibility, reveal to me the future I seek. Guide me to the timeline that serves my highest good." Allow your mind to become a screen, ready to receive impressions, images, or sensations of possible future outcomes.
5. **Observe:** In your mind's eye, allow images or scenes to unfold. These may appear as quick flashes, detailed visions, or symbolic representations. Simply observe without judgment, trusting that Vega's energy is guiding you to the knowledge you need.

6. **Returning:** When you are ready, visualize the light retracting from your third eye, returning to Vega. Ground yourself by focusing on your breath and the Earth beneath you.
7. **Reflect:** Open your eyes and write down any images or sensations you experienced. Over time, review these reflections to identify patterns and guide your decisions.

Tips: Use this ritual during waxing or full moons to amplify its visionary power.

3. Alternate Dimensions Meditation with the Pleiades

The Pleiades, or the Seven Sisters, are a star cluster associated with mysticism, spiritual knowledge, and connections to other realms. This meditation allows you to tap into alternate dimensions or parallel realities, expanding your understanding of the universe and your place within it.

Tools Needed:

- Seven small candles (to represent the stars of the Pleiades)
- A piece of labradorite or moldavite (for interdimensional exploration)

Instructions:

1. **Create Your Space:** Arrange the seven candles in a circle around your meditation space. Light the candles and place the labradorite in the center.
2. **Visualizing the Pleiades:** Close your eyes and imagine the Pleiades cluster in the night sky, glowing with a soft, mystical light. Focus on the seven stars, feeling their energy forming a circle of light around you.
3. **Journey to Another Dimension:** As you breathe, visualize a swirling vortex of light forming at the center of the Pleiades. Mentally say, "Pleiades, stars of other realms, open the path to alternate dimensions. Guide me to the reality that expands my consciousness."
4. **Entering the Vortex:** Imagine stepping into the vortex of light. As you move through it, feel yourself shifting into an alternate dimension. Allow images, sensations, and feelings to arise. You may experience different landscapes, beings, or realities that offer new perspectives on your life and the universe.

5. **Exploring:** Spend a few moments exploring this dimension. Notice any symbols, messages, or insights that stand out to you.
6. **Returning:** When you are ready, visualize the vortex drawing you back to the present. Slowly return to your physical body, grounding your energy by focusing on your breath.
7. **Reflect:** Write down any impressions or insights you received during your journey. This practice helps you integrate the knowledge from alternate dimensions into your current reality.

Tips: Perform this meditation during celestial events, such as equinoxes or solstices, to enhance its interdimensional effects.

Working with Celestial Events for Time Travel

Certain celestial events, like eclipses, meteor showers, and planetary alignments, create potent energy fields that facilitate star-based time travel and exploration of different timelines.

4. Solar Eclipse Time Travel Ritual

A solar eclipse represents a time of transformation, revealing hidden truths and opening pathways to new timelines. This ritual uses the energy of a solar eclipse to explore your future or alternate paths in life.

Instructions:

1. **Prepare Your Space:** During a solar eclipse, find a quiet place where you can sit comfortably.
2. **Visualize the Eclipse:** Close your eyes and imagine the eclipse above you. See the sun's light being partially obscured, creating a ring of glowing light.
3. **Set Your Intention:** Mentally state your intention, such as "Reveal to me the future possibilities" or "Guide me to an alternate path that aligns with my highest good."
4. **Entering the Eclipse:** Visualize a beam of light descending from the eclipse, surrounding you. Imagine this light creating a doorway in front of you, leading to another timeline or dimension. When you are ready, step through the doorway and explore.
5. **Observe:** Allow images, symbols, or sensations to arise, representing potential futures or alternate realities. Stay open to the experience without forcing it.
6. **Returning:** Visualize yourself stepping back through the doorway, returning to the present. Ground yourself by focusing on your breath and the Earth beneath you.

Tips: Keep a journal nearby to record any insights or visions received during the ritual.

Conclusion

Star Magic offers a profound way to explore the dimensions of time through the ancient light of the stars. By tapping into celestial timelines with stars like Sirius, Vega, and the Pleiades, you can access past lives, gain glimpses of future potentials, and explore alternate realities, expanding your understanding of the universe and your soul's journey.

Through meditation, visualization, and rituals, you harness the stars' timeless energy to uncover hidden wisdom, heal past wounds, and align with your highest path. As you practice star-based time travel, you will find that the stars are not only guides in the night sky but also beacons of infinite possibilities that transcend the boundaries of time and space. Embrace the magic of the stars, and let their light guide you through the labyrinth of timelines, revealing the vast potential that lies within and beyond you.

Chapter 29: Cosmic Boundaries—Ethics and Responsibility in Star Magic

Star Magic, like any form of mystical practice, is a powerful tool that can bring about profound changes and transformations in one's life. However, with this power comes great responsibility. The stars have been guiding humanity for millennia, offering light, wisdom, and energy. When working with the cosmic forces of the stars, it is crucial to approach the practice with respect, integrity, and a deep understanding of the potential consequences of one's actions. In Star Magic, ethics, consent, protection, and intention are the foundational principles that guide responsible practice, ensuring that the use of stellar energy aligns with the highest good.

This chapter delves into the ethical considerations and responsibilities inherent in Star Magic. It discusses the importance of setting clear intentions, seeking consent, respecting free will, protecting oneself and others, and understanding the impact of working with cosmic energies. By adhering to these principles, practitioners can engage in Star Magic in a way that is empowering, beneficial, and in harmony with the universe.

The Ethical Use of Star Energy

Star Magic is not just a set of practices; it is a spiritual path that involves interaction with the cosmic forces of the universe. The energy of the stars is potent, and its misuse can lead to unintended consequences. Therefore, ethical conduct is paramount to ensure that Star Magic is used wisely, respectfully, and with the right intentions.

1. Intention: The Core of Ethical Practice

In Star Magic, intention is the driving force behind every ritual, meditation, and spell. The energy you put into your practice, guided by your intentions, determines the outcome of your work.

- **Setting Clear and Positive Intentions:** Always approach star-based practices with clear, positive intentions that aim to benefit yourself, others, and the world. Avoid intentions driven by selfish desires, revenge, manipulation, or harm, as these can create imbalances and negative karmic repercussions.
- **Aligning with the Stars:** The stars embody various energies, such as healing, wisdom, courage, and transformation. Before invoking a star's energy, reflect on whether your intention aligns with the star's natural attributes and cosmic rhythm. For example, calling upon Sirius for wisdom or healing is in harmony with its energy, while attempting to manipulate its power for control over others is not.

Example: If you wish to use Star Magic to enhance a relationship, set an intention that focuses on mutual growth, harmony, and love, rather than trying to control the other person's actions or emotions.

2. Consent: Honoring Free Will

Consent is a fundamental aspect of ethical Star Magic. When performing rituals or spells that involve others, it is essential to seek their consent and respect their free will. The stars may offer guidance and support, but they do not condone interference in another's path without permission.

- **Personal Consent:** Always ensure you are fully willing and ready to engage in a star-based ritual or spell. Never perform Star Magic if you feel uncertain, pressured, or fearful, as this can lead to negative or unintended results.
- **Seeking Consent from Others:** When using Star Magic in any context that involves another person (e.g., healing, protection, relationship work), obtain their explicit consent. Without permission, even well-intentioned magic can infringe on their free will and may lead to karmic consequences.

- **Energetic Consent:** If you are working with a star, constellation, or celestial entity, take a moment to attune to its energy and ask for permission to connect with it. Stars are ancient and conscious entities, and acknowledging their presence with respect sets the foundation for a harmonious relationship.

Example: Before performing a healing ritual using the energy of the Pleiades for a friend, ask them if they are open to receiving this cosmic support. Respect their answer, even if they decline.

Establishing Cosmic Boundaries

Setting boundaries is a vital part of responsible Star Magic practice. Boundaries protect you from unwanted energies and help maintain the integrity of your work. They also prevent your energy from inadvertently affecting others in ways you did not intend.

1. Protection: Shielding Yourself and Others

When working with cosmic energies, it is important to establish protective boundaries to safeguard your energy field and that of others. The stars can be both illuminating and intense; their energy needs to be channeled responsibly.

- **Personal Shields:** Before beginning any Star Magic practice, create an energetic shield around yourself. Visualize a sphere of light (golden, white, or the color associated with the star you are working with) enveloping your body, forming a protective barrier that only allows positive energy to pass through.
- **Protective Talismans:** Use crystals such as labradorite, selenite, or black tourmaline as protective talismans during your rituals. Charge these stones with star energy to create a constant protective field around you.
- **Ethical Protection Spells:** When casting protection spells for others, ensure you have their permission and use stars known for their protective qualities, like Aldebaran or Antares. Clearly state

that the protection is meant to support the person's well-being, not to control their circumstances.

Example: Before performing a star meditation, visualize a sphere of light from the star you are connecting with (e.g., a blue sphere for Sirius) surrounding you. This shield will help you absorb only the star's positive, beneficial energy and deflect any unwanted or disruptive influences.

2. Energetic Boundaries: Preventing Energy Overreach

When using star energy, it is important to be mindful of the ripple effects your actions can have on the cosmic web. Every thought, intention, and spell sends vibrations through the universe, affecting not just you but also others around you.

- **Contain Your Energy:** During rituals, visualize your energy and intention remaining within the boundary you have set. Avoid sending out energy that could inadvertently impact others unless your spell explicitly includes them and you have their consent.
- **Closing and Sealing:** After every star ritual or meditation, close the energetic space you have created. Visualize the star's light retracting back into the cosmos, and mentally affirm that the energy of the ritual is now sealed. This act of closure prevents any lingering energies from affecting you or others unknowingly.

Example: After a manifestation ritual using the energy of the Milky Way, visualize a silver light sealing the energy of your work within a sphere, ensuring it only affects the areas you have intended.

Working with Stars: Respect and Responsibility

The stars are ancient, wise, and conscious entities. When invoking their energy, you are entering into a relationship with the cosmos. Treating the stars with respect and responsibility is crucial to maintaining a harmonious connection.

1. Respecting Star Energies

- **Acknowledgment:** Before invoking the energy of a star or constellation, take a moment to acknowledge its presence. Express gratitude for its light, wisdom, and guidance. This acknowledgment fosters a respectful relationship and aligns your practice with the universe's natural harmony.
- **Mindful Invocations:** Use star energy with the awareness that it is a powerful force. Avoid invoking star energies for frivolous or selfish reasons, and never use them to harm others. The stars' energy is meant to guide, heal, and transform, not to control or manipulate.
- **Timing and Harmony:** Align your work with natural cosmic rhythms, such as moon phases, star alignments, and celestial events. This practice not only enhances the potency of your work but also shows respect for the cosmic order.

Example: When invoking Regulus for strength and courage, begin by saying, "Regulus, Heart of the Lion, I honor your light and strength. I call upon your energy to empower my spirit and guide me with courage." Such words demonstrate respect for the star's presence.

2. Responsibility in Teaching and Sharing Star Magic

If you are guiding others in Star Magic, it is your responsibility to teach the importance of ethical practice, consent, and protection. Share the knowledge of how to work with cosmic energies responsibly, emphasizing the power and potential impact of star-based rituals.

- **Educate on Boundaries:** Teach others how to establish energetic boundaries, create protective shields, and work with star energies in a way that respects both their own and others' autonomy.
- **Empower Others:** Encourage those you teach to develop their personal relationship with the stars, empowering them to make their own decisions about how they use Star Magic. Promote self-awareness, reflection, and personal integrity in every aspect of the practice.

Example: When teaching someone to perform a star-based healing ritual, instruct them on the importance of obtaining consent, grounding their energy, and closing the ritual space afterward to prevent any unintended energy exchange.

Navigating Karmic Consequences in Star Magic

The universe operates on principles of balance and karma. Every action, intention, and spell you perform creates ripples in the cosmic web, returning to you in some form. When practicing Star Magic, being aware of the potential karmic consequences helps guide your actions responsibly.

1. Harm None Principle

In Star Magic, adhere to the principle of "harm none." This means refraining from any magical work that could cause harm, loss, or suffering to others. Always ask yourself, "Will this action support the greater good, or could it potentially cause harm?"

- **Positive Intentions:** Focus your star magic on positive outcomes, such as healing, growth, and self-empowerment, rather than controlling others or interfering with their free will.
- **Reflection:** Before performing a ritual, take a moment to reflect on its potential consequences. Consider how the energy you send out may affect others and the universe. If there is any doubt or uncertainty, reconsider or modify your intention.

Example: When performing a manifestation ritual using the energy of Vega, phrase your intention in a way that does not impose on others' lives, such as "I manifest abundance and joy in my life" rather than "I will receive money from a specific person."

2. Addressing Unintended Consequences

Despite the best intentions, sometimes star-based work may have unintended effects. If you sense that a ritual has caused disruption or imbalance, take responsibility to correct it.

- **Cleansing and Rebalancing:** Perform a cleansing ritual using star energy (such as Sirius for purification) to clear any negative vibrations. Visualize cosmic light restoring harmony to the situation.
- **Reflect and Learn:** Use the experience as an opportunity to reflect on your practice. Ask yourself what you can learn from the situation to guide future actions more responsibly.

Example: If you perform a spell with Aldebaran's energy for strength but notice increased tension in your relationships, use the light of Sirius to cleanse the energy and restore balance, reflecting on how to refine your intentions in the future.

Conclusion

Star Magic is a profound and powerful practice that requires a deep sense of ethics, responsibility, and respect for the cosmic forces at play. By setting clear, positive intentions, honoring consent, protecting your energy, and respecting the ancient power of the stars, you align yourself with the universe's harmony and ensure that your work contributes to the greater good. Remember that every action in Star Magic sends ripples through the cosmic web, affecting not just you but also the world around you. Embrace the power of the stars with an open heart, mindful of the boundaries and responsibilities that come with wielding their energy. In doing so, you create a practice that is not only magical but also balanced, ethical, and aligned with the infinite wisdom of the cosmos. Let the stars be your guide, lighting your path as you journey through the vast expanse of the universe with integrity, awareness, and respect.

Chapter 30: Aligning with the Cosmic Order—Finding Your Place in the Universe

The universe is an intricate tapestry woven with the threads of stars, planets, galaxies, and all forms of life. Each of us is a unique strand in this cosmic web, with a purpose that aligns with the greater flow of the universe. Understanding and embracing your place in this vast design can bring a profound sense of purpose, peace, and direction. In Star Magic, the stars serve as guides and mirrors, reflecting your inner essence and helping you align with your life's path. By working with star energies, celestial events, and the cosmic flow, you can discover your unique role in the universe and align yourself with its rhythms to live a life of harmony, growth, and fulfillment.

This chapter explores how to use Star Magic to uncover your life's purpose, align with your true self, and flow effortlessly with the universe. It provides detailed techniques, rituals, and meditations for connecting with the stars, understanding their influence on your destiny, and finding your place in the grand cosmic design.

The Cosmic Order and Personal Alignment

The universe operates in cycles, rhythms, and patterns, from the movements of the stars and planets to the phases of the moon. This cosmic order influences everything, including our lives, emotions, and experiences. When you align yourself with these cosmic currents, you create a harmonious flow in your life, allowing you to manifest your true desires and fulfill your purpose.

Key Concepts in Aligning with the Cosmic Order:

- **Cosmic Flow:** The universe is constantly moving and evolving. Aligning with its flow means recognizing the natural rhythms in your life, understanding the cycles you are experiencing, and working in harmony with these patterns.

- **Personal Resonance:** Each person resonates with certain stars, constellations, and celestial energies. By discovering which cosmic forces align with your essence, you can understand your purpose and how to express it in the world.
- **Life's Purpose:** The stars can help you uncover your life's purpose, whether it involves personal growth, creativity, service, or spiritual development. By attuning to their energy, you can gain insights into your true calling.

Preparing for Cosmic Alignment

Before beginning practices to align with the cosmic order, take time to create a space and mindset conducive to inner exploration and cosmic connection.

1. Create a Cosmic Altar: Set up an altar that represents the universe's vastness and your connection to it. Include star charts, candles, symbols of infinity, crystals (such as selenite, amethyst, and clear quartz), and personal items that represent your goals, desires, and aspirations.

2. Reflect on Your Current State: Before attempting to align with the cosmic order, spend time reflecting on where you currently are in life. Ask yourself:

- What areas of my life feel out of balance or disconnected?
- What am I seeking to change or understand?
- What do I feel drawn to in terms of career, relationships, or personal development?

3. **Clear and Ground:** Use cleansing tools like sage, palo santo, or incense to clear your space of negative energy. Ground yourself by visualizing roots growing from your feet into the Earth, providing stability as you explore the vastness of the universe.

Techniques for Aligning with the Cosmic Flow

The following techniques guide you in working with the stars to discover your purpose, align with your true self, and find your unique place in the universe. These practices involve meditation, star-based rituals, and cosmic introspection exercises that help you attune to the cosmic order and integrate it into your life.

1. Discovering Your Guiding Star

Each person has a star or constellation that resonates with their soul's essence and purpose. Finding your guiding star can provide a source of inspiration, strength, and direction in your life.

Tools Needed:

- Star chart or a star app to help identify stars and constellations
- A piece of labradorite or moonstone (to enhance intuition)
- A journal and pen

Instructions:

1. **Set Up Your Space:** Place the labradorite on your altar and have your star chart or app nearby. Sit comfortably, close your eyes, and take deep breaths to relax and center yourself.
2. **Meditation:** Visualize the night sky above you, filled with countless stars. Allow your mind to drift, feeling the vastness of the cosmos surrounding you.
3. **Intention:** Mentally set the intention to connect with your guiding star. Say silently, "I call upon the star that aligns with my essence. Reveal yourself to me, and guide me on my path."

4. **Connecting:** In your mind's eye, scan the sky and notice which star or constellation draws your attention. It may shine brighter, have a specific color, or emit a particular energy. Allow yourself to feel its presence and energy.
5. **Identify:** Open your eyes and use your star chart or app to identify the star or constellation you felt connected to. Write its name and any impressions you received in your journal.
6. **Reflect:** Research the qualities, mythology, and astrological significance of the star or constellation. Reflect on how these traits resonate with your personality, dreams, and life's purpose.

Tips: Perform this meditation under a clear night sky for a deeper connection with the stars.

2. The Cosmic Alignment Ritual with Regulus

Regulus, known as the "Heart of the Lion," is a powerful star in the constellation Leo that embodies courage, leadership, and self-expression. This ritual uses Regulus' energy to help you align with your personal power and cosmic purpose.

Tools Needed:

- Gold or yellow candle (to represent Regulus' energy)
- A piece of citrine or sunstone (for empowerment and clarity)
- A star chart showing the constellation Leo
- A small piece of paper and a pen

Instructions:

1. **Prepare Your Space:** Light the candle and place the citrine on your altar. Lay out the star chart with Leo and focus on Regulus.
2. **Setting Intention:** On the piece of paper, write down your intention for the ritual, such as "I seek to align with my highest purpose and the universe's flow."

3. **Visualizing Regulus:** Close your eyes and visualize Regulus shining brightly in the night sky. See its golden light forming a beam that descends toward you, filling your heart with warmth, strength, and courage.
4. **Chanting:** While holding the citrine, chant, "Regulus, Heart of the Lion, align me with the cosmic flow. Guide me to my true purpose; help me find my place and grow."
5. **Drawing Cosmic Energy:** Imagine the light of Regulus expanding within your heart, illuminating your inner self. Feel this energy aligning your thoughts, emotions, and spirit with the universe's rhythm.
6. **Reflection:** Open your eyes and write down any feelings, insights, or images that came to you during the ritual.
7. **Closing:** Blow out the candle, keeping the citrine as a talisman to remind you of your alignment with Regulus' guiding light.

Tips: Perform this ritual during the waxing moon to amplify its power of growth and alignment.

3. Moon Phase Alignment for Personal Growth

The moon's phases represent different cycles of growth, release, and renewal. By aligning your actions and intentions with these lunar phases, you harmonize with the universe's flow and enhance your progress toward your goals.

Instructions:

1. **New Moon (Intention Setting):** During the new moon, set intentions for what you wish to manifest in alignment with your cosmic purpose. Write down your goals and dreams, focusing on how they resonate with your inner self.
2. **Waxing Moon (Building Energy):** As the moon waxes, take action toward your goals. Channel the growing energy of the moon to build momentum and strength in your pursuits. Use star magic rituals to amplify your progress.

3. **Full Moon (Clarity and Realization):** During the full moon, reflect on your achievements and insights. Meditate with stars like Sirius or Vega to gain clarity about your path and understand how your actions align with your purpose.
4. **Waning Moon (Release and Adjustment):** As the moon wanes, focus on releasing anything that no longer serves you. Perform cleansing rituals with stars like Antares or the Pleiades to let go of doubts, fears, or obstacles blocking your alignment with the universe.

Tips: Keep a moon journal to track your intentions, actions, reflections, and releases throughout each lunar cycle.

4. Astrological Timing and Cosmic Flow

Understanding your astrological birth chart is another way to align with the cosmic order. The positions of the stars and planets at the time of your birth reveal insights into your personality, strengths, and life path.

- **Identify Key Astrological Aspects:** Use your birth chart to identify the stars, planets, and zodiac signs that strongly influence your life. For example, if you have a prominent placement in Leo, connecting with stars like Regulus or constellations like Orion may resonate deeply with your purpose.
- **Celestial Events:** Pay attention to celestial events, such as eclipses, meteor showers, and planetary transits, to align your star magic practices with the universe's rhythm. These events can serve as catalysts for personal growth and transformation.

Example: If an eclipse is occurring in the sign of Taurus, and you have significant Taurus placements in your chart, use this energy to explore and align with your values, self-worth, and material goals.

Aligning Actions with Cosmic Purpose

Once you have identified your guiding stars, connected with cosmic energies, and gained clarity on your purpose, the next step is to align your daily actions with the universe's flow.

1. Morning Cosmic Alignment Visualization

Start each day by connecting with your guiding star and setting an intention to align with the cosmic flow.

Instructions:

1. **Visualize:** Close your eyes and visualize your guiding star shining brightly above you. Imagine its light forming a beam that enters your crown, filling your body with its energy.
2. **Set an Intention:** Mentally state, "Today, I align my thoughts, actions, and energy with the cosmic flow. I trust the universe to guide me to my purpose."
3. **Affirmation:** Repeat an affirmation that resonates with your purpose, such as "I move in harmony with the stars" or "I am in tune with the universe's rhythm."

2. Cosmic Journaling

Regularly journal about your experiences with star magic, cosmic alignment, and the insights you receive. Use prompts like:

- What guidance have the stars offered me recently?
- How have I felt in alignment or out of sync with the universe?
- What actions can I take to align more closely with my purpose?

Tips: Review your journal entries periodically to identify patterns, growth, and areas that need more focus.

Conclusion

Aligning with the cosmic order means recognizing and embracing your unique role in the grand design of the universe. The stars, with their ancient wisdom and energy, serve as guides that help you discover your life's purpose and navigate your journey. Through star-based meditation, rituals, and alignment practices, you can connect with the cosmic flow, harmonizing your actions, intentions, and spirit with the universe's rhythm. By finding your guiding star, working with celestial energies, and aligning with natural cycles like the moon phases, you uncover the deeper layers of your being and move confidently along your path. Embrace the stars as your companions in this journey of discovery, allowing their light to illuminate your purpose and guide you toward a life of harmony, fulfillment, and cosmic alignment.

Chapter 31: Star Magic for Creativity and Inspiration

Creativity is a boundless force that flows through every aspect of the universe, from the formation of stars and galaxies to the growth of life on Earth. The stars themselves are beacons of inspiration, radiating energy that can spark the imagination and open channels of creativity within us. In Star Magic, the stars serve as cosmic muses, guiding artists, writers, musicians, and creators of all kinds to connect with their inner wellspring of inspiration. By channeling the energy of the stars, you can unlock new levels of creativity, break through creative blocks, and infuse your work with the universe's vibrant power.

This chapter explores how to use Star Magic to enhance creativity and inspiration. It provides detailed rituals, meditations, and visualizations tailored for creators who wish to connect with stellar power to fuel their creative endeavors. Whether you're a writer seeking the right words, an artist searching for inspiration, or a musician looking for the perfect melody, the stars can help guide and enhance your creative process.

The Stars as Cosmic Muses

The stars have inspired countless works of art, literature, music, and invention throughout human history. Their light, energy, and beauty evoke a sense of wonder and mystery, opening the mind to new ideas and perspectives. In Star Magic, each star and constellation carries a unique energy that can be channeled to enhance different aspects of creativity.

Key Stars and Constellations for Creativity:

- **Vega:** In the constellation Lyra, Vega is known for its association with harmony, artistic inspiration, and beauty. Channeling Vega's energy can enhance creativity in music, writing, and visual arts.

- **Sirius:** The brightest star in the night sky, Sirius represents clarity, insight, and spiritual illumination. It can help writers and artists access deeper truths and express them through their work.
- **The Pleiades:** This cluster of stars, often called the Seven Sisters, embodies nurturing and creative energy. It is especially beneficial for those working on projects that involve storytelling, fantasy, and nurturing themes.
- **Orion:** The constellation of Orion is associated with strength, focus, and the pursuit of goals. Artists and creators can call upon Orion's energy to overcome creative blocks and channel their inspiration into tangible results.

Preparing for Star-Infused Creativity

Before beginning any star-based rituals or meditations for creativity, it's important to create a conducive environment that fosters inspiration and connection with stellar energy.

1. Create a Creative Altar: Set up an altar dedicated to creativity and inspiration. Include items like candles, star maps, crystals (such as amethyst for intuition, citrine for creativity, and clear quartz for amplification), and symbols that represent your artistic pursuits (pens, paintbrushes, musical instruments, etc.). Add images of stars or constellations that resonate with you.

2. Set Your Creative Intentions: Reflect on what you hope to achieve in your creative endeavors. Do you seek inspiration for a new project? Are you trying to break through a creative block? Write down your intentions in a journal to clarify your focus.

3. Cleanse and Ground: Cleanse your creative space using sage, palo santo, or incense to remove any stagnant or negative energy. Ground yourself by visualizing roots extending from your feet into the Earth, anchoring you as you connect with the cosmic flow of creativity.

Star Magic Rituals for Creativity

The following rituals and meditations are designed to help you channel the energy of the stars to enhance your creativity and bring new inspiration into your work. Each practice aligns with the unique energy of specific stars and constellations to open creative channels and empower your artistic expression.

1. Vega's Harmony Ritual for Artistic Inspiration

Vega, a bright star in the constellation Lyra, is associated with harmony, beauty, and artistic inspiration. This ritual helps you connect with Vega's energy to enhance your creativity in music, writing, or visual arts.

Tools Needed:

- Blue or silver candle (to represent Vega's energy)
- A piece of sodalite or amethyst (to enhance creativity and intuition)
- A star chart or image of the constellation Lyra
- Art supplies (e.g., sketchbook, pen, paintbrush)

Instructions:

1. **Prepare Your Space:** Light the candle and place the sodalite or amethyst on your altar. Have your art supplies and star chart or image of Lyra nearby.
2. **Setting Intention:** Close your eyes and take deep breaths. Focus on your intention to channel artistic inspiration. Say aloud, "Vega, star of harmony and beauty, I call upon your energy to inspire my creativity and open my heart to artistic expression."
3. **Visualizing Vega:** In your mind's eye, visualize Vega shining brightly in the night sky. See its blue-silver light descending toward you, enveloping you in a sphere of creative energy.
4. **Channeling Inspiration:** Hold the sodalite or amethyst in your hands and visualize Vega's light entering your mind, filling it with

new ideas, images, and inspirations. Feel this light flowing down through your arms and hands, imbuing your art supplies with its energy.
5. **Creative Expression:** Begin to create. Whether you're drawing, painting, writing, or playing music, allow Vega's light to guide your hands, opening a flow of inspiration. Don't overthink; simply let the energy move through you.
6. **Closing:** When you feel ready, blow out the candle and place the sodalite or amethyst on your altar. Thank Vega for its guidance and inspiration.

Tips: Perform this ritual whenever you feel creatively blocked or when starting a new artistic project.

2. Sirius Clarity Meditation for Writers

Sirius, the brightest star, embodies clarity, insight, and the illumination of truth. This meditation helps writers connect with Sirius to clear mental fog, find the right words, and access deeper layers of inspiration.

Tools Needed:

- White candle (to represent Sirius)
- A piece of clear quartz (to enhance mental clarity)
- Journal or writing pad and pen

Instructions:

1. **Set Up Your Space:** Light the candle and place the clear quartz on your altar. Sit comfortably with your journal or writing pad in front of you.
2. **Grounding:** Close your eyes and visualize roots extending from your feet into the Earth, grounding you.
3. **Connecting with Sirius:** Imagine the night sky above you. See Sirius, the brightest star, radiating a brilliant white light. Visualize

this light forming a beam that descends toward your crown, filling your mind with clarity and insight.
4. **Clarity of Thought:** As you breathe in the light of Sirius, feel it dissolving any mental blocks, doubts, or distractions. Allow the light to open a clear channel between your thoughts and the page in front of you.
5. **Free Writing:** Open your eyes and begin to write freely. Let Sirius' energy guide your words, exploring any ideas, emotions, or stories that come to mind. Don't worry about structure or grammar—simply let the flow of inspiration guide your pen.
6. **Affirmation:** After writing, close your eyes and say, "Sirius, star of illumination, I thank you for the clarity and insight you have brought to my words."
7. **Closing:** Blow out the candle and keep the clear quartz on your writing desk to continue receiving Sirius' energy.

Tips: Use this meditation before starting a new writing project or when you need to overcome writer's block.

3. Pleiadian Dream Visualization for Creative Insight

The Pleiades star cluster, known as the Seven Sisters, embodies nurturing and creative energy. This visualization exercise is designed to help you tap into the Pleiades' energy for creative insights, particularly in storytelling, fantasy, and dreamlike creations.

Tools Needed:

- Seven small candles (to represent the stars of the Pleiades)
- A piece of moonstone (to enhance intuition and dreamlike creativity)

Instructions:

1. **Set Up Your Space:** Arrange the seven candles in a circle around your meditation space. Light the candles and place the moonstone in the center.
2. **Visualizing the Pleiades:** Close your eyes and imagine the Pleiades cluster in the night sky, glowing with a soft, mystical light. Visualize this light forming a swirling mist around you, filled with dreamlike colors and shapes.
3. **Entering the Creative Dream:** See yourself stepping into this mist, feeling the nurturing and creative energy of the Pleiades enveloping you. As you walk through the mist, notice images, symbols, or stories that begin to form around you. These are the seeds of your creative inspiration.
4. **Gathering Inspiration:** Spend a few moments exploring the mist, gathering any ideas, images, or feelings that stand out. Trust your intuition and allow the Pleiades' energy to guide you.
5. **Returning:** When you are ready, visualize the mist gently receding, bringing the creative energy of the Pleiades back into your heart. Open your eyes and note down any insights or ideas in your journal.
6. **Closing:** Extinguish the candles, thanking the Pleiades for their guidance and inspiration.

Tips: Perform this visualization before bedtime to enhance your dream creativity or during the waxing moon to amplify its nurturing energy.

Enhancing Creative Flow with Star Magic

In addition to specific rituals, there are daily practices and affirmations that can help maintain a steady flow of creativity by aligning you with the stars.

4. Cosmic Morning Affirmations for Creativity

Start your day by aligning with stellar energy to enhance your creative flow.

Instructions:

1. **Visualize:** Close your eyes and visualize a star (Vega, Sirius, or another star that resonates with you) shining above you. Imagine its light filling you with vibrant, creative energy.
2. **Affirmations:** Mentally or verbally repeat affirmations, such as:
   - "I am a vessel of cosmic creativity."
   - "The stars inspire my imagination and guide my hands."
   - "I channel the light of the universe into my art."
3. **Feel the Energy:** As you say each affirmation, feel the energy of the star entering your body, filling you with inspiration and confidence for your creative work.

5. Moon Phase Creativity Alignment

Aligning your creative work with the moon phases can enhance your productivity and inspiration.

- **New Moon:** Use this phase to set creative intentions, start new projects, and explore fresh ideas.
- **Waxing Moon:** During the waxing moon, focus on developing your ideas, building momentum, and bringing your creative vision to life.
- **Full Moon:** The full moon is a time of heightened energy and expression. Use this phase to showcase your work, share your creations, and reflect on your progress.
- **Waning Moon:** During the waning moon, focus on refining, editing, and clearing any creative blocks. Let go of what no longer serves your artistic process.

Tips: Keep a lunar journal to track how the different moon phases affect your creativity and productivity.

Conclusion

The stars are more than celestial bodies; they are cosmic muses, guiding and inspiring creativity in all its forms. By connecting with the energy of stars like Vega, Sirius, and the Pleiades, you can open channels of inspiration, break through creative blocks, and infuse your work with the universe's beauty and power. Through star-based rituals, meditations, and daily alignment practices, you tap into the endless well of creativity that flows through the cosmos. Embrace the stars as partners in your creative journey, allowing their light to spark your imagination, illuminate your vision, and guide you in bringing your artistic dreams to life. Let Star Magic be your key to unlocking the boundless creativity that lies within you, as you weave the cosmic energies into the fabric of your art, writing, music, and every form of self-expression.

Chapter 32: Star Magic for Abundance and Prosperity

The universe is filled with endless energy and possibilities, and the stars are radiant sources of this abundance. Throughout history, celestial bodies have been viewed as symbols of wealth, growth, and prosperity. In Star Magic, the stars provide a powerful means to attract abundance and financial success, serving as cosmic beacons that can align you with the flow of prosperity. By harnessing their energy through rituals, spells, and meditations, you can open pathways to wealth, attract new opportunities, and manifest your desires for financial stability and growth.

This chapter delves into how to use Star Magic for attracting abundance and prosperity. It includes detailed rituals, spells, and practices that draw on the energy of specific stars and constellations associated with wealth, luck, and success. By aligning with the stars, you can tap into the universe's boundless flow of prosperity and invite financial abundance into your life.

Stars and Constellations of Prosperity

In Star Magic, certain stars and constellations are renowned for their connection to abundance, prosperity, and success. Their light symbolizes the wealth of the cosmos, offering guidance and support for manifesting financial goals.

Key Stars and Constellations for Prosperity:

- **Aldebaran:** Located in the constellation Taurus, Aldebaran is known as the "Eye of the Bull" and is associated with wealth, success, and material abundance. It embodies the energy of determination, strength, and prosperity.
- **Regulus:** Known as the "Heart of the Lion" in the constellation Leo, Regulus is linked to fame, leadership, and the power to attract wealth and success through confidence and courage.

- **Capella:** This bright star in the constellation Auriga is associated with fortune, prosperity, and the nurturing of financial resources.
- **Orion's Belt:** The three stars of Orion's Belt symbolize a direct path to success and achievement, helping you focus on your goals and manifest prosperity.

Preparing for Star-Based Abundance Rituals

Before conducting any rituals for abundance and prosperity, it's essential to prepare your space and mindset to effectively channel the energy of the stars.

1. Create an Abundance Altar: Set up an altar dedicated to wealth and prosperity. Include items such as green or gold candles, coins, star charts, crystals (like citrine for wealth, green aventurine for luck, and pyrite for financial success), and symbols of abundance (plants, a bowl of coins, a money jar).

2. Set Clear Financial Intentions: Reflect on what you wish to attract in terms of wealth and prosperity. Do you seek a new job, financial stability, or increased income? Write down your financial goals and intentions in a journal to focus your energy.

3. Cleanse and Ground: Cleanse your space using sage, palo santo, or incense to remove negative energy. Ground yourself by visualizing roots growing from your feet into the Earth, anchoring you in the present moment and the material world.

Rituals and Spells for Attracting Abundance with Star Magic

The following rituals and spells help you channel the energy of the stars to manifest abundance and financial prosperity. Each practice draws on the power of specific stars or constellations associated with wealth, aligning your energy with the cosmic flow of success.

1. Aldebaran's Wealth Ritual

Aldebaran, a bright star in the constellation Taurus, is known for its strong connection to wealth, success, and material prosperity. This ritual harnesses Aldebaran's energy to attract abundance and fortify your financial goals.

Tools Needed:

- Green or gold candle (to represent abundance)
- A piece of citrine or pyrite (to attract wealth)
- A star chart or image of the constellation Taurus
- A small bowl of coins or cash
- A piece of paper and a pen

Instructions:

1. **Set Up Your Altar:** Place the candle, citrine, bowl of coins, and star chart of Taurus on your altar. Sit comfortably in front of your altar and light the candle.
2. **Setting Intention:** On the piece of paper, write down your specific financial goal or intention. This could be an amount of money you wish to manifest, a job opportunity, or a general increase in abundance.
3. **Connecting with Aldebaran:** Close your eyes and visualize Aldebaran shining brightly in the night sky. See its light forming a golden beam that descends toward you, enveloping you in its prosperous energy.
4. **Channeling Prosperity:** Hold the citrine in your hands and visualize Aldebaran's light entering the stone, charging it with the energy of wealth and success. As you hold this vision, repeat the affirmation: "Aldebaran, Eye of the Bull, guide me to abundance and success. I attract wealth, prosperity, and financial growth with your light."

5. **Placing Intentions:** Place the paper with your financial goal under the bowl of coins on your altar. This symbolizes the grounding of your intention in material wealth.
6. **Affirmation:** Repeat the affirmation three times, focusing on the feeling of abundance flowing into your life. Feel Aldebaran's energy surrounding you and filling your aura with golden light.
7. **Closing:** Blow out the candle and keep the citrine or pyrite with you as a talisman to attract wealth. Place the bowl of coins on your desk or in a prominent place to serve as a reminder of your intention.

Tips: Perform this ritual during a waxing moon to amplify the energy of growth and abundance.

2. Regulus' Power of Success Spell

Regulus, the "Heart of the Lion" in the constellation Leo, embodies the energy of confidence, leadership, and the power to attract success and wealth. This spell uses Regulus' energy to boost your self-assurance and open the flow of prosperity into your life.

Tools Needed:

- Gold or yellow candle (to represent Regulus' energy)
- A piece of tiger's eye or sunstone (for confidence and success)
- A small mirror

Instructions:

1. **Set Up Your Space:** Light the candle and place the tiger's eye on your altar. Hold the mirror in your hands and sit comfortably.
2. **Visualizing Regulus:** Close your eyes and imagine the constellation Leo, with Regulus shining brightly at its heart. Visualize a golden beam of light descending from Regulus and surrounding you, filling you with courage, confidence, and the power to attract success.

3. **Empowering Spell:** Look into the mirror and see Regulus' light glowing around you, making you radiant and powerful. As you gaze into your reflection, repeat the spell: "Regulus, star of power and might, I shine with the light of prosperity and success. I am confident; I am strong. Wealth flows to me in endless song."
4. **Channeling Confidence:** Feel the energy of Regulus entering your solar plexus, boosting your confidence and aligning you with the flow of abundance. Imagine this energy spreading through your entire being, dissolving any doubts or fears about wealth and success.
5. **Closing:** Blow out the candle and carry the tiger's eye with you to continue channeling Regulus' energy.

Tips: Use this spell before important meetings, interviews, or financial decisions to attract success and confidence.

3. Capella's Fortune Meditation

Capella, a bright star in the constellation Auriga, is associated with fortune, wealth, and the nurturing of financial resources. This meditation helps you connect with Capella's energy to attract abundance and maintain financial stability.

Tools Needed:

- Green or white candle (to represent Capella)
- A piece of jade or green aventurine (for luck and prosperity)

Instructions:

1. **Set Up Your Space:** Light the candle and place the jade on your altar. Sit comfortably and close your eyes, taking deep breaths to center yourself.
2. **Visualizing Capella:** In your mind's eye, see Capella shining brightly in the night sky, radiating a warm, golden light. Visualize

this light forming a beam that descends toward you, enveloping you in its nurturing energy.
3. **Channeling Abundance:** Hold the jade in your hands and feel Capella's light entering your heart, filling you with a sense of warmth, security, and prosperity. As you breathe, imagine this light spreading through your body, awakening your inner ability to attract and nurture wealth.
4. **Affirmation:** Mentally repeat the affirmation: "Capella, star of fortune and light, nurture my wealth and guide my way. Abundance flows to me with ease, and I grow prosperous every day."
5. **Meditate:** Spend a few moments in silence, focusing on the feeling of abundance surrounding you. See your financial goals manifesting effortlessly, supported by Capella's energy.
6. **Closing:** When you are ready, open your eyes and blow out the candle. Place the jade on your altar or carry it with you to continue receiving Capella's nurturing energy.

Tips: Perform this meditation during the full moon to harness the energy of abundance and illumination.

Star Spells for Financial Opportunities

In addition to specific rituals, there are simple star spells you can use to attract financial opportunities and prosperity.

4. Orion's Belt Manifestation Spell

Orion's Belt, with its three aligned stars, symbolizes focus, success, and direct paths to achievement. This spell helps you manifest financial opportunities by aligning with the energy of Orion's Belt.

Instructions:

1. **Set Your Intention:** Write down a specific financial opportunity you wish to manifest, such as a new job, investment success, or a business deal.
2. **Visualize:** Close your eyes and visualize Orion's Belt shining brightly in the sky. See its three stars aligning perfectly with your intention, creating a direct path toward your financial goal.
3. **Chant:** Hold your hands over your heart and chant, "Orion's Belt, align with me. Guide my path to prosperity. Opportunities arise, success I see. Wealth flows freely, so mote it be."
4. **Release:** Visualize your intention being sent into the universe, carried by the light of Orion's stars.
5. **Affirmation:** Repeat daily until the opportunity manifests, using the power of Orion's Belt to maintain focus and alignment.

Daily Practices for Attracting Abundance

Incorporate these daily practices into your routine to align with the flow of abundance and prosperity.

5. Morning Prosperity Visualization

Begin each day by visualizing a star of abundance, such as Aldebaran or Regulus, shining above you. Imagine its light filling you with the energy of wealth, success, and confidence. Repeat affirmations like:

- "I am aligned with the flow of abundance in the universe."
- "Wealth and prosperity come to me easily and effortlessly."
- "I attract financial success in all my endeavors."

Conclusion

The stars are powerful sources of abundance, radiating energy that can help you attract wealth, success, and financial prosperity. By aligning with stars like Aldebaran, Regulus, and Capella, you can tap into the universe's boundless flow of wealth and bring your financial goals into reality. Through star-based rituals, spells, and meditations, you can channel cosmic energy to attract new opportunities, increase your income, and create a stable foundation for your financial future. As you practice Star Magic for abundance, remember that prosperity is a reflection of the universe's infinite potential. Let the stars guide you on your journey to wealth, success, and a life filled with the riches of the cosmos.

Chapter 33: Ritual Tools in Star Magic

Star Magic is a practice steeped in symbolism and cosmic energy, utilizing specific tools to harness and direct the power of the stars effectively. Each tool has its own unique properties, serving as a conduit to channel celestial energies during rituals, meditations, and spellwork. From star maps that guide you to the stars' positions to crystals that amplify your connection to stellar energy, these tools help you align with the universe and enhance your magical practices.

This chapter provides a comprehensive guide to the essential tools used in Star Magic. It covers how to choose, cleanse, and consecrate these tools, as well as how to use them in ritual work. Whether you are new to Star Magic or a seasoned practitioner, understanding the purpose and proper use of these tools will deepen your connection with the stars and amplify the power of your rituals.

Essential Tools in Star Magic

Here are the key tools used in Star Magic rituals, each serving a unique purpose in your practice. They facilitate a deeper connection with stellar energy, focus your intentions, and enhance the overall effectiveness of your magic.

1. Star Maps and Star Charts

Purpose: Star maps and charts are fundamental in Star Magic, as they help you locate and work with specific stars, constellations, and celestial events. They serve as guides, allowing you to identify the stars' positions in the sky and align your rituals with their energies.

- **How to Use:** Use star maps during rituals to visualize the stars you are invoking. For example, when performing a ritual to channel the energy of Sirius, place a star map showing the constellation Canis Major on your altar. As you connect with the star, focus on its location on the map to strengthen your intention.
- **Choosing a Star Map:** Choose a detailed star map that includes major stars, constellations, and celestial events like eclipses and

meteor showers. Consider investing in a physical star chart or a digital star map application to provide real-time star positions.
- **Customization:** Personalize your star map by marking stars and constellations that resonate with you. This adds a layer of intention to your practice and makes the map a unique tool in your Star Magic rituals.

2. Crystals for Star Magic

Purpose: Crystals serve as amplifiers and conduits of stellar energy. Each crystal has its own vibration that corresponds with certain stars, constellations, and magical intentions. By using crystals, you can enhance your connection to specific star energies and direct them more effectively in your rituals.

- **Key Crystals in Star Magic:**
    - **Clear Quartz:** Amplifies energy and intention. It is versatile and can be used to connect with any star or celestial energy.
    - **Amethyst:** Enhances intuition and spiritual insight. Ideal for connecting with stars associated with wisdom and clarity, like Sirius.
    - **Citrine:** Attracts abundance, success, and positivity. Use in rituals involving stars like Aldebaran, which embody prosperity.
    - **Moonstone:** Associated with the moon and feminine energy, aiding in rituals connected to moon phases and nurturing stars like the Pleiades.
    - **Labradorite:** Protects and opens pathways for interdimensional exploration, making it suitable for working with stars linked to other realms, like the Pleiades.
    - **Selenite:** Cleanses energy and creates a connection with higher realms, perfect for channeling celestial light during star-based meditation.

- **How to Use:** Place crystals on your altar during rituals to align with the energy of the stars you are invoking. Hold a crystal during meditation to amplify your connection with the star's vibration. For example, when channeling Vega's creative energy, hold an amethyst or place it next to your art supplies.
- **Consecrating Crystals:** Cleanse your crystals with moonlight, sage, or running water. Consecrate them by holding the crystal in your hands, focusing on your intention, and saying, "I consecrate you as a conduit of [star's name] energy. May you amplify and guide this light in my rituals."

3. Candles in Star Magic

Purpose: Candles are used in Star Magic to represent the light and energy of specific stars, bringing their cosmic power into the ritual space. The flame serves as a focal point, helping you concentrate on your intention and connect with the stellar energy you are invoking.

- **Color Correspondences:** Choose candle colors that correspond to the star or celestial energy you wish to work with:
    - **White:** Universal, purity, moonlight, Sirius.
    - **Blue:** Wisdom, spiritual insight, Vega.
    - **Gold:** Wealth, success, Regulus, Aldebaran.
    - **Green:** Abundance, growth, Capella.
    - **Silver:** Mysticism, moon energy, the Pleiades.
- **How to Use:** Light candles at the beginning of your rituals to open a connection with the star's energy. For example, when working with Sirius for insight, light a white candle and focus on its flame to visualize Sirius' light illuminating your mind.
- **Consecrating Candles:** Before using a candle, consecrate it by anointing it with oil (like lavender or frankincense) and stating your intention. Hold the candle and say, "I consecrate this candle in the name of [star's name]. May its light guide this ritual and channel the star's energy."

4. Wands for Directing Stellar Energy

Purpose: Wands are tools used to direct and focus energy during rituals. In Star Magic, a wand helps you channel the light and power of the stars, directing it toward specific intentions or areas in your life.

- **Choosing a Wand:** Select a wand made from materials that resonate with you. Crystal-tipped wands (amethyst, quartz) are excellent for focusing stellar energy. Wooden wands from trees associated with certain star energies (e.g., oak for strength, willow for intuition) are also powerful.
- **How to Use:** Use the wand to draw star symbols, constellations, or sigils in the air during rituals. Point the wand toward your crystals, candles, or other tools to direct the star's energy where you need it. For example, when invoking Orion's energy, use the wand to trace the shape of Orion's Belt in the air.
- **Consecrating the Wand:** To consecrate your wand, hold it under the night sky and say, "By the stars above, I consecrate this wand as a channel of stellar power. May it guide and direct the light of the cosmos in my rituals." Pass the wand through the smoke of sage or incense to seal its energy.

5. Incense and Herbs

Purpose: Incense and herbs are used to cleanse the ritual space, purify the energy, and invoke specific celestial qualities. Their smoke symbolizes the bridge between the earthly and cosmic realms.

- **Incense Correspondences:**
    - **Frankincense:** Spiritual connection, Sirius.
    - **Sandalwood:** Grounding, strength, Orion.
    - **Jasmine:** Creativity, beauty, Vega.
    - **Lavender:** Calm, protection, the Pleiades.
- **Herbal Offerings:** Herbs such as rosemary, sage, and bay leaves can be used as offerings to the stars. Place them on your altar or

burn them as incense to enhance the connection with celestial energies.
- **How to Use:** Light incense during your rituals to cleanse the space and invoke the star's energy. For example, when calling upon the Pleiades, burn lavender incense to open a channel of nurturing, mystical energy.
- **Consecrating Incense and Herbs:** To consecrate incense or herbs, hold them in your hands and state your intention: "I consecrate this [incense/herb] to purify and channel the energy of [star's name]. May its scent bridge the gap between earth and sky."

6. Sigils and Symbols

Purpose: Sigils and symbols represent specific stars, constellations, and intentions in Star Magic. They serve as a visual link to the celestial energy you are invoking and can be drawn, carved, or placed on your altar.

- **Creating Sigils:** Draw a sigil that represents your intention, incorporating star symbols (e.g., a star, constellation, or the star's astrological glyph). For example, when working with Regulus, create a sigil that includes a lion's mane or heart symbol to reflect the star's power.
- **Using Sigils:** Place the sigil on your altar, carve it into a candle, or draw it on your body with oil to connect with the star's energy. In rituals, visualize the sigil glowing with starlight, activating its power.
- **Consecrating Sigils:** Before using a sigil, consecrate it by holding it under the light of the star it represents. Say, "I consecrate this sigil in the name of [star's name]. May it serve as a channel of your light and power in my work."

Consecrating Your Ritual Tools

Consecration is the process of dedicating your tools to Star Magic, infusing them with your intention and the energy of the stars. Consecrated tools become powerful conduits for stellar energy, enhancing the effectiveness of your rituals and spellwork.

1. General Consecration Ritual:

1. **Gather Your Tools:** Place all the tools you wish to consecrate on your altar (e.g., candles, crystals, wand, star maps).
2. **Cleanse the Tools:** Use sage, palo santo, or incense to cleanse each tool, waving the smoke around them to remove any lingering energies.
3. **Call Upon the Stars:** Light a candle representing a guiding star (e.g., Sirius for insight, Aldebaran for abundance). Close your eyes and visualize the star shining above you.
4. **Infuse with Energy:** Hold each tool one by one, focusing on your intention and the star's energy. Say, "I consecrate this [tool] to serve as a conduit of the stars. May it guide, protect, and amplify the power of the cosmos in my rituals."
5. **Seal the Energy:** Visualize the star's light surrounding each tool, sealing its energy. When finished, blow out the candle, thanking the star for its guidance.

Using Consecrated Tools in Rituals

Once your tools are consecrated, they become powerful allies in your Star Magic practice. Use them in your rituals to channel stellar energy, set intentions, and manifest your desires. Keep your tools on your altar, and cleanse and recharge them regularly under moonlight or starlight to maintain their potency.

Conclusion

Ritual tools are essential components of Star Magic, serving as channels through which you can focus and direct the energy of the stars. By using tools like star maps, crystals, candles, wands, incense, and sigils, you create a tangible connection to celestial forces, enhancing the effectiveness of your magical work. Properly cleansing and consecrating your tools is crucial to align them with the cosmic energies you wish to invoke, transforming them into potent instruments of power. As you work with these tools, you deepen your relationship with the stars, empowering your rituals, spells, and meditations. Let your tools become extensions of your intention and connection to the cosmos, guiding you on your journey through the vast expanse of Star Magic.

Chapter 34: Star Magic and the Elemental Forces

The universe operates in harmony through the interplay of cosmic and elemental forces. In Star Magic, working solely with stellar energy provides immense power and guidance, but when combined with the elemental energies—Earth, Air, Fire, and Water—it becomes a holistic and balanced magical practice. The elements represent fundamental aspects of existence, each contributing unique qualities and energies to support the manifestation of intentions, the alignment with cosmic cycles, and the grounding of celestial energies into the physical realm.

This chapter explores how to integrate the energies of the stars with the four elements to create a comprehensive approach to Star Magic. You will learn how to balance these energies in your rituals, understand their unique properties, and use them to enhance your connection with the stars. By aligning star magic with elemental forces, you create a dynamic and harmonized practice that deepens your spiritual growth, strengthens your magical workings, and grounds celestial power into your daily life.

The Four Elements in Star Magic

In the realm of Star Magic, the elements are more than natural forces—they are conduits for channeling the stars' energy into tangible forms. Each element has a distinct relationship with celestial energy, influencing how star magic is manifested and experienced.

1. Earth: The Foundation and Grounding Force

- **Qualities:** Stability, nurturing, growth, abundance, physicality
- **Correspondence:** Earth provides the grounding necessary to anchor celestial energy into the material world. It represents the physical realm, the resources we draw upon, and the growth we experience.
- **Elemental Symbols:** Stones, crystals, salt, soil, plants, herbs, pentacles

- **Star Associations:** Aldebaran (wealth, strength), Capella (fortune, nurturing), Taurus (earthly stability)

In Star Magic: Earth energy stabilizes and grounds the often ethereal nature of star energy. When you work with stars like Aldebaran, known for its connection to abundance and strength, invoking Earth energy helps manifest prosperity in physical forms, such as wealth, health, and security.

2. Air: The Breath and Mind

- **Qualities:** Intellect, communication, inspiration, clarity, movement
- **Correspondence:** Air governs the mind, thoughts, ideas, and communication. It is the breath of life that carries the intentions of star magic through space and time.
- **Elemental Symbols:** Incense, feathers, wind, smoke, bells, swords
- **Star Associations:** Sirius (wisdom, spiritual insight), Vega (artistic inspiration), Gemini (communication, versatility)

In Star Magic: Air energy amplifies the intellectual and communicative aspects of stellar energy. When connecting with stars like Sirius for spiritual insight or Vega for creative inspiration, invoking Air helps to clear the mind, facilitate mental clarity, and carry cosmic messages.

3. Fire: The Spark of Passion and Transformation

- **Qualities:** Passion, courage, transformation, willpower, creativity
- **Correspondence:** Fire represents the power of transformation, the drive to pursue goals, and the spark of creativity. It burns away the old to make way for the new, aligning with the stars' fiery light.
- **Elemental Symbols:** Candles, flames, sun, wands, swords

- **Star Associations:** Regulus (courage, leadership), Antares (passion, change), Leo (confidence, expression)

In Star Magic: Fire energy aligns with the dynamic, creative force of stars. When invoking stars like Regulus for courage and success, or Antares for transformation, Fire enhances the ritual's intensity and empowers your intentions to manifest with boldness and vitality.

4. Water: The Flow of Emotions and Intuition

- **Qualities:** Emotions, intuition, healing, reflection, fluidity
- **Correspondence:** Water is the element of emotions, intuition, and the subconscious. It represents the flow of life and the ability to adapt and nurture.
- **Elemental Symbols:** Water, seashells, cups, mirrors, moon phases
- **Star Associations:** The Pleiades (nurturing, creativity), Pisces (dreams, spirituality), Cancer (emotional depth)

In Star Magic: Water energy enhances the intuitive and emotional aspects of stellar energy. When working with the Pleiades for nurturing creativity or Pisces for dream exploration, invoking Water allows you to flow with the star's guidance, nurturing spiritual growth and emotional healing.

Balancing the Elements with Stellar Energy in Rituals

Balancing the elements with star energy creates a holistic practice, grounding your cosmic work, expanding your consciousness, igniting your intentions, and deepening your emotional and spiritual connection. Here's how to integrate each element into your Star Magic rituals.

1. Invoking Earth: Grounding Star Energy

Purpose: Incorporating Earth energy into your rituals grounds the celestial power, making it tangible and helping to manifest your intentions in the physical world.

How to Use:

- **Crystals:** Place grounding crystals like hematite, obsidian, or black tourmaline on your altar. When invoking stars associated with abundance like Aldebaran, hold a piece of citrine or green aventurine to anchor the energy of prosperity.
- **Salt Circle:** Create a circle of salt around your ritual space to symbolize Earth's grounding force. Visualize the light of the star descending and merging with the circle, stabilizing the cosmic energy.
- **Soil and Plants:** Add soil, stones, or small plants to your altar when performing rituals for growth or stability. For example, during a ritual with Capella, place a small plant on your altar as an offering to the star's nurturing energy.

Ritual Example: For a prosperity ritual with Aldebaran, bury a coin or crystal in a small pot of soil. As you invoke the star's energy, visualize it entering the soil, grounding into the Earth, and transforming into tangible abundance.

2. Invoking Air: Clarifying and Amplifying Intentions

Purpose: Air brings clarity, movement, and communication to star rituals, helping carry your intentions to the cosmos and bringing inspiration.

How to Use:

- **Incense:** Burn incense like lavender, frankincense, or sandalwood to invoke Air. Visualize the smoke carrying your intentions to the stars, particularly when seeking guidance from Sirius or Vega.
- **Feathers:** Place feathers on your altar to symbolize the Air element. During rituals for mental clarity or communication, hold a feather and wave it through the air, visualizing it sweeping away mental fog and opening a channel to the star's wisdom.

- **Wind Chimes:** Use wind chimes or bells to create vibrations that align with the celestial energies. Their sound represents the movement of Air, aiding in connecting with stars associated with intellect and inspiration.

Ritual Example: During a meditation with Sirius for wisdom, light incense and allow its smoke to swirl around you. As you inhale the scent, visualize the smoke entering your mind, clearing it of distractions and aligning your thoughts with the star's clarity.

3. Invoking Fire: Energizing and Transforming Intentions

Purpose: Fire adds passion, power, and transformative energy to your star rituals, empowering your will to manifest desires.

How to Use:

- **Candles:** Light candles in colors that correspond with the star's energy (e.g., gold for Regulus, red for Antares). Use the flame as a focal point to draw in the star's fiery power.
- **Burning Sigils:** Create a sigil that represents your intention and the star you are working with. Hold it in your hands, focusing on your desire, then burn it in the candle flame to release the energy into the universe.
- **Wands:** Use a wand to direct fiery energy during your ritual. When invoking stars like Regulus for courage, trace the star's symbol in the air with the wand, visualizing it glowing with fiery light.

Ritual Example: For a transformation ritual with Antares, carve a sigil into a red candle, representing your intention for change. As the candle burns, visualize the flame consuming the old and igniting new possibilities, powered by Antares' energy.

4. Invoking Water: Deepening Intuition and Emotional Connection

Purpose: Water enhances the emotional, intuitive aspects of star magic, allowing you to flow with the cosmic energy and gain insights from the stars.

How to Use:

- **Bowls of Water:** Place a bowl of water on your altar to represent the element. For rituals involving stars like the Pleiades, add a few drops of essential oil (lavender or jasmine) to the water, stirring it clockwise to invoke nurturing energy.
- **Moon Water:** Use moon-charged water for rituals involving lunar energies or stars associated with intuition. Sprinkle it around your ritual space to purify and invite the star's energy.
- **Scrying:** Use a bowl of water as a scrying tool during rituals to connect with stars that govern dreams and the subconscious. Gaze into the water to receive messages or visions from the stars.

Ritual Example: For a dream-enhancing ritual with the Pleiades, place a bowl of water under the moonlight to charge it. During the ritual, anoint your forehead with the moon water and visualize the Pleiades' energy flowing into your dreams, opening pathways to cosmic wisdom.

Creating a Balanced Ritual Space

Incorporating all four elements into your star rituals creates a balanced space that enhances the flow of celestial energy. Here's how to set up a balanced elemental ritual space:

1. **Earth:** Place grounding stones or a small bowl of salt in the northern part of your altar.
2. **Air:** Set incense, feathers, or a bell in the eastern part of your altar to represent the Air element.

3. **Fire:** Position candles in the southern part of your altar, selecting colors that correspond to the star's energy you are invoking.
4. **Water:** Place a bowl of water or a seashell in the western part of your altar to invoke the element of Water.

As you perform your ritual, acknowledge each element, thanking them for their presence and support. Visualize them harmonizing with the star's energy, creating a balanced and powerful field for your magical work.

Elemental Meditation with Star Energy

To align with the elemental forces and stellar energies, practice this meditation:

1. **Grounding with Earth:** Visualize roots extending from your body into the earth, grounding you. Feel the stability and strength of Earth anchoring you.
2. **Breathing with Air:** Inhale deeply, drawing in the light of a star like Sirius. Imagine the Air around you becoming infused with its energy, clearing your mind and opening your thoughts.
3. **Igniting with Fire:** Visualize a flame within your heart, fueled by the star's light. Feel this fire empowering your intentions, filling you with confidence and determination.
4. **Flowing with Water:** Imagine a wave of starlight flowing through your body, washing away doubts and filling you with peace. Feel the Water element connecting you emotionally to the cosmic energy.

Conclusion

Incorporating the elemental forces into your Star Magic practice creates a holistic approach that aligns your work with the balance and harmony of the universe. Earth grounds celestial energy into tangible forms, Air clarifies and carries intentions, Fire ignites and transforms, and Water deepens intuition and emotional flow. By understanding and invoking these elements, you not only enhance the effectiveness of your star rituals but also create a balanced magical practice that reflects the interconnectedness of all things. Let the stars and elements guide you on your path, as you embrace the cosmic dance of energy, intention, and transformation in your journey of Star Magic.

Chapter 35: Advanced Star Magic Techniques

Star Magic is a multifaceted practice that offers limitless possibilities for growth, transformation, and cosmic alignment. While foundational rituals and meditations are powerful, advanced techniques provide deeper levels of engagement with celestial energies, allowing seasoned practitioners to explore the complexities of the universe. These techniques include working with multi-star alignments, invoking rare celestial events, and combining Star Magic with other mystical practices for a more integrated and dynamic magical experience.

This chapter delves into advanced Star Magic techniques, offering detailed methods for those ready to expand their practice. You will learn how to work with the energies of multiple stars simultaneously, invoke the rare and potent energies of unique celestial events, and incorporate Star Magic into other mystical practices like astrology, tarot, and elemental magic. By mastering these advanced methods, you will elevate your practice to new heights and deepen your connection with the cosmos.

Multi-Star Alignments: Working with Constellations and Star Clusters

Working with individual stars is powerful, but aligning with multiple stars within constellations or star clusters can create a more dynamic and potent flow of energy. Each star within a constellation or cluster brings a unique influence, and combining their energies allows for multi-layered magical workings.

1. Harmonizing with Constellations

Purpose: Aligning with the energy of an entire constellation enhances your intentions by drawing upon the combined power of its stars. This method is ideal for rituals seeking a comprehensive impact on various aspects of life, such as transformation, protection, or wisdom.

How to Work with Constellations:

- **Choose the Constellation:** Select a constellation that aligns with your purpose. For example, **Orion** is known for strength, focus, and the pursuit of goals, while **Lyra** (which contains Vega) is associated with artistic inspiration and harmony.
- **Visualizing the Constellation:** Begin by visualizing the constellation in the night sky. Imagine its stars connected by lines of light, forming the constellation's shape.
- **Multi-Star Invocation:** As you visualize the constellation, call upon each star individually. For example, when working with **Orion**, invoke **Betelgeuse** for power, **Rigel** for success, and **Bellatrix** for warrior strength. Visualize each star's energy flowing toward you, combining into a single, harmonious force.
- **Drawing the Constellation:** Use a wand, finger, or athame to trace the shape of the constellation in the air or on your altar, invoking its full energy. State, "By the power of [Constellation's Name], I call upon your light to [state your intention]. May your stars align and guide this work."

Ritual Example: For a ritual of strength and determination, align with Orion by lighting three candles to represent **Betelgeuse**, **Rigel**, and **Bellatrix**. As you light each candle, call upon the star's unique energy, allowing them to blend into a potent force that empowers your intentions.

2. Star Cluster Energy: The Pleiades and Hyades

Purpose: Star clusters like the **Pleiades** and **Hyades** offer a concentrated field of energy that can be harnessed for specific magical purposes, such as nurturing creativity, enhancing intuition, and facilitating emotional healing.

How to Work with Star Clusters:

- **Connect with the Cluster:** Visualize the cluster as a group of stars radiating a unified light. For the **Pleiades**, imagine the stars as a swirling vortex of nurturing, mystical energy.
- **Group Energy Alignment:** Place seven candles in a circle to represent the **Pleiades**. As you light each candle, call upon the collective energy of the cluster, stating, "Pleiades, stars of nurturing and creation, surround me with your guiding light. Unite your energies to [state your intention]."
- **Multi-Channel Meditation:** During meditation, visualize yourself surrounded by the stars of the cluster, their combined energy creating a field of light that envelops you. Feel the unique qualities of each star contributing to the overall energy of the cluster.

Ritual Example: When invoking the Pleiades for emotional healing, light seven blue candles in a circle. As you sit within the circle, imagine the stars of the Pleiades shining above you, their energies merging into a soothing wave of light that washes over you, bringing comfort and renewal.

Invoking Rare Celestial Energies

Rare celestial events, such as planetary alignments, meteor showers, eclipses, and supernovas, provide unique and potent energies that can be harnessed for specific magical purposes. Advanced practitioners can use these energies to amplify their rituals, set intentions for profound transformation, and access higher realms of consciousness.

1. **Planetary Alignments: Merging Planetary and Stellar Energies**

Purpose: When planets align with specific stars, their combined energies create a powerful synergy that can be used to enhance magical workings. For example, a conjunction of **Jupiter** with **Aldebaran** may signify a time of increased prosperity and expansion.

How to Use Planetary Alignments:

- **Track Alignments:** Use astrological software or star maps to track upcoming planetary alignments with significant stars. Note the alignment's date, zodiac sign, and the themes associated with both the planet and the star.
- **Dual Invocation:** During the alignment, invoke both the star and the planet. For instance, during a **Venus-Sirius** conjunction, light a white candle for **Sirius** and a pink candle for **Venus**. State, "I call upon the union of Venus and Sirius. May their combined energies bring love, wisdom, and spiritual growth."
- **Channeling the Synergy:** Meditate during the alignment, visualizing the star and planet merging their energies into a beam of light that flows toward you. Direct this light into a specific area of your life, such as relationships, finances, or spiritual growth.

Ritual Example: For a **Jupiter-Aldebaran** alignment, create a ritual focused on abundance. Light a green candle for **Aldebaran** and a purple candle for **Jupiter**. Invoke their energies to blend and infuse your financial goals with growth and success.

2. Eclipses: Shadow and Light in Star Magic

Purpose: Eclipses are powerful celestial events that bring sudden shifts, revelations, and opportunities for transformation. During a solar or lunar eclipse, the stars' energy is intensified, offering a unique window for deep magical work.

How to Use Eclipses in Rituals:

- **Preparation:** Begin preparing for an eclipse ritual at least three days before the event. Reflect on areas of your life that need change or illumination.
- **Eclipse Invocation:** During the eclipse, invoke stars associated with shadow work and transformation, such as **Antares** or **Algol**. State, "Under the shadow of the eclipse, I call upon [star's name] to reveal what is hidden and transform what no longer serves me."
- **Shadow and Light Visualization:** Visualize the energy of the eclipse merging with the star's light, creating a vortex of shadow and illumination. Step into this vortex, allowing it to cleanse, reveal, and transform your intentions.

Ritual Example: During a **lunar eclipse**, invoke **Antares** for transformation. Light a red candle and visualize the moon's shadow mingling with Antares' fiery energy, burning away old patterns and igniting the spark of renewal.

3. Meteor Showers: Harnessing Sudden Bursts of Energy

Purpose: Meteor showers are periods when the Earth passes through the debris of comets, resulting in a celestial display of shooting stars. These events symbolize sudden inspiration, bursts of energy, and the swift manifestation of intentions.

How to Work with Meteor Showers:

- **Timing:** Perform meteor shower rituals during the peak nights of the event. The **Perseids** in August and the **Geminids** in December are particularly potent.
- **Wishing Ritual:** As you see a shooting star, hold a crystal (such as clear quartz) in your hand and make a wish. State your intention clearly, feeling the meteor's energy carry it into the cosmos.
- **Meteor Magic Bowl:** Fill a bowl with water and place it under the sky during the meteor shower to absorb its energy. Use this water in future rituals for swift manifestation and inspiration.

Ritual Example: During the **Perseids**, sit under the stars with a piece of clear quartz. As you see a meteor, hold the quartz and state your wish aloud, visualizing the meteor's light infusing the quartz with the power to bring your wish to fruition.

Combining Star Magic with Other Mystical Practices

For seasoned practitioners, integrating Star Magic with other mystical systems—such as astrology, tarot, and elemental magic—creates a multifaceted and comprehensive approach to magic. These combinations deepen your practice and allow for more intricate and personalized workings.

1. **Astrology and Star Magic: Personalizing Rituals**

Purpose: Use your astrological birth chart to identify prominent stars, zodiac signs, and planetary influences in your life. This insight personalizes your Star Magic rituals to align with your innate cosmic energy.

How to Combine:

- **Natal Star Connection:** Identify stars that align with significant placements in your birth chart (e.g., **Regulus** conjunct your Sun). Create rituals that invoke these stars to enhance the qualities they bring to your life.
- **Transits:** Track current astrological transits involving stars, such as when a planet passes over a fixed star in your chart. Use these transits for ritual work that corresponds to the transit's energy (e.g., a **Venus-Aldebaran** transit for attracting abundance in relationships).

Ritual Example: If your natal Moon is aligned with **Sirius**, create a monthly ritual during the full moon to invoke Sirius' energy for emotional clarity and spiritual growth.

2. **Tarot and Star Magic: Divination and Guidance**

Purpose: Combining tarot with Star Magic offers a method of receiving guidance from the stars. Tarot spreads can be tailored to reflect star energies, providing insights into the cosmic forces at play in your life.

How to Combine:

- **Star Tarot Spread:** Create a tarot spread inspired by a constellation, such as the **Orion Spread**, with each card representing a star in Orion. Draw cards to gain insights on areas of life that align with the star's attributes (e.g., **Betelgeuse** for power, **Rigel** for success).

- **Stellar Card Ritual:** After drawing a tarot card, invoke a star that resonates with the card's meaning. For example, if you draw **The Star** card, invoke **Vega** for inspiration and hope.

Ritual Example: For an **Orion Spread**, draw cards and place them in the shape of Orion's Belt. Use the cards' meanings to explore different aspects of strength, focus, and goal achievement, then invoke Orion's stars to guide your path.

3. Elemental Magic: Balancing Star Energy

Purpose: Incorporating elemental forces into Star Magic rituals enhances their power and creates a balanced flow of energy.

How to Combine:

- **Elemental Stars:** Identify stars that correspond to the four elements (e.g., **Aldebaran** for Earth, **Sirius** for Air, **Regulus** for Fire, **Pleiades** for Water). Invoke these stars during elemental rituals to amplify their energy.
- **Four-Element Star Circle:** Create a circle with candles representing the four elements, placing symbols of each element on your altar. Invoke a star for each element, visualizing the circle filling with balanced, celestial energy.

Ritual Example: For a balanced ritual, invoke **Aldebaran** (Earth), **Sirius** (Air), **Regulus** (Fire), and the **Pleiades** (Water). Visualize their energies merging into a sphere of light, enveloping you with the universe's harmony and power.

Conclusion

Advanced Star Magic techniques open the door to a deeper, more intricate connection with the cosmos. By working with multi-star alignments, invoking rare celestial energies, and integrating other mystical practices, you create a comprehensive approach that reflects the dynamic and interconnected nature of the universe. These advanced methods empower you to work with the stars on a multi-dimensional level, amplifying the impact of your intentions and aligning you more profoundly with cosmic forces. Embrace these techniques as part of your ongoing journey through the vast expanse of Star Magic, where the stars are not just celestial bodies but living energies that guide, transform, and illuminate your path.

Chapter 36: Becoming a Star Mage

After journeying through the mysteries, rituals, and techniques of Star Magic, you have reached the point of transformation—becoming a Star Mage. This is a calling that goes beyond merely practicing magic; it's about embodying the energy of the stars, living in alignment with the cosmos, and using celestial power to guide, heal, and inspire both yourself and others. Stepping into the role of a Star Mage requires responsibility, discipline, and a deep understanding of the universe's rhythms.

This final chapter empowers you to fully embrace your role as a Star Mage. It outlines the responsibilities you carry, the skills you need to develop, and the knowledge you must master. It also provides guidance on how to integrate Star Magic into your daily life, deepen your practice, and share your wisdom with others. Becoming a Star Mage is not just about learning rituals; it's about embodying the cosmic wisdom and nurturing the magic within you to its fullest potential.

The Role of a Star Mage

A Star Mage is not merely a practitioner of magic but a guardian and interpreter of celestial energies. This role encompasses various aspects, from performing rituals to guiding others in their cosmic journeys. As a Star Mage, you serve as a bridge between the heavens and the earthly realm, using star energy to bring about harmony, insight, and transformation.

1. Keeper of Cosmic Knowledge

A Star Mage is a lifelong student and keeper of cosmic wisdom. This involves understanding the movements of stars, constellations, and celestial events, as well as their impact on the physical and spiritual worlds.

- **Astrological Awareness:** A Star Mage must continuously study celestial patterns, star positions, and cosmic alignments. Understanding astrology, particularly fixed stars and their influence on personal and collective energies, is crucial to mastering star magic.

- **Star Histories and Myths:** Knowing the myths, histories, and spiritual significance of stars and constellations allows you to connect more deeply with their energies. For example, understanding the mythological background of **Orion** or the **Pleiades** enhances your ability to invoke and work with these stars effectively.
- **Stellar Energies:** Familiarize yourself with the specific energies each star carries—whether it be **Sirius** for wisdom and spiritual illumination or **Regulus** for courage and leadership. This knowledge forms the foundation for crafting precise and potent rituals.

2. Master of Rituals and Techniques

To become a Star Mage, you must master a diverse range of rituals, meditations, and magical techniques. This includes working with the stars in harmony with the elements, lunar phases, planetary alignments, and rare celestial events.

- **Star Alignment Rituals:** Proficiency in aligning with individual stars, constellations, and star clusters is essential. Develop the skill to craft your own rituals tailored to specific needs, whether for healing, abundance, or spiritual growth.
- **Multi-Star Workings:** As a Star Mage, you should be comfortable invoking the energies of multiple stars simultaneously, combining their powers for complex magical workings.
- **Advanced Practices:** Master advanced techniques, such as invoking rare celestial energies during eclipses or meteor showers. These practices elevate your magic, allowing you to channel potent cosmic forces for profound transformation.

Responsibilities of a Star Mage

With great power comes great responsibility. A Star Mage must approach their practice with integrity, respect, and mindfulness of the cosmic energies they are channeling. As a guardian of star magic, it is your duty to use this power ethically and for the greater good.

1. Respect for Celestial Energies

The stars are ancient, conscious entities that deserve reverence and respect. A Star Mage honors this by approaching each ritual, meditation, and invocation with gratitude and mindfulness.

- **Acknowledging the Stars:** Before invoking a star, always take a moment to acknowledge its presence and energy. Speak words of respect, expressing your intention and gratitude. For example, when invoking **Sirius**, say, "Sirius, brightest of stars, I honor your light and wisdom. Guide me as I seek your energy."
- **Ethical Use of Magic:** Use the power of the stars responsibly, focusing on intentions that align with the highest good. Avoid manipulating others or using star magic for harmful purposes. Remember, the energy you send out into the universe returns to you.

2. Serving as a Guide and Healer

A Star Mage often acts as a guide for others, helping them connect with star energies and understand the cosmic forces at work in their lives.

- **Sharing Knowledge:** Share your knowledge of star magic with others, whether through teaching, writing, or leading group rituals. Your insights can help others navigate their own spiritual paths and understand the influence of the stars on their lives.
- **Healing and Support:** Use your skills to offer healing and support. Whether through energy work, star-based meditations, or rituals, your role as a Star Mage includes helping others align with their true selves and the universe's rhythm.

3. Maintaining Cosmic Harmony

A key responsibility of a Star Mage is to work in harmony with the universe's natural cycles and rhythms.

- **Aligning with Cosmic Cycles:** Observe lunar phases, planetary movements, and star alignments in your daily life and magical practice. This alignment ensures that your actions and intentions resonate with the universe's flow, increasing their power and efficacy.
- **Balancing Energies:** Use your knowledge of the elements to balance the cosmic energies you channel. Grounding stellar energy with Earth, harmonizing it with Air, igniting it with Fire, and flowing with Water creates a balanced practice that reflects the interconnectedness of all things.

Skills to Develop as a Star Mage

To fully embody the role of a Star Mage, certain skills need to be developed and honed over time. These skills will enhance your practice and deepen your connection with the stars.

1. Astrological Proficiency

A Star Mage must be adept at reading and interpreting astrological charts, focusing particularly on the influence of fixed stars, constellations, and celestial events.

- **Star Chart Interpretation:** Learn how to read star maps and astrological charts to track the positions of stars and planets. This skill allows you to identify auspicious times for rituals, align with celestial energies, and understand the impact of cosmic events on both a personal and collective level.
- **Personal Star Alignment:** Study your birth chart to identify stars that have a significant influence on your life. Use this knowledge to create personalized rituals that harness the power of these stars to support your growth and development.

2. Ritual Crafting

Develop the ability to create and adapt rituals based on the energy you wish to invoke and the celestial patterns present at any given time.

- **Custom Rituals:** Design your own star rituals, incorporating elements that resonate with your intentions. For example, if crafting a ritual for abundance, you might choose to work with **Aldebaran** during a waxing moon phase, using green candles, citrine, and soil to ground the star's energy.
- **Versatility:** Be flexible and innovative in your ritual work. Combine star magic with other mystical practices, such as tarot, astrology, or elemental magic, to create multi-dimensional experiences.

3. Energy Sensitivity and Control

A Star Mage must be sensitive to energy, able to sense and direct the flow of celestial forces.

- **Meditative Focus:** Regular meditation is essential to heighten your sensitivity to stellar energies. Practice connecting with stars through visualization and breathwork, learning to distinguish the unique vibrations of each celestial body.
- **Energy Manipulation:** Develop the skill to direct energy using tools like wands, crystals, and sigils. Practice techniques such as drawing down starlight, casting circles, and creating protective barriers to manage the flow of energy in your rituals.

4. Inner Reflection and Self-Mastery

Mastering Star Magic begins with mastering oneself. Self-awareness, emotional intelligence, and spiritual discipline are crucial for any Star Mage.

- **Journaling:** Keep a journal of your rituals, experiences, and insights. Documenting your star magic practice helps you track your progress, recognize patterns, and gain deeper self-understanding.
- **Self-Reflection:** Regularly reflect on your intentions and the results of your magical workings. This practice ensures that you

remain aligned with the highest good and continue to grow in wisdom and power.

Integrating Star Magic into Daily Life

To truly become a Star Mage, you must integrate star magic into your daily routine. This continuous practice strengthens your connection to the stars and weaves their energy into every aspect of your life.

1. Daily Cosmic Alignment

Start each day by aligning with the stars. Begin your morning with a brief meditation, visualizing a star that resonates with your intention for the day.

- **Morning Star Meditation:** Choose a star to guide you for the day. For example, if you need clarity and insight, visualize **Sirius** shining its light upon you. Breathe in its energy, feeling it fill you with wisdom and focus.
- **Daily Affirmation:** State an affirmation that aligns with the star's energy, such as "I align with the wisdom of Sirius. My mind is clear, my path is illuminated."

2. Rituals for Moon Phases and Seasons

Incorporate lunar phases and seasonal cycles into your star magic practice.

- **Lunar Rituals:** Perform rituals in harmony with the moon's phases. During the new moon, set intentions with stars like **Aldebaran** for new beginnings. During the full moon, invoke stars like **Vega** to illuminate truths and enhance creativity.
- **Seasonal Celebrations:** Align your practice with seasonal changes. For example, during the spring equinox, work with stars associated with growth and renewal, such as **Capella** or the **Pleiades**.

3. Nightly Star Reflection

End your day with a moment of reflection under the stars.

- **Starlight Bath:** Stand outside or by a window, gazing at the night sky. Visualize the stars pouring their light down upon you, washing away stress and filling you with cosmic energy.
- **Gratitude:** Express gratitude to the stars you have worked with, thanking them for their guidance and support throughout the day.

Sharing Star Magic with Others

As a Star Mage, part of your role may involve teaching, guiding, and sharing your knowledge with others. This can take many forms, from leading group rituals to writing books or creating courses on star magic.

1. Teaching and Leading Rituals

If you feel called, offer your knowledge to others through teaching. Lead star magic rituals for groups, guiding participants through the process of connecting with celestial energies.

- **Group Rituals:** Design group rituals that focus on shared intentions, such as manifesting community abundance through the energy of **Aldebaran**. Provide guidance on how to invoke star energies, use ritual tools, and align with the cosmic flow.
- **Workshops and Courses:** Host workshops or create courses on star magic to teach others about the stars, constellations, celestial events, and how to work with these energies in their own lives.

2. Writing and Creating Resources

Contribute to the body of star magic knowledge by writing articles, books, or creating online content.

- **Educational Content:** Share your insights through blogs, videos, or social media, offering tips, techniques, and information on the stars and their magical uses.
- **Creating Guides:** Write in-depth guides on star magic topics, such as working with multi-star alignments, combining star magic with astrology, or crafting advanced rituals.

Conclusion

Becoming a Star Mage is a journey of learning, growth, and deep cosmic connection. It is about stepping into your role as a conduit of celestial energies, a keeper of cosmic wisdom, and a guardian of star magic. By embodying the knowledge, skills, and responsibilities outlined in this chapter, you align with the universe's rhythm and empower yourself to manifest your desires, guide others, and live in harmony with the stars. Remember, being a Star Mage is not just about performing rituals; it is about living in alignment with the cosmos, embracing your role as a bridge between the heavens and Earth, and using the infinite power of the stars to illuminate your path and the paths of those around you. As you move forward, continue to explore the mysteries of the universe, deepen your practice, and let the stars guide you in every step of your magical journey.

Appendix A: Glossary

In the study and practice of Star Magic, numerous terms arise from astrology, astronomy, and mystical traditions. This glossary provides comprehensive definitions to enhance your understanding of these terms, serving as a quick reference guide for both novice and seasoned practitioners. It includes key concepts, celestial phenomena, star-related terminology, and tools used in rituals, ensuring you are well-equipped with the knowledge needed to navigate the vast world of Star Magic.

Aldebaran: A bright red star in the constellation Taurus, known as the "Eye of the Bull." Associated with wealth, success, and determination, Aldebaran's energy is often invoked in rituals for prosperity and strength.

Alignment: The positioning of planets, stars, or celestial bodies in relation to each other, often creating powerful energetic influences. In Star Magic, alignments are used to amplify magical intentions and connect with specific cosmic forces.

Amulet: A magical object, often a piece of jewelry or a crystal, believed to contain protective powers. In Star Magic, amulets can be charged with star energy to serve as a source of guidance, luck, or protection.

Antares: A red supergiant star in the constellation Scorpius, known as the "Heart of the Scorpion." It symbolizes transformation, passion, and power, often used in rituals for deep change and personal growth.

Ascendant (Rising Sign): The zodiac sign that was rising on the eastern horizon at the time of an individual's birth. It represents one's outward behavior, appearance, and how they present themselves to the world.

Astrology: The study of the movements and positions of celestial bodies (such as stars, planets, and the moon) and their influence on human affairs and natural phenomena.

Betelgeuse: A bright, red supergiant star in the constellation Orion. Associated with power, strength, and the warrior spirit, it is invoked for rituals related to courage, determination, and overcoming obstacles.

Capella: The brightest star in the constellation Auriga, associated with prosperity, fortune, and the nurturing of financial resources. It is often used in rituals for growth, abundance, and stability.

Celestial Events: Phenomena that occur in the sky, including solar and lunar eclipses, meteor showers, planetary alignments, and supernovae. These events provide potent energies that can be harnessed for magical practices.

Chakras: Energy centers within the human body, each corresponding to different aspects of physical, emotional, and spiritual well-being. In Star Magic, chakras may be aligned with specific stars to enhance their vibrational energy.

Circle Casting: The practice of creating a sacred space or protective boundary for magical work. In Star Magic, a circle may be cast using elements (Earth, Air, Fire, Water) or by invoking specific stars and constellations.

Clear Quartz: A versatile crystal known for its ability to amplify energy and intentions. In Star Magic, clear quartz can be used to enhance the connection with stellar energies and strengthen the impact of rituals.

Conjunction: In astrology, a conjunction occurs when two or more celestial bodies align closely in the sky, creating a powerful blending of their energies. Conjunctions with stars are significant in Star Magic for amplifying their effects.

Constellation: A group of stars that forms a recognizable pattern in the night sky, often named after mythological characters, animals, or objects. Constellations like Orion, Leo, and the Pleiades are frequently invoked in Star Magic rituals.

Crystals: Minerals with specific vibrational properties, often used in magical practices to amplify intentions, protect energy, and channel star power. Common crystals in Star Magic include amethyst, citrine, selenite, and moonstone.

Divination: The practice of seeking knowledge and guidance through supernatural means, often using tools like tarot cards, astrology charts, or scrying. In Star Magic, divination may involve interpreting the positions and movements of stars and constellations.

Eclipse: A celestial event that occurs when one body, such as the moon or sun, passes into the shadow of another. Solar and lunar eclipses are considered powerful times for magic, revealing hidden truths and opening pathways for transformation.

Elemental Magic: A branch of magic that involves working with the four elements—Earth, Air, Fire, and Water. In Star Magic, elemental forces are invoked to balance and ground celestial energies during rituals.

Equinox: An astronomical event occurring twice a year when the day and night are of equal length. The spring and autumn equinoxes are considered significant in Star Magic for rituals related to balance, renewal, and alignment with cosmic cycles.

Fixed Stars: Stars that appear to remain in a fixed position in relation to other celestial bodies. These stars, such as Sirius, Regulus, and Aldebaran, hold specific magical properties and are invoked in Star Magic to channel their energies.

Full Moon: The lunar phase when the moon is fully illuminated. In Star Magic, the full moon is a time of heightened energy, clarity, and manifestation, making it ideal for rituals that seek to amplify intentions or bring matters to fruition.

Invocation: A magical practice in which a practitioner calls upon a deity, spirit, star, or celestial energy for guidance, support, or power. In Star Magic, invocation often involves focusing on a specific star or constellation and inviting its energy into the ritual.

Labradorite: A crystal known for its iridescent qualities and ability to enhance intuition, protection, and interdimensional exploration. In

Star Magic, labradorite is used to connect with mystical stars and otherworldly energies.

Lunar Phases: The changing appearances of the moon as it orbits the Earth, including new moon, waxing moon, full moon, and waning moon. Each phase carries different energies and influences magical workings in Star Magic.

Meteor Shower: A celestial event when numerous meteors appear to radiate from a single point in the sky. In Star Magic, meteor showers symbolize sudden inspiration, bursts of energy, and swift manifestation.

Moon Water: Water that has been left under the moonlight to absorb its energy. Moon water is used in Star Magic for purification, healing, and rituals involving stars that correspond to lunar qualities.

Multi-Star Alignment: A practice in Star Magic where the energies of multiple stars or an entire constellation are invoked simultaneously to create a more dynamic and potent magical effect.

Natal Chart: An astrological chart that maps the positions of the stars, planets, and celestial bodies at the exact time and location of an individual's birth. In Star Magic, natal charts reveal significant star alignments that influence personal energies and magical work.

New Moon: The lunar phase when the moon is not visible from Earth. The new moon symbolizes new beginnings, intention-setting, and the planting of seeds for future growth.

Orion: A prominent constellation named after the hunter in Greek mythology. Known for its association with strength, focus, and the pursuit of goals, Orion's stars are often invoked in rituals for empowerment and success.

Pentacle: A symbol often used in magical practices, consisting of a five-pointed star within a circle. It represents the balance of the five elements (Earth, Air, Fire, Water, and Spirit) and can be used in Star Magic rituals to ground stellar energies.

Pleiades: A cluster of stars known as the "Seven Sisters," associated with nurturing, creativity, and mysticism. The Pleiades' energy is invoked in Star Magic for emotional healing, intuition, and dream work.

Regulus: A bright star in the constellation Leo, known as the "Heart of the Lion." Associated with courage, leadership, and success, Regulus is often invoked for rituals that seek to empower, inspire, and attract recognition.

Retrograde: A period when a planet appears to move backward in its orbit from the perspective of Earth. Retrograde periods, particularly those of Mercury, Venus, and Mars, have significant effects on communication, relationships, and action in Star Magic practices.

Scrying: A method of divination that involves gazing into a reflective surface, such as water, mirrors, or crystals, to receive messages, visions, or insights. In Star Magic, scrying can be used to connect with stellar energies and gain cosmic guidance.

Sigil: A symbolic representation of an intention, star, or celestial energy, often drawn or carved during rituals to channel specific powers. In Star Magic, sigils are used to focus star energies and enhance the potency of magical workings.

Sirius: The brightest star in the night sky, located in the constellation Canis Major. Known for its association with wisdom, spiritual insight, and illumination, Sirius is invoked in Star Magic for clarity, enlightenment, and deepening one's spiritual journey.

Solar Eclipse: A celestial event that occurs when the moon passes between the Earth and the sun, temporarily blocking the sun's light. Solar eclipses are considered times of powerful transformation, new beginnings, and the unveiling of hidden truths in Star Magic.

Star Map: A chart or diagram that shows the positions of stars and constellations in the sky. Star maps are essential tools in Star Magic for locating and working with specific stellar energies.

Starlight Bath: A practice in which a practitioner visualizes themselves being bathed in the light of a particular star or stars to absorb their energy and qualities. This technique is often used for cleansing, healing, or empowerment in Star Magic.

Supernova: The explosive death of a star, releasing a tremendous amount of energy into the universe. In Star Magic, supernovas symbolize dramatic transformation, release, and the creation of new potentials.

Tarot: A deck of cards used for divination, guidance, and introspection. In Star Magic, tarot cards can be incorporated into rituals to provide insights related to celestial energies, star alignments, and cosmic influences.

Talisman: An object infused with magical energy and intended to attract specific outcomes, such as protection, love, or prosperity. In Star Magic, talismans can be charged with star energy to serve as conduits of stellar power.

Wand: A tool used in magical practices to direct and channel energy. In Star Magic, wands may be used to trace star symbols, invoke celestial energies, and focus the flow of star power during rituals.

Waxing Moon: The lunar phase following the new moon, when the moon is increasing in illumination. The waxing moon is associated with growth, expansion, and the manifestation of intentions.

Waning Moon: The lunar phase after the full moon, when the moon is decreasing in illumination. The waning moon is a time for release, letting go of what no longer serves, and preparing for new beginnings.

This glossary serves as a comprehensive guide to the terms and concepts encountered in the practice of Star Magic. Familiarizing yourself with these definitions will deepen your understanding and enhance your ability to work with the stars effectively. As you continue your journey as a Star Mage, let this glossary be a companion, reminding you of the vast and intricate web of cosmic forces you are now a part of.

Appendix B: Charts

Charts are invaluable tools for any Star Mage. They provide detailed information on star positions, planetary correspondences, and astrological aspects, enabling you to plan and perform rituals in harmony with cosmic energies. This appendix offers a collection of charts to support your practice, serving as a quick reference to the celestial patterns that influence Star Magic. These charts include the positions of key fixed stars, planetary correspondences with both astrological signs and celestial bodies, moon phases, and important astrological aspects. By consulting these charts, you can align your rituals with the most potent cosmic forces for your specific intentions.

1. Fixed Star Positions and Correspondences

This chart provides the current approximate positions of key fixed stars, their zodiac signs, degrees, and magical correspondences. Fixed stars have a profound influence on Star Magic practices, each possessing unique energy that can be invoked in rituals.

Fixed Star	Constellation	Zodiac Sign	Approximate Degree	Magical Correspondence
Aldebaran	Taurus	Taurus	9°	Wealth, prosperity, success

Fixed Star	Constellation	Zodiac Sign	Approximate Degree	Magical Correspondence
Antares	Scorpius	Scorpio	10°	Transformation, passion, power
Betelgeuse	Orion	Gemini	28°	Strength, courage, focus
Capella	Auriga	Gemini	21°	Fortune, nurturing, growth

Fixed Star	Constellation	Zodiac Sign	Approximate Degree	Magical Correspondence
Regulus	Leo	Leo	29°	Leadership, courage, fame
Sirius	Canis Major	Cancer	14°	Wisdom, spiritual insight, illumination
Vega	Lyra	Capricorn	15°	Artistic inspiration, harmony, beauty

Fixed Star	Constellation	Zodiac Sign	Approximate Degree	Magical Correspondence
Pleiades	Taurus	Taurus	29°	Nurturing, creativity, mysticism
Spica	Virgo	Libra	23°	Abundance, talent, protection
Algol	Perseus	Taurus	26°	Shadow work, intensity, banishing

How to Use:

- Use this chart to identify the current zodiac sign and degree of key fixed stars when planning your rituals.

- Incorporate the fixed star's magical correspondence into your intention. For example, when performing a ritual for abundance, invoke **Spica** or **Aldebaran** by focusing on their position in the zodiac and aligning with their energy.

2. **Planetary Correspondences and Their Influence in Star Magic**

Planets have distinct energies that interact with the stars, influencing your magical work. This chart lists each planet, its astrological associations, and its primary influence in Star Magic.

Planet	Zodiac Signs Ruled	Magical Influence	Associated Stars
Sun	Leo	Vitality, self-expression, confidence	Regulus (Leo), Aldebaran (Taurus)
Moon	Cancer	Emotions, intuition, subconscious	Sirius (Cancer), Pleiades (Taurus)

Planet	Zodiac Signs Ruled	Magical Influence	Associated Stars
Mercury	Gemini, Virgo	Communication, intellect, adaptability	Capella (Gemini), Spica (Virgo)
Venus	Taurus, Libra	Love, beauty, harmony, attraction	Aldebaran (Taurus), Vega (Capricorn)
Mars	Aries, Scorpio	Action, courage, passion, assertiveness	Antares (Scorpio), Betelgeuse (Gemini)
Jupiter	Sagittarius, Pisces	Expansion, luck, growth, abundance	Aldebaran (Taurus), Spica (Libra)

Planet	Zodiac Signs Ruled	Magical Influence	Associated Stars
Saturn	Capricorn, Aquarius	Structure, discipline, responsibility	Vega (Capricorn), Sirius (Cancer)
Uranus	Aquarius	Innovation, change, independence	Regulus (Leo), Capella (Gemini)
Neptune	Pisces	Spirituality, dreams, intuition	Pleiades (Taurus), Spica (Libra)
Pluto	Scorpio	Transformation, power, rebirth	Antares (Scorpio), Algol (Taurus)

How to Use:

- Select a planet that corresponds with your ritual's intention. For example, to attract love, work with **Venus** and invoke stars such as **Aldebaran** or **Vega** that align with Venus' influence.
- Combine planetary energy with fixed stars to create a multi-layered magical effect, like invoking **Mars** and **Antares** for a ritual focused on courage and transformation.

3. Moon Phases and Their Energies

The moon's phases significantly impact Star Magic practices, each phase offering unique energy that can be harnessed to amplify your intentions.

Moon Phase	Description	Magical Energy
New Moon	No visible moon in the sky	New beginnings, intention-setting, planting seeds
Waxing Crescent	Slightly visible crescent moon	Growth, expansion, attracting new opportunities

Moon Phase	Description	Magical Energy
First Quarter	Half-moon visible	Action, decision-making, overcoming obstacles
Waxing Gibbous	Nearly full moon	Refinement, focus, manifesting desires
Full Moon	Fully illuminated moon	Clarity, power, culmination, illumination
Waning Gibbous	Begins to decrease in illumination	Release, gratitude, reflection
Last Quarter	Half-moon decreasing	Letting go, breaking habits, banishment

Moon Phase	Description	Magical Energy
Waning Crescent	Thin crescent before new moon	Surrender, rest, preparation for new cycles

How to Use:

- Align your rituals with the moon phase that corresponds to your intention. For example, conduct rituals for new beginnings and goal setting during the **New Moon**, while performing release and banishment rituals during the **Waning Moon**.
- Enhance moon phase rituals by invoking stars associated with lunar energy, such as **Sirius** (for the full moon) or the **Pleiades** (for nurturing and intuition).

4. Astrological Aspects and Their Influence on Star Magic

Astrological aspects describe the angles formed between planets and stars, influencing how their energies interact. Understanding these aspects helps you harness celestial dynamics in your magical practices.

Aspect	Degrees	Influence
Conjunction	0°	Merging of energies, amplification, intensity
Sextile	60°	Harmony, opportunity, cooperative flow
Square	90°	Tension, challenge, motivation for change
Trine	120°	Balance, natural ease, effortless support
Opposition	180°	Polarity, balance, potential for conflict

How to Use:

- **Conjunctions:** Use conjunctions to merge energies of stars and planets. For example, during a **Sun-Regulus conjunction**, invoke both the Sun's vitality and Regulus' courage to empower self-expression rituals.
- **Trines:** Take advantage of trines for harmonious and effortless workings. When a trine occurs between **Jupiter** and **Aldebaran**, use this alignment for abundance and prosperity rituals.
- **Squares and Oppositions:** These aspects present challenges but offer growth. Use squares to confront obstacles, invoking stars like **Antares** for transformation, and oppositions for balancing energies in your life.

5. Planetary Hours and Days for Star Magic

Each day and hour is ruled by a specific planet, influencing the type of magic that is most effective during that time.

Day	Planetary Ruler	Ideal Magical Work
Sunday	Sun	Vitality, success, confidence, prosperity

Day	Planetary Ruler	Ideal Magical Work
Monday	Moon	Intuition, emotions, healing, dreams
Tuesday	Mars	Courage, strength, action, protection
Wednesday	Mercury	Communication, intellect, travel, commerce
Thursday	Jupiter	Abundance, growth, luck, prosperity

Day	Planetary Ruler	Ideal Magical Work
Friday	Venus	Love, beauty, harmony, friendship
Saturday	Saturn	Structure, discipline, protection, banishment

How to Use:

- Perform star rituals during the planetary hour or day that aligns with your intention. For example, to perform a ritual for love and attraction, conduct it on **Friday** (Venus' day) during a **Venus** hour for added power.
- Combine planetary days with fixed star energies. For a ritual invoking **Sirius** for wisdom, choose **Monday** (ruled by the Moon) to enhance intuitive and spiritual aspects.

6. Seasonal Star Alignments

Stars and constellations are more visible and energetically accessible during certain times of the year. Use this chart to plan star rituals in harmony with the seasons.

Season	Visible Stars/Constellations	Energetic Influence
Spring	Orion, Pleiades, Aldebaran	Growth, renewal, creativity, strength
Summer	Vega, Sirius, Regulus	Illumination, vitality, leadership, inspiration
Autumn	Antares, Capella, Andromeda	Transformation, abundance, balance
Winter	Betelgeuse, Gemini (Castor and Pollux)	Reflection, inner strength, guidance

How to Use:

- Plan seasonal rituals that correspond with the energy of visible stars. During **Summer**, invoke **Sirius** or **Vega** for rituals of illumination and inspiration.
- Use seasonal changes to align with your personal growth. For example, invoke **Orion** during **Spring** for rituals focused on strength, renewal, and setting new goals.

Conclusion

These charts serve as essential references for planning, timing, and enhancing your Star Magic practices. By understanding the positions of fixed stars, aligning with planetary energies, working with lunar phases, interpreting astrological aspects, and incorporating seasonal cycles, you can craft rituals that are in harmony with the cosmic forces at play. Keep these charts close at hand as you explore the mysteries of the universe, using them to guide your magical work and deepen your connection with the stars.

Appendix C: Suggested Books

The study and practice of Star Magic, astrology, astronomy, and cosmic mysticism are vast and multifaceted, drawing from ancient wisdom and modern understanding of the cosmos. This curated list of books provides further reading for those looking to deepen their knowledge and expand their practice. The selected works encompass topics including fixed stars, celestial movements, astrology, cosmic spirituality, and the magical properties of stars, planets, and the universe. Whether you are a novice or a seasoned Star Mage, these books will guide you on your journey through the mysteries of the stars and the universe.

1. Star Magic and Fixed Stars

"The Fixed Stars and Constellations in Astrology" by Vivian E. Robson

- **Overview:** A classic and comprehensive exploration of fixed stars, this book dives into the astrological influence of stars and constellations. Robson provides detailed descriptions of over 100 fixed stars, including their mythological backgrounds, influences, and astrological significances.
- **Why Read It:** Essential for understanding the unique energies of the stars you invoke in Star Magic rituals, this book offers insights into how fixed stars interact with planetary influences and zodiac signs.

"Brady's Book of Fixed Stars" by Bernadette Brady

- **Overview:** A modern classic that focuses on the practical application of fixed stars in astrology. Brady provides detailed information on each fixed star's mythology, astrological influence, and significance in personal and mundane astrology.

- **Why Read It:** This book is invaluable for those who wish to integrate fixed stars into their astrological charts and rituals, offering a practical guide to aligning with star energies.

"Star Lore: Myths, Legends, and Facts" by William Tyler Olcott

- **Overview:** An exploration of star myths, legends, and historical references across different cultures. Olcott provides an in-depth look at constellations, detailing their mythological backgrounds and symbolic meanings.
- **Why Read It:** Understanding the myths and legends associated with stars and constellations enriches your Star Magic practice, allowing you to connect with their energies on a deeper, more symbolic level.

2. Astrology and Celestial Influences
"Parker's Astrology: The Definitive Guide to Using Astrology in Every Aspect of Your Life" by Julia and Derek Parker

- **Overview:** A comprehensive introduction to astrology, covering natal charts, planetary movements, zodiac signs, houses, aspects, and transits. The book includes easy-to-follow explanations and practical examples.
- **Why Read It:** Essential for any Star Mage looking to understand how astrological forces interact with star energies, aiding in personalizing star rituals and aligning with planetary influences.

"Astrology for the Soul" by Jan Spiller

- **Overview:** A deep dive into the influence of the lunar nodes in astrology, particularly focusing on North and South Node placements and their spiritual lessons.

- **Why Read It:** This book provides insights into cosmic destiny and life path, helping you integrate lunar influences into your Star Magic practice, especially when working with moon phases and eclipses.

"The Only Astrology Book You'll Ever Need" by Joanna Martine Woolfolk

- **Overview:** An accessible yet detailed guide to the fundamentals of astrology, including zodiac signs, planets, houses, and aspects. It also offers practical advice on interpreting charts.
- **Why Read It:** For those new to astrology, this book offers a solid foundation, making it easier to incorporate astrological knowledge into your Star Magic rituals.

3. Astronomy and Celestial Movements
"The Practical Astronomer" by Will Gater and Anton Vamplew

- **Overview:** An informative and visually rich guide to stargazing and observing celestial objects. It includes star charts, guides to identifying constellations, and tips on how to use telescopes.
- **Why Read It:** This book is an excellent resource for Star Mages who want to connect with the stars through direct observation, enhancing their practice with real-time celestial alignment.

"NightWatch: A Practical Guide to Viewing the Universe" by Terence Dickinson

- **Overview:** A popular guide to the night sky, offering clear star maps, guides to the phases of the moon, and information on planets and constellations. It is an ideal companion for amateur astronomers.

- **Why Read It:** This book aids in understanding the physical aspects of the stars and their positions, enriching the star maps used in Star Magic and allowing you to time rituals with cosmic events more precisely.

"The Stars: A New Way to See Them" by H.A. Rey

- **Overview:** A classic work on stargazing that presents constellations in a way that is easy to identify. Rey's diagrams help you find and recognize constellations with clear and engaging illustrations.
- **Why Read It:** As a Star Mage, recognizing constellations is key to your practice. This book provides the foundational knowledge needed to identify stars and constellations, allowing for more effective star invocations.

4. Cosmic Mysticism and Spirituality
"The Secret Teachings of All Ages" by Manly P. Hall

- **Overview:** A comprehensive exploration of ancient spiritual, mystical, and esoteric knowledge, including the astrological mysteries, celestial deities, and star-based mythologies from various cultures.
- **Why Read It:** For those seeking a deeper spiritual context, this book provides rich insights into the cosmic mysteries, helping you integrate Star Magic with broader mystical traditions.

"The Book of the Moon" by Maggie Aderin-Pocock

- **Overview:** An exploration of the moon's influence on Earth, covering its phases, cycles, and cultural significance. It blends scientific facts with mythological narratives to offer a holistic view of the moon's role in human life.

- **Why Read It:** Understanding the moon's influence is crucial in Star Magic, especially when working with lunar phases. This book enhances your knowledge of the moon's mysteries, aiding in moon-related rituals and magic.

"Mysticism: The Preeminent Study in the Nature and Development of Spiritual Consciousness" by Evelyn Underhill

- **Overview:** A profound study of mysticism, exploring the spiritual journey, stages of enlightenment, and the soul's connection to the cosmos.
- **Why Read It:** For Star Mages interested in the spiritual dimension of their practice, this book provides a deep dive into the nature of mystical experiences, offering insights into the cosmic consciousness accessed through star magic.

5. Magical Practices and Tools
"The Modern Witchcraft Guide to the Wheel of the Year" by Judy Ann Nock

- **Overview:** This guide explores the Wheel of the Year's seasonal cycles and their corresponding magical practices. It includes rituals, meditations, and activities to connect with each season's energies.
- **Why Read It:** Aligning Star Magic with the Wheel of the Year enhances your practice by synchronizing with natural cycles. This book provides ideas for incorporating star energy into seasonal rituals.

"The Crystal Bible" by Judy Hall

- **Overview:** A comprehensive guide to crystals and gemstones, detailing their properties, uses, and correspondences.

- **Why Read It:** Since crystals play a significant role in Star Magic, this book helps you choose the right stones to amplify star energy and enhance your rituals.

"High Magic: Theory and Practice" by Frater U.D.

- **Overview:** A practical manual for advanced magical practices, including techniques for invocation, evocation, and working with cosmic forces.
- **Why Read It:** While not focused exclusively on Star Magic, this book provides valuable techniques for energy work, ritual structure, and the magical mindset, all of which are applicable to star-based practices.

6. Star Magic and Advanced Practices
"The Cosmic Doctrine" by Dion Fortune

- **Overview:** A complex work that explores the esoteric principles of the universe, including the flow of cosmic energies, the structure of the cosmos, and spiritual evolution.
- **Why Read It:** For advanced Star Mages, this book offers a profound understanding of cosmic principles, enhancing your ability to work with star energies on a metaphysical level.

"Astrological Magic: Basic Rituals & Meditations" by David Rankine and Sorita d'Este

- **Overview:** A practical guide to performing astrological magic, including rituals, meditations, and methods for harnessing planetary and stellar energies.
- **Why Read It:** This book bridges the gap between astrology and magic, providing techniques for incorporating star energies into

rituals and offering methods for creating your own star-based spells and meditations.

"The Complete Magician's Tables" by Stephen Skinner

- **Overview:** A comprehensive reference of correspondences, including planetary, elemental, and zodiacal associations, as well as magical symbols and deities.
- **Why Read It:** For advanced practitioners, this book is an invaluable resource for finding correspondences to fine-tune your star magic rituals, helping you align with the correct energies for your intentions.

How to Use This List

- **Beginner Star Mages:** Start with foundational astrology and astronomy books to build your understanding of celestial movements and star positions. Books like "Parker's Astrology" and "The Practical Astronomer" provide an essential knowledge base.
- **Intermediate Practitioners:** Explore texts on fixed stars and cosmic mysticism, such as "The Fixed Stars and Constellations in Astrology" by Vivian E. Robson, to deepen your connection with stellar energies.
- **Advanced Star Mages:** Delve into complex works like "The Cosmic Doctrine" by Dion Fortune and "Astrological Magic" by David Rankine and Sorita d'Este to master the integration of star magic with other mystical practices.

Conclusion

This list of suggested books offers a range of perspectives and depths on the study of stars, astrology, astronomy, and cosmic mysticism. Whether you seek to expand your astrological knowledge, deepen your spiritual connection with the cosmos, or refine your magical practices, these books provide valuable insights and practical techniques to support your journey as a Star Mage. Explore these texts, let them guide you, and integrate their wisdom into your ongoing practice of Star Magic.

Appendix D: Journal Entry

Journaling is an essential practice for Star Mages, as it allows you to document your experiences, insights, and results from your Star Magic practices. By recording each ritual, meditation, and interaction with the stars, you create a valuable resource that reflects your growth, enhances your self-awareness, and provides insights for refining your magical techniques. This guided journal entry is designed to help you capture the details of your Star Magic work systematically, ensuring that you document not only the practical aspects but also your intuitive feelings, cosmic connections, and any manifestations that arise.

This journal entry format is divided into multiple sections, guiding you through each stage of your ritual or meditation. By reflecting on your intentions, the energies invoked, the tools used, and the outcomes experienced, you deepen your understanding of how star energies interact with your life and how you can harness them more effectively in the future.

Guided Journal Entry: Exploring the Cosmos Through Star Magic

1. Date and Time of Ritual

- **Date:**
- **Start Time:**
- **End Time:**

Why Record This: The date and time can affect the energies present during your ritual. Noting this information helps you identify patterns related to astrological alignments, moon phases, and other celestial influences.

2. Celestial Influences

- **Moon Phase:**
    - ◈ New Moon
    - ◈ Waxing Crescent
    - ◈ First Quarter
    - ◈ Waxing Gibbous
    - ◈ Full Moon
    - ◈ Waning Gibbous
    - ◈ Last Quarter
    - ◈ Waning Crescent
- **Visible Constellations/Stars:**
- **Astrological Aspects:** (E.g., Sun conjunct Regulus, Venus trine Aldebaran)
- **Current Season:**

Why Record This: Understanding the celestial influences at play during your ritual provides context for the energies you are working with and can explain any unique experiences you encounter.

3. Intention of the Ritual or Meditation

- **What is your main goal or intention for this practice?** (E.g., Attract abundance, gain clarity, release negative energy)
- **Why is this intention important to you at this time?**

Why Record This: Setting a clear intention focuses your energy and aligns it with the star's power. Reflecting on your intention also deepens your connection to the ritual's purpose and enhances your ability to manifest desired outcomes.

4. Stars and Constellations Invoked

- **Stars/Constellations:** (List the stars or constellations you focused on during the ritual, e.g., Aldebaran, Orion, Pleiades)
- **Magical Correspondences:**
    - **Aldebaran:** Wealth, success
    - **Orion:** Strength, focus
    - **Pleiades:** Creativity, intuition

Why Record This: Documenting which stars and constellations you invoke helps you track which celestial energies resonate most powerfully with you and how they influence your magical workings.

5. Tools and Items Used

- **Candles:** (List colors, scents, or shapes, e.g., green candle for abundance)
- **Crystals:** (E.g., Citrine, amethyst, moonstone)
- **Incense/Herbs:** (E.g., Frankincense for spiritual connection, sage for cleansing)
- **Sigils/Symbols:** (Did you create or use specific sigils related to the stars or intention? If so, describe or sketch them below.)
- **Other Tools:** (E.g., wand, altar, star map)

Why Record This: The tools used during your ritual influence the energy you work with. Documenting them allows you to see which combinations of tools amplify or complement the star energies you invoke.

6. Ritual/Meditation Steps

- **Outline the steps you took during your ritual or meditation.** (Include how you cast the circle, invoked the stars, and any specific actions performed.)
- **Did you incorporate any specific chants, invocations, or affirmations?** Write them below.

Why Record This: Detailing the steps of your ritual helps you replicate successful practices in future sessions and adjust techniques that may not have worked as intended.

7. Physical and Emotional State Before the Ritual

- **Physical:** (E.g., Tired, energetic, calm)
- **Emotional:** (E.g., Anxious, hopeful, peaceful)

Why Record This: Your physical and emotional state can affect how you connect with star energies. Noting this information provides insights into how your well-being interacts with your magical practice.

8. Experiences During the Ritual

- **What sensations did you experience?** (E.g., warmth, tingling, pressure)
- **Did you see, hear, or sense anything unusual?** (E.g., star-like lights, whispers, feelings of presence)
- **Were there any moments of heightened energy or clarity?**

Why Record This: Recording your experiences during the ritual helps you identify how different star energies manifest and communicate with you, enhancing your ability to work with them in the future.

9. Messages or Insights Received

- **Did you receive any messages, visions, or insights during the ritual?**
- **How do these messages relate to your intention or current situation?**

Why Record This: Often, rituals can yield profound insights or guidance. Documenting these messages allows you to revisit them later and interpret their meanings more deeply.

10. Outcome and Results

- **Did you notice any immediate changes or effects after the ritual?**
- **Have there been any subsequent events, signs, or synchronicities that align with your intention?**
- **Do you feel a shift in your mindset, emotions, or energy?**

Why Record This: Tracking the results of your rituals helps you assess their effectiveness, learn from your experiences, and refine your techniques for future practices.

11. Reflections and Adjustments

- **What aspects of the ritual worked well?**
- **Were there any parts that felt out of alignment or ineffective?**
- **What would you do differently next time?**

Why Record This: Reflection is key to growth in your practice. By assessing what worked and what didn't, you gain a clearer understanding of how to adjust your methods to better align with your intentions and the star energies you are working with.

12. Affirmations for Moving Forward

- **What affirmations can you carry forward to maintain the energy of this ritual?** (E.g., "I align with the prosperity of Aldebaran," "The Pleiades nurture my creativity and intuition.")

Why Record This: Affirmations help to sustain the energy and focus of your ritual in the days following. By reinforcing the star energies you've invoked, you keep your intention active and aligned with the cosmos.

Summary:

This guided journal entry format encourages you to capture every detail of your Star Magic practice, from the astrological influences to the tools used, and the experiences encountered. By documenting your intentions, experiences, and reflections, you create a comprehensive record of your journey as a Star Mage. Over time, your journal becomes a valuable resource that helps you refine your techniques, recognize patterns in cosmic influences, and deepen your connection with the universe.

Use this format as a template for each of your rituals, meditations, and magical workings. Regularly review past entries to identify successful practices, understand how different star energies affect you, and witness your growth as a practitioner of Star Magic. Your journal is not just a record—it is a mirror reflecting the evolution of your cosmic journey, guiding you toward ever-greater mastery of the stars.

Message from the Author:

I hope you enjoyed this book, I love astrology and knew there was not a book such as this out on the shelf. I love metaphysical items as well. Please check out my other books:

-Life of Government Benefits

-My life of Hell

-My life with Hydrocephalus

-Red Sky

-World Domination:Woman's rule

-World Domination:Woman's Rule 2: The War

-Life and Banishment of Apophis: book 1

-The Kidney Friendly Diet

-The Ultimate Hemp Cookbook

-Creating a Dispensary(legally)

-Cleanliness throughout life: the importance of showering from childhood to adulthood.

-Strong Roots: The Risks of Overcoddling children

-Hemp Horoscopes: Cosmic Insights and Earthly Healing

- Celestial Hemp Navigating the Zodiac: Through the Green Cosmos

-Astrological Hemp: Aligning The Stars with Earth's Ancient Herb

-The Astrological Guide to Hemp: Stars, Signs, and Sacred Leaves

-Green Growth: Innovative Marketing Strategies for your Hemp Products and Dispensary

-Cosmic Cannabis

-Astrological Munchies

-Henry The Hemp

-Zodiacal Roots: The Astrological Soul Of Hemp

- **Green Constellations: Intersection of Hemp and Zodiac**

-Hemp in The Houses: An astrological Adventure Through The Cannabis Galaxy

-Galactic Ganja Guide
Heavenly Hemp
Zodiac Leaves
Doctor Who Astrology
Cannastrology
Stellar Satvias and Cosmic Indicas
Celestial Cannabis: A Zodiac Journey
AstroHerbology: The Sky and The Soil: Volume 1
AstroHerbology:Celestial Cannabis:Volume 2
Cosmic Cannabis Cultivation
The Starry Guide to Herbal Harmony: Volume 1
The Starry Guide to Herbal Harmony: Cannabis Universe: Volume 2
Yugioh Astrology: Astrological Guide to Deck, Duels and more
Nightmare Mansion: Echoes of The Abyss
Nightmare Mansion 2: Legacy of Shadows
Nightmare Mansion 3: Shadows of the Forgotten
Nightmare Mansion 4: Echoes of the Damned
The Life and Banishment of Apophis: Book 2
Nightmare Mansion: Halls of Despair
Healing with Herb: Cannabis and Hydrocephalus
Planetary Pot: Aligning with Astrological Herbs: Volume 1
Fast Track to Freedom: 30 Days to Financial Independence Using AI, Assets, and Agile Hustles
Cosmic Hemp Pathways
How to Become Financially Free in 30 Days: 10,000 Paths to Prosperity
Zodiacal Herbage: Astrological Insights: Volume 1
Nightmare Mansion: Whispers in the Walls
The Daleks Invade Atlantis
Henry the hemp and Hydrocephalus

10X The Kidney Friendly Diet

Cannabis Universe: Adult coloring book

Hemp Astrology: The Healing Power of the Stars

Zodiacal Herbage: Astrological Insights: Cannabis Universe: Volume 2

Planetary Pot: Aligning with Astrological Herbs: Cannabis Universes: Volume 2

Doctor Who Meets the Replicators and SG-1: The Ultimate Battle for Survival

Nightmare Mansion: Curse of the Blood Moon

The Celestial Stoner: A Guide to the Zodiac

Cosmic Pleasures: Sex Toy Astrology for Every Sign

Hydrocephalus Astrology: Navigating the Stars and Healing Waters

Lapis and the Mischievous Chocolate Bar

Celestial Positions: Sexual Astrology for Every Sign

Apophis's Shadow Work Journal: : A Journey of Self-Discovery and Healing

Kinky Cosmos: Sexual Kink Astrology for Every Sign

Digital Cosmos: The Astrological Digimon Compendium

Stellar Seeds: The Cosmic Guide to Growing with Astrology

Apophis's Daily Gratitude Journal

Cat Astrology: Feline Mysteries of the Cosmos

The Cosmic Kama Sutra: An Astrological Guide to Sexual Positions

Unleash Your Potential: A Guided Journal Powered by AI Insights

Whispers of the Enchanted Grove

Cosmic Pleasures: An Astrological Guide to Sexual Kinks

369, 12 Manifestation Journal

Whisper of the nocturne journal(blank journal for writing or drawing)
The Boogey Book
Locked In Reflection: A Chastity Journey Through Locktober
Generating Wealth Quickly:
How to Generate $100,000 in 24 Hours

If you want solar for your home go here: https://www.harborsolar.live/apophisenterprises/

Get Some Tarot cards: https://www.makeplayingcards.com/sell/apophis-occult-shop

Get some shirts: https://www.bonfire.com/store/apophis-shirt-emporium/

Instagrams:
@apophis_enterprises,
@apophisbookemporium,
@apophisscardshop
Twitter: @apophisenterpr1
Tiktok:@apophisenterprise
Youtube: @sg1fan23477, @FiresideRetreatKingdom

Podcast: Apophis Chat Zone: https://open.spotify.com/show/5zXbrCLEV2xzCp8ybrfHsk?si=fb4d4fdbdce44dec

Newsletter: https://apophiss-newsletter-27c897.beehiiv.com/

Milton Keynes UK
Ingram Content Group UK Ltd.
UKHW032317121024
449481UK00012B/457